Emma Ewing

The art of cookery

A manual for homes and schools

Emma Ewing

The art of cookery
A manual for homes and schools

ISBN/EAN: 9783744785990

Printed in Europe, USA, Canada, Australia, Japan

Cover: Foto ©Lupo / pixelio.de

More available books at **www.hansebooks.com**

ART OF COOKERY

A MANUAL FOR HOMES AND SCHOOLS

BY

EMMA P. EWING

Superintendent of the Chautauqua School of Cookery, formerly Professor of Domestic Economy in the Iowa State Agricultural College, and of Household Science in Purdue University, Indiana.

THE BOWEN-MERRILL COMPANY
PUBLISHERS
INDIANAPOLIS, INDIANA

PREFACE.

A GREAT need exists in our homes and schools for more intelligent instruction in regard to the preparation of food. This book was written to supply that need. In it the principles underlying the art of cookery are clearly explained. And with its aid any person of ordinary intelligence ought to be able to select, prepare, and serve, in a scientific and skilful manner, such articles of food as are in general use.

CONTENTS.

PART I.—MARKETING.

CHAPTER.		PAGE.
	INTRODUCTION	7
I.	HOW TO SELECT MEAT	10
II.	HOW TO SELECT VEGETABLES	15

PART II.—FOOD MATERIALS.

	INTRODUCTION	17
III.	CARE OF FOOD MATERIALS	18
IV.	PREPARATION OF FOOD MATERIALS	20

PART III.—METHODS OF COOKING.

	INTRODUCTION	33
V.	BROILING	34
VI.	BAKING	46
VII.	BOILING	65
VIII.	STEAMING	81
IX.	STEWING	84
X.	SOUP-MAKING	100
XI.	MEAT SAUCES	126
XII.	FRYING	136
XIII.	SICK-ROOM COOKERY	156
XIV.	CANNING, PRESERVING, AND PICKLING	163

PART IV.—MIXING.

	INTRODUCTION	179
XV.	BREAD-MAKING	182

CHAPTER.		PAGE.
XVI.	Pastry and Pie	213
XVII.	Puddings	227
XVIII.	Cake-making	247
XIX.	Delicate Desserts	254
XX.	Sherbets, Water Ices, and Ice Creams	260

PART V.—SEASONING.

	Introduction	263
XXI.	Salad-making	268
XXII.	Entrées and Side Dishes	283
XXIII.	Boned Meats	307
XXIV.	Eggs and Omelets	311

PART VI.—SERVING AND GARNISHING.

	Introduction	315
XXV.	Carving	316
XXVI.	Bills of Fare	319

THE ART OF COOKERY.

PART I.—MARKETING.

INTRODUCTION.

For the benefit of housekeepers and students of cookery a few general rules are here given in regard to marketing and the selection of food materials.

The methods of cutting up calves, sheep, and hogs are so similar, in a general way, to that of cutting up beef cattle—the main difference being in the fewer number of cuts on account of the smaller size of the animals—that the rules which are applicable in the selection of the best cuts of beef are applicable also in the selection of the best cuts in any of these smaller animals.

The method of cutting up a beef, as illustrated in the plate, is that which is followed by the best butchers in New York and Chicago, and is the one in most general use in this country. The divisions marked with the letter S are generally used as steak. The figures 2 and 3 along the top of the back denote the number of ribs in each cut or roast, as there designated.

The name by which each piece is called, as **marked** on the illustration, is given in the following list :

1, S, Thick sirloin.
2, Second cut, or middle ribs.
3, S, Small end sirloin.

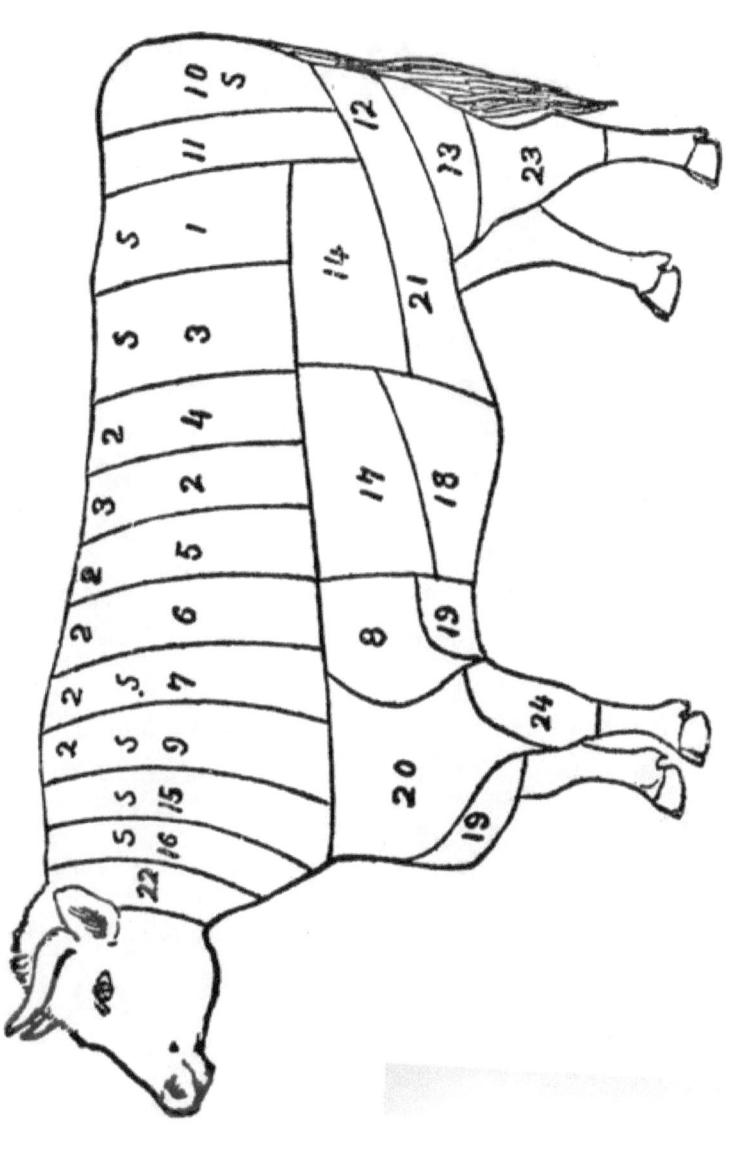

4, First cut rib.
5, Third cut, or thick rib.
6, First cut chuck rib.
7, S, Second cut chuck rib.
8, S, Cross rib.
9, S, Third cut chuck.
10, S, Rump.
11, Face of rump.
12, First cut round.
13, Second cut round.
14, Top of sirloin.
15, S, Neck piece.
16, Second neck piece.
17, Plate piece.
18, Navel piece.
19, Brisket.
20, Shoulder clod.
21, Flank piece.
22, Third cut of neck.
23, Leg.
24, Shin.

CHAPTER I.

HOW TO SELECT MEAT.

To Select Beef.—Cattle from four to eight years of age furnish the best beef. The flesh of young animals is less rich in flavor and nutrition, and loses more weight in cooking than that of mature age. Good beef has a dark red color when first cut, which changes to a lighter shade after a few minutes' exposure to the air. It looks juicy, is fine grained, smooth, firm, and, at the same time, elastic to the touch. It has a fair proportion of fat about the kidneys and overlying the loin and ribs, while the lean or muscular portions are ingrained and marbled with dots and streaks of fat. A very dark color indicates an old animal, a pale, moist muscle a very young one, and a bluish or dark red color poor beef.

Those portions of a beef containing the greatest amount of tenderloin are generally considered the choicest, consequently they command the highest price. But, as a matter of fact, the sirloin, rump, ribs, and some other cuts, although less tender, contain more juice, flavor, and nutrition than the tenderloin.

The fore quarter of a beef contains a larger proportion of bone to meat, and is less tender, than the hind quarter, but is quite equal to it in juiciness and flavor. Backward from the head, in the fore quarters, and upward from the legs in both fore and hind quarters, the quality and price of the meat increases.

The best steak is the porterhouse steak, cut from the loin of an animal where the tenderloin is largest. It contains both tenderloin and sirloin, separated by a small bone, and is frequently called a pin-bone steak. Further back the pin-bone centers in a cross-bone at the top, and a cut from there is often called a T-bone steak. Steaks cut forward from the porterhouse steaks have no separating bone in them, but are nevertheless called porterhouse steaks by many butchers, and are not infrequently given that name even when cut so far forward that there is not a semblance of tenderloin about them. When the pin-bone or T-bone is removed from a porterhouse steak, and it is divided into two parts, these parts are known respectively as tenderloin steak and sirloin steak. As has already been said, the tenderloin is the tenderest portion of a beef; but many people prefer a sirloin to a tenderloin steak on account of its being more juicy and richer flavored. After the loin, the rump steaks are the best. The round is very inferior for broiling, as the juices are so thin and exposed that it is difficult to keep them from flowing out while the meat is cooking, and leaving it dry and tasteless. Round steak is better cooked as Salisbury or Hamburger steak, or sautéd and braised.

The first, second, and third cut ribs, as shown on the chart, make prime roasts. The rump also makes an excellent roast. The chuck ribs do not make nearly so good a roast as either of the other cuts mentioned. But the portions that are best for steaks furnish the finest roasts. And while sirloin is considered best for a large roast, nothing can be choicer for a small one than porterhouse.

To Select Veal.—Milk-fed calves that are from six to eight weeks of age make the best veal. The fat about the kidneys of such calves is white and the flesh is white and firm. The hind quarter is the choicest and generally sells for a few cents a pound more than the fore quarter. The loin makes the fattest and finest chops. Cutlets are usually taken from the leg. The fillet is also taken from the leg. Roasts are selected from the loin, the breast, the shoulder, and the leg.

The pancreatic glands, or sweetbreads, are two small lumps of flesh that are found in the lower throat and near the heart of the calf. They seldom weigh more than half a pound, and their function is to assimilate the oily portions of the food of the young animal. In milk-fed calves the sweetbreads are composed largely of assimilated cream and are very tender and delicate in flavor, but as the calves increase in age they become tough and worthless. The sweetbread nearest the heart is plump and oval in form, while that from the throat is longer and less compact. There is little difference, however, in their flavor or delicacy.

To Select Mutton.—The best mutton is that in which the fat is abundant, white, clear, and solid, the leg bones white, the scored skin on the fore quarters red, and the lean meat juicy and firm and of a dark red color.

To Select Lamb.—In selecting lamb choose that which has hard, white fat on the back and about the kidneys, and has pinkish-hued bones.

To Select Pork.—The lean of the best pork is of a delicate red color, juicy, firm, and fine grained. The fat is white and the skin thin and pearly. When the skin is thick the pig is old.

To Select Ham.—Medium-sized hams weighing from eight to twelve pounds are usually the best. Hams should be plump and round, with short tapering shanks and small bones. The fat should be white and firm, and the skin thin and not wrinkled.

To Select Poultry.—A moderate sized turkey is more apt to be young than a larger one, and a hen is preferable to a gobbler, being generally plumper, fatter, and more delicate in flavor. The legs of a turkey should be black and smooth and the breast-bone soft and pliable. If the legs are rough, the breast-bone hard, and the skin tough, the turkey is old. When turkeys or other fowls are fresh the eyes are bright and full, and the feet and legs limber. The breast of a goose should be plump and white, and the feet yellow and flexible. If the windpipe is soft the goose is young. Capons are the greatest delicacies known in the poultry line, as they retain the tenderness of young chickens while having the size and flavor of mature fowls. To judge the age of a chicken press with the finger on the breast-bone at the point nearest the tail, and if the bone is soft and pliable the chicken is young. Poultry that is dark and slimy is stale and unfit for food.

To Select Eggs.—Fresh eggs look clear and semi-transparent in a strong light, and if lifted in the hand feel heavier than eggs that are stale. If eggs are dropped into a bucket or pan of water those that are perfectly fresh will sink to the bottom and rest on their sides, those that are stale will stand obliquely in the water, while those that are positively bad will take an upright position and float. Cold-storage eggs should be avoided, as they usually have a sour, musty flavor that renders them very undesirable for most culinary purposes.

To Select Fish.—In selecting fish choose only those with firm flesh, stiff fins, lively red gills, and full, clear eyes.

CHAPTER II.

HOW TO SELECT VEGETABLES.

CONSIDERABLE care should be observed in the selection of vegetables, as most green vegetables are very perishable, and lose their flavor and become unhealthful when they wilt or grow stale. A few general rules are given for the selection of such as are in most common use.

To Select Potatoes.—Those that have the most perfect skin and are heaviest for their size are always the best.

To Select Cabbage.—The firmest and heaviest heads of cabbage are best.

To Select Cauliflower.—Select large, solid heads that are creamy white. Wilted leaves and dark flowers are indications of staleness.

To Select Squash.—Hubbard and other varieties of fall and winter squash, and also pumpkins, should be selected by weight. The heavier a squash or pumpkin is in proportion to size the tenderer and richer flavored it is apt to be.

To Select Turnips.—Medium-sized turnips are generally sweetest, provided they are firm, heavy, and free from green spots.

To Select Carrots, Parsnips, and Salsify.—These all belong in the same family of vegetables, and are best when unwilted, solid, heavy, and free from side roots.

To Select Cucumbers.—Select those of medium size that are dark green in color and very plump and firm.

To Select Spinach.—Spinach should be bright green in color, unwilted, and crisp.

To Select Celery.—Dwarf is much finer flavored than mammoth. But whatever variety is selected it should be white, firm, and crisp.

To Select Lettuce.—Head lettuce is much superior to that known as "cut lettuce," and the more firm and solid the heads are the more tender and delicate flavored the lettuce will be.

To Select Egg Plant.—The large, oval-shaped purple is the best. If fresh the egg will be firm and the skin brilliant.

To Select Tomatoes.—Smooth, firm, heavy tomatoes are the least watery and the finest flavored.

To Select Onions.—Thin-skinned, solid onions are always the best. The mildest of any of the different varieties is the large Spanish onion.

To Select Peas and Beans.—Green peas and string beans should be young and freshly picked.

To Select Green Corn.—The cobs should be well filled and the grains plump and milky.

To Select Berries and Fruits.—A dry surface is a pretty sure indication of freshness in strawberries, raspberries, and blackberries; and plumpness, brightness of skin, and freedom from spots of decay are the most reliable indications of freshness in such fruits as apples, peaches, plums, cherries, grapes, etc.

PART II.—FOOD MATERIALS.

INTRODUCTION.

It is quite as important to know how to take care of food materials as it is to select them, and in a majority of homes the loss incurred through ignorance or carelessness in this respect is very great. Consequently every housekeeper should be acquainted with the best methods of taking care of all kinds of food materials before and after they have been cooked, so as to avoid waste in this direction. Ignorance in selecting, caring for, and preparing their food materials has impoverished, and is impoverishing, many families.

CHAPTER III.

CARE OF FOOD MATERIALS.

ALL kinds of meat and poultry should be kept in a cool, dry atmosphere and should be suspended from hooks in such a manner as not to rest against anything. The choicest portion of the fowl or joint of meat should, when suspended, hang lowest, therefore turkeys, chickens, etc., should be hung by the feet, and a leg of lamb, mutton, or other animal by the shank-bone.

It is unsafe to keep veal or fresh pork any length of time, and both meats are better to be cooked while fresh.

A turkey can safely hang three or four days in a cool, dry atmosphere, but chickens and other fowls do not improve after hanging twenty-four hours. Of course, in a well-ventilated ice-chamber the time they can be allowed to hang, without detriment, may be lengthened considerably. The best and most modern authorities approve of drawing all poultry and game before it is hung. It should not, however, be washed until shortly before it is to be cooked.

Fresh fish should not be allowed to soak any length of time in cold water. They should be kept cold and dry, and are better to be cooked as soon as possible after being caught.

Milk and cream should be kept apart from all foods

that emit odors, and should be closely covered. Butter also should be kept where it cannot absorb odors, and, if kept in large quantities, should be covered with brine, or with several inches of dry salt. A great deal of milk, cream, and butter is ruined by being put in a refrigerator or closet, with a variety of other articles whose odors they quickly absorb.

All cooked foods should be stored in glass, china, or earthen-ware vessels, and should be carefully covered.

Eggs should be kept in a cool, dry atmosphere. If eggs are packed in dry salt, pointed end down, they may be kept in good condition for several weeks.

Fruits and vegetables, as a general rule, keep best in a cool, dry atmosphere. Lettuce, cress, celery, and parsley are best preserved by being wrapped in a towel or napkin wrung out of cold water, then in paper, and kept in a cool place.

Berries and all soft, small fruits should be picked over carefully and scattered on plates, or sheets of white paper. They should not be piled high in deep dishes until shortly before they are to be served.

Imperfectly ripened, or partly green, tomatoes may be ripened very perfectly by being wiped dry, wrapped in paper or cloth, placed in a basket lined with paper or cloth to exclude the light, and set in a warm place for twenty-four hours.

CHAPTER IV.

PREPARATION OF FOOD MATERIALS.

THE proper preparation of food materials—both those which are to be cooked and those which are to be served uncooked—is so important a matter that every housekeeper, cook, and student of cookery should have a practical knowledge of how to prepare, as well as how to select, all the various food materials and articles of food that are likely to be included in the ordinary bill of fare.

To Pick a Fowl.—Fowls that are picked dry are considered superior to those whose feathers are removed by scalding, but as the latter method of taking the feathers from fowls of nearly all kinds is the one in general use and is much easier and quicker than dry picking, it is the method here given: Hold the fowl by the feet or legs, plunge it in very hot water, and draw it out again almost instantly. Repeat the process several times, until the feathers are thoroughly soaked and can be pulled out easily. Then take the fowl in the left hand, and with the right hand pluck out the feathers, stripping them from the legs down toward the head. After all the feathers have been removed, rub out the pin feathers with a coarse cloth, and singe off the hairs over a blaze of alcohol or gas.

To Draw a Fowl.—Cut off the head of the fowl, if

it has not already been removed. Slit the skin the full length of the neck at the back, and carefully loosen it from the neck and craw. Cut off the neck about an inch from the body, and remove the craw and windpipe, being careful not to tear the skin of the fowl. Insert a sharp-pointed knife in front of, and close to, the tail and cut through the skin around the vent and outside the entrail. Lift up the skin below the breast-bone of the fowl, leaving a strip an inch in width above the vent. Cut crosswise two inches and make an opening large enough to insert two fingers, with which carefully draw out the entire contents of the body of the fowl. Separate the heart, liver, and gizzard from the entrails. Remove the gall-sack from the liver very carefully, and open and empty the gizzard.

To Draw a Bird.—This is the best and easiest way of drawing a bird or young chicken that is to be broiled: Insert a small sharp-pointed knife between the shoulder and the backbone and cut down the back the entire length of the fowl or bird—being careful not to cut into the entrails. Lay the fowl or bird open and remove the contents of the body.

To Wash a Fowl.—Dissolve a teaspoonful of soda in two quarts of water, and with a brush or cloth wash the skin of the fowl very thoroughly. Rinse the inside with the soda water. Wash the giblets also. Rinse all in cold water and wipe dry with a soft towel.

To Prepare a Fish.—To remove the scales from a fish use a stiff-bladed knife, and scrape from the tail toward the head. If the fish is to be stuffed and baked **trim off** the fins and open the belly about one third the length of the fish, beginning near the tail. Remove the entrails, wash and rinse the fish well, and dry with a soft towel. If the fish is to be broiled, open it down the belly the entire length of the fish, and unless it is to be boned, cut through the bones close to the backbone, and deep enough into the fish to allow it to lie flat and wide open.

To Bone a Fish.—Cut off its head and insert the point of the boning-knife close to the backbone, under the small bones that lie near the inside surface of the fish. Slip the knife under these bones and carefully lift them from the fish, leaving the meat as little disturbed or broken as possible. With a round-pointed, dull-bladed knife scrape the flesh away from the backbone and the bones that project into the fish therefrom, until they can be lifted away clear of flesh; then with the blade of the knife smooth and pack together the flesh that has been disturbed by removing them. It is not advisable to bone small fish, and all fish, as well as meats of every kind, are of finer flavor when cooked with the bones left in them.

To Prepare Soup-Bones.—Remove the skin from soup-bones, instead of washing them, and make deep incisions, quite near together, in the lean meat, with a knife.

To Prepare a Roast of Beef.—Remove the outer skin, and with a moist cloth wipe the surface on the inside of the cut wherever it has been exposed to dust. All joints of meat should be prepared in the same manner as beef, and should not be wet or washed when it is possible to make them clean by removing the outer skin and wiping them.

To Prepare a Leg of Mutton or Lamb.—The outer skin should always be carefully removed from both mutton and lamb before either of them are cooked. This is more important in the preparation of mutton and lamb than in the preparation of other meats, as mutton and lamb are both liable to have an unpleasant, woolly flavor when boiled or roasted, unless the outer skin has first been removed.

To Prepare Steak or Chops.—Remove the outer skin and all superfluous fat and bones. As the fat of veal and lamb is much more delicate than that of beef and mutton a larger quantity of it can be left on the former than on the latter meats.

To Prepare Breakfast Bacon.—Cut off the dried and hardened surface from as much of a piece of breakfast bacon as is needed. Lay the bacon, skin side down, on a meat board and cut in thin slices down to the rind, until the desired number is obtained, then turn the knife under the slices and separate them from the rind.

To Prepare Sliced Ham.—Remove the outer rind, also a very thin strip along the inner edge of each slice, as those portions have a rank flavor, and are dirty from exposure.

To Prepare a Ham for Boiling or Baking.—Lay the ham, skin side down, in a large pan, pour over it a quart of hot, and several quarts of cold, water. Add a large spoonful of soda to the water, and with a brush scrub the ham thoroughly all over, then rinse in clean water and soak ten or twelve hours, in sufficient water to cover it, with the skin side up.

To Prepare a Dried Tongue.—A dried, smoked

tongue should be prepared in the same manner as a ham.

To Prepare Salted Fish.—Soak the fish, skin side up, in cold water ten or twelve hours, or long enough to freshen it sufficiently, then hang in a cool place to drain and become dry enough to broil readily.

To Prepare Liver.—Skin the liver, cut it in slices half an inch thick, soak half an hour in cold salt water, and dry with a soft towel.

To Prepare Sweetbreads.—Put in cold salt water, and let them soak an hour.

To Prepare Potatoes.—If the potatoes are to be baked or boiled in their skins, wash clean, using a small brush to scrub them with, and remove, with a knife, all specks or blemishes. In paring potatoes use a small, thin-bladed, sharp-pointed knife, drop the potatoes as soon as pared into cold water, and let them remain there until needed for cooking. This keeps them from exposure to the air, and prevents their becoming discolored.

To Prepare Turnips, Carrots, Etc.—Cut or slice the turnips in pieces before paring, unless they are to be cooked whole. Instead of scraping the skin from carrots, parsnips, and salsify it is easier and better to remove a thin paring by cutting from the top, lengthwise of the vegetable. Carrots, parsnips, and salsify should, like potatoes, be dropped in water as soon as pared.

To Prepare Squashes.—Squashes of the hard-shelled variety should be washed or scrubbed until perfectly clean, and then be cut with a saw into pieces the size desired for baking or steaming. Pumpkins and squashes of the soft-shelled varieties should be divided into pieces easily handled, before they are pared.

To Shell Peas.—Pick up the pods with the left hand and press the thumb of the right hand upon the front of the lower end of the pod—the forefinger of the right hand supporting the pod beneath—until it splits open. Then slip the thumb into the opening, run it up the entire length of the pod, and scrape out the peas into a dish or pan beneath the hand. Shelled peas should not be allowed to drop into the dish containing the pods.

To String Beans.—To remove the strings from green snap beans bend the sharp point at the lower end of the pod backward until it breaks, and, with it still attached, remove the string along the back of the pod, breaking off with it the stem at the opposite end. Instead of breaking the pods separately between the fingers, a handful of them may be taken at a time and cut with a knife upon a board much more expeditiously.

To Wash Asparagus.—Take each stalk by the cut end and swash it back and forward in a large pan of water. Tie the washed stalks in bunches of six or eight in each bunch, with a white cotton string; place the green tips evenly together and cut off the opposite ends of the stalks, thus making the bunches of a uniform length.

To Prepare Cabbage or Cauliflower.—Cut off the roots and remove the outside leaves, then divide the heads into quarters and lay face downward in cold salted water for half an hour before cooking. Salt water is said to induce worms and bugs to come from their hiding places in vegetables and float upon the water.

To Prepare Spinach, Etc.—Cut off the roots and

pick off the dead leaves from spinach, dandelion, and other greens, carefully examine for insects and worms, throw into salted water, let remain for half an hour, then wash each bunch or head singly in a large pan of clean water. Spinach, dandelions, and other greens washed by the handful and crowded together in quantities in the water when washed are usually gritty and unpalatable when cooked.

To Prepare Celery.—Remove the coarse outside stems and pare the root. Divide the stalk into halves—if large into quarters—and trim off all leaves that are not ornamental or edible.

To Prepare Lettuce.—Cut off the root and remove the outside leaves from each head. Then remove the other leaves one by one and place them in cold water. Rinse carefully, lay in a fine wire basket, and swing in a draft of air to dry off, or lay on a coarse towel and shake gently until dry. Keep in a cool place until served. Cress, chicory, sorrel, and all salad leaves should be washed and dried in a similar manner.

To Prepare Cucumbers.—Lay the cucumbers upon ice, or in cold water, until half an hour before serving, then pare and slice upon broken ice. Just before serving drain off the water. Cucumbers should never be soaked in salted water, as salt renders them tough and indigestible.

To Prepare Tomatoes.—Lay the tomatoes, stem end down, in a basin or bowl, and pour boiling water over them until they are completely covered with it. Let stand half a minute, then drain it off, and fill the bowl with cold water. Renew the water several times, if necessary, but do not handle the tomatoes until quite cold. As soon as the tomatoes are cold the skins can be removed quite easily. If the tomatoes are to be used raw lay them upon ice until just before serving, when the skins can be removed and the tomatoes sliced.

To Prepare Bread and Cracker Crumbs.—As different kinds of crumbs are required for different purposes the various methods of preparing them are here given:

Crumbs No. 1.—To prepare crumbs for stuffing meats, poultry, etc., remove the crust from a loaf of stale bread, break the loaf in the middle, and rub the jagged or rough edges against each other until the bread is rubbed into tolerably fine crumbs.

Crumbs No. 2.—Crumbs for scolloping meats, oysters, fish, etc., should be prepared in the same manner as those for stuffing meats and poultry, and should then be rubbed through a coarse sieve.

Crumbs No. 3.—To prepare crumbs that are to be used in frying, take pieces of dry bread, crusts, or crackers, lay upon a molding board, and, with a rolling-pin, crush and roll them into very fine crumbs. Sift before using.

Stuffing for Poultry.—Season to taste with salt and pepper the desired quantity of Crumbs No. 1, and moisten lightly with melted butter. If additional seasoning be desired, minced parsley, celery, or onion may be used.

Stuffing for Veal.—Season to taste with salt and pepper the desired quantity of Crumbs No. 1, or with salt, pepper, and lemon-thyme, or with salt, pepper, and a combination of grated lemon-peel and nutmeg, or ground mace—using half as much nutmeg or mace as lemon-peel, and moisten well with melted butter. Crumbs No. 1 seasoned with salt and pepper and a little sage or sweet marjoram, and moistened with melted butter, may be used for stuffing pork.

Stuffing for Fish.—Use the same seasoning and prepare in the same manner as for veal.

To Remove the Skins from Peaches and Plums.—The skins may be removed from peaches, plums, grapes, and some other fruits, in the same way they are removed from tomatoes, but success depends greatly upon the exact condition of the fruit. And as the skins of all these fruits can frequently be peeled off readily without the aid of boiling water it is always advisable to experiment with a small quantity of the fruit before deciding upon which is the easiest method of removing them.

To Pare Peaches.—Cut the peaches in halves, remove the halves from the pits by twisting or "wringing" them in opposite directions, and pare the halves.

To Prepare Apples.—Begin to pare an apple at the large or stem end, and pare round and round until the other end is reached. When the desired number of apples have been pared, cut them into halves, then into quarters, and then remove the core from each quarter by following with a small knife the natural outline of the core. Large apples of irregular form can be pared more readily after they are divided into quarters. Apples and most other fruits become discolored by exposure to the air, after they are pared, consequently they should not be pared any length of time before they are put to cook; but when they are—as circumstances frequently render it necessary for them to be—they should always be covered with several folds of towel wrung out of cold water.

To Pick Over Berries.—Pour from the basket or box, upon a large white plate, enough berries to cover the surface, then remove all poor berries and dirt from the plate and carefully slip the berries into a dish. Repeat this process until all the berries have been picked over. Berries are so easily bruised and crushed that they should never be piled high in deep bowls until they are ready to be served.

To Hull Strawberries.—Take each berry between the thumb and fingers of the left hand, gather up the hull and stem with the thumb and forefinger of the right hand, and by a gentle twist remove them, leaving the berry unbruised or uninjured in the least.

To Wash Berries.—With rare exceptions, berries, currants, and all small fruit should be washed before they are served. For washing them, use an earthen bowl, larger at the top than at the bottom, and that will hold at least a gallon. Fill the bowl nearly full of cold water. Slip the berries carefully from the plates upon which they were laid when picked over into the water, and with the hands lift and stir them gently, so as to free them of dirt and dust. Pour off the light dirt that rises to the surface of the water, and, with the hands, lift the berries into a flat-bottomed sieve, and let them drain a few minutes. If more than a quart of berries is to be washed, pour those in the sieve into the dish from which they are to be served, and proceed in a similar manner with those remaining unwashed.

To Wash Rice.—Pick over the quantity of rice needed, put it in a bowl, cover with tepid water, lift in the hands and rub the kernels briskly against each other to remove the starch. Rinse in cold water several times, or until the water ceases to look milky, then drain and put at once to cook.

To Wash Oranges and Lemons.—Before oranges and lemons are used they should be well scrubbed with a small, stiff brush, in warm water, then be rinsed in cold water and wiped dry.

MANAGEMENT OF A COAL FIRE.

To start a fresh coal fire in a range, lay in a sufficient quantity of dry kindlings, add a little coal, open the drafts, and light the kindlings. Be careful to have the kindlings burning briskly, and the coal well ignited, before any more coal is added, and also not to let the fire get under too great headway before the dampers are closed. Only a small quantity of coal should be put on at a time, and when it is fairly ignited more should be added, until the requisite degree of heat is obtained. When a steady, continuous heat is wanted for baking, the front damper should be closed, or nearly so, and an occasional sprinkle of fresh coal added to the fire. The fire-box should never be packed so full of coal as to cause the griddles and top of the stove to grow red-hot. When the fire is not wanted for active use in cooking, a little coal should be put on and all the dampers closed. Unless the stove is perfectly air tight, which is seldom the case, it will, when thus closed, burn slowly and reduce the coal to ashes, leaving scarcely any cinders or clinkers; and when fresh coal is put on and the dampers are opened, the fire will be bright and clear and ready for use in a few minutes. It is very important in the management of a coal fire to avoid exposing the live coal to the air, or keeping too strong a draft on the stove. Exposure of burning coal to the air deadens and turns it to cinder in a short time, and when the draft is very strong it causes a greater combustion of fuel than is necessary, carries off heat that should be utilized, and soon fills the stove with clinkers.

PART III.—METHODS OF COOKING.

INTRODUCTION.

AT FIRST glance the methods of cooking seem almost innumerable. But upon careful examination it will be found that there are only four, namely: broiling, baking, boiling, and frying. All other methods are merely nominal, being modifications, variations, or combinations of these four primary methods. It will also be found upon examination that the action going on within the article being cooked is very similar in character, whether the article is being broiled, baked, boiled, or fried. But the flavor and digestibility, as well as the nutritive value of various articles of food are very differently affected by the different methods of cooking.

CHAPTER V.

BROILING.

BROILING is one of the most perfect methods of cooking many articles of food, and may be accomplished quite successfully, without either broiler or gridiron, on a bed of live coals or over a clear blaze. Broiling is the sudden searing and browning of the surface of food; and a steak or chop to be perfectly broiled must have its surface instantly seared or cooked. This instantaneous searing, or surface cooking, hardens the albumen and forms a coating which shuts in the juices of the article being broiled; provided it is turned frequently enough to keep the seared surfaces intact during the process.

Where much broiling is to be done a charcoal burner is very desirable; but the light wire broiler or toaster that opens and closes with hinges and can be held in the hand—of which nearly all shapes and sizes are manufactured—is so convenient and so admirably adapted to the purpose that it is difficult to imagine how any one who understands the elementary principles of cooking, and knows anything about the management of a fire, should care to seek an easier or a better method of broiling for the average family than that afforded by an ordinary range or cook-stove and a wire broiler. With one of these broilers, which can be held in the hand and turned quickly, at pleasure, steaks, chops, poultry, game, fish, oysters—in fact, any article of food that it is advisable to broil—can, when the fire is in proper condition, be broiled over the fire in a common range or cook-stove in about as perfect a manner as it is possible to broil food.

How to Broil.—Have a clear, bright fire in the range. Open the main damper so as to create a good draft and allow the escape of smoke or gas. Remove one of the front griddles and place the article to be broiled in the broiler, and over the open griddle-hole. Turn the broiler frequently to keep the meat from burning, to prevent the juice from being forced through its seared surfaces by the heat, and to allow it to cook evenly on both sides. If the drippings from the fat of the meat create a blaze, withdraw the broiler an instant until the blaze subsides. A deep cover laid over the meat will retain the heat and facilitate the broiling. When the fire becomes dull—if coal is used—add a sprinkle of fresh coal, replace the griddle, and use the other end of the stove, which, having been protected from the air, will be clear and bright. Where but one griddle is removed at a time a portion of the fire can be kept always in good condition, and by adopting this method broiling can be carried on continuously as long as desired. When a wood fire is used for broiling, the wood must be kept blazing brightly, or the coals glowing vigorously, all the time. If the wood is dry and sufficiently fine, and is kept burning briskly, almost any article of food can be broiled over it very perfectly, and without being either burned or smoked. Gas, either natural or artificial, when rightly managed, makes an excellent broiling fire.

To Broil a Steak.—Trim neatly by removing with a sharp knife the outer skin and superfluous fat. Fill the broiler compactly, after greasing it, adjusting the meat to the size of the griddle-hole of the stove. Hold close down to the coals or blaze an instant until the under surface of the meat is seared. Turn and sear the other side in a similar manner. Then, by frequent turnings, allow the inside to cook gradually, and the outside to brown nicely without becoming hardened. The intense heat applied to the under surface of meat in broiling drives the juices toward the opposite surface, and unless the broiler is turned frequently enough to keep both surfaces well seared the juices will be forced out and the meat rendered dry, tough, and innutritious.

Some like steak rare, others well done, and tastes differ so widely that the exact time necessary for broiling a steak cannot be given. A steak an inch thick will cook rare in eight minutes, medium in ten minutes, and well done in twelve minutes, and during the process of cooking the broiler should be turned at least twenty times. A thinner steak requires a shorter, and a thicker steak a longer time to broil. One can determine the condition of a steak pretty correctly in this manner: Press upon it with the point of a spoon or a dull knife blade. If the resistance to the pressure is firm the steak is uncooked. If the resistance is slight the steak is rare. If there is no resistance it is well done. When a steak is sufficiently cooked it should be served at once. The usual method of serving a steak is to lay it on a warm platter upon which has been placed a small quantity of butter, salt, and pepper; but it is quite customary to serve a steak without seasoning, thus permitting the eater to season according to inclination.

A popular cook-book, after giving some sensible directions for broiling a steak, adds, "It should when broiled be well seasoned, placed on a piping hot platter, and another hot platter placed over it and left there for ten minutes to draw out a nice, rich gravy." In its proper place "a nice, rich gravy" is undoubtedly a good thing, but most people consider it superfluous with a tender, juicy, perfectly broiled steak; and especially so when it is manufactured of juices drawn, expressly for that purpose, from the steak. A broiled steak should never be placed upon "a piping hot platter," lest it get overcooked and have the juices drawn out; but as soon as broiled it should be put upon a warm plate or platter and kept at a moderate, even temperature. So treated it will remain for ten or fifteen minutes in nearly as perfect condition as when removed from the broiler.

Fresh meats should not be seasoned before they are put to broil, or while broiling; neither should the surface be cut or broken during the process of broiling. The juices are extracted and the meat rendered dry and tasteless by such practices.

To Broil Chops.—Mutton chops should have most of the fat removed from them and should be trimmed neatly, and broiled and served like beefsteak. A mutton chop should be at least an inch thick.

Lamb chops should be trimmed, broiled, and served like mutton chops. As the fat of lamb is more delicate than the fat of mutton, a larger quantity of fat should be left on a lamb than on a mutton chop. Lamb chops are frequently served on thin slices of dry toast.

Veal and pork chops may be broiled, like mutton or lamb chops, but the best method of cooking is to sauté or braise them.

To Broil Sweetbreads.—If the sweetbreads are young soak them an hour in cold salted water, then cut in slices and broil over the fire, in a wire broiler. If they are old and tough, place them in boiling water, cook until tender—from half an hour to two hours, according to age—remove from the fire, place in cold water to harden, and, when perfectly cold, wipe dry, slice, and broil.

To Broil Tripe.—Dry the pieces of tripe on a towel, brush them on both sides with melted butter, to induce rapid browning, lay on a wire broiler, place over the fire, and turn two or three times, or until nicely browned and perfectly heated all through. Baste with butter and serve on a warm platter. Tripe should always be boiled or stewed before it is broiled.

To Broil Liver.—Dust the slices of prepared liver with flour, dip in melted butter, place in the broiler, and broil and serve like beefsteak.

To Broil a Chicken.—Lay the prepared chicken on a towel, flatten with a rolling-pin, put in a wire broiler, place over the fire inside down, and let it remain in that position until well seared, then turn the broiler over, sear the skin side, and so turn and sear alternately until thoroughly broiled. Lift to a warm platter, season, and serve.

A small, young chicken—and no other should be

cooked in this manner—will broil over a brisk fire in from fifteen to twenty minutes; but unless the fire is bright and in good condition the chicken will be imperfectly cooked, and as a consequence will be stringy and comparatively tasteless.

To Broil Prairie Chicken.—Both prairie chicken and grouse can be broiled in the same manner as chicken.

To Broil a Quail.—Have ready some melted butter in a heated platter. Dip the prepared quail in the butter. Drain and lay in the broiler over bright coals. Remove occasionally and dip in, or baste with, the butter. As soon as the bird is an even brown all over, take it from the broiler, add a sprinkle of salt and pepper to the butter left from basting, and pour the mixture over the bird. This makes a dainty dish for an invalid.

If a number of quails are to be broiled, plunge them for half a minute into fat or oil at frying temperature, drain, place in a broiler, and broil over a bright fire. The quail is such a dry-meated bird that none of its juices should be lost in cooking; and as this hot oil bath shuts them in very effectually it is quite a desirable accessory in broiling quail.

To Broil a Fish.—Place the prepared fish in a wire broiler, put it over a brisk fire, skin side up, and when the inside is well seared turn the broiler over and sear the skin side. After both sides have been seared, continue turning the broiler as frequently as necessary, thus searing the two sides alternately, until the fish is thoroughly cooked.

To Broil Oysters.—Roll the oysters in fine bread crumbs, dip in melted butter, lay in a wire broiler, and cook quickly over a brisk fire, turning the broiler as often as necessary.

To Broil Ham.—Cut the slices of ham rather thin, place them in a wire broiler, and broil over a quick fire, turning frequently, till both sides are nicely browned.

To Broil Tomatoes.—Select tomatoes not over ripe, wash, wipe, and slice in thick slices. Season with salt, sugar, and pepper, roll in fine bread crumbs, or in flour, dip in melted butter, and broil in a wire broiler over a clear fire.

To Toast Bread.—When a slice of bread is placed near a clear fire it gradually browns or toasts. The same method of cooking that is termed broiling when applied to meats is termed toasting when applied to bread. Broiling must therefore be varied somewhat in its application to different articles. The heat applied to a steak when first put to broil cannot be too intense, for the best results are obtained when the surface is seared or cooked instantly. But in toasting or broiling bread this is not the case. The application of heat to the slice of bread in order to toast it properly should be gradual, as the object is not to shut in the moisture which the bread contains but to drive it out, and gradually dry and brown the surface of the bread. Bread is toasted to divest it of moisture, as well as to brown and give it a peculiar flavor. Toasting converts the insoluble starch in bread into a soluble substance called dextrine, which after being moistened by the saliva is easily digested. For this reason bread properly toasted agrees better with weak stomachs than any other kind of bread. But if the slices are thick and are carelessly held before **or**

over a very hot fire, the outside becomes quickly browned and toughened, the moisture is driven in, instead of being evaporated, and the toast is rendered clammy and indigestible. To make good toast it is necessary to observe these directions: Cut the bread in even slices about half an inch in thickness. Slightly dry them in the oven, or before the fire. Put each slice on a toasting fork, or in a wire broiler, and hold it before or over a clear bright fire of coals, but at a sufficient distance from them to allow it to brown evenly without burning. When the surface of one side becomes a rich golden color, turn and toast the other side in a similar manner. Serve in a toast rack, or on a warm plate. Be careful not to pile the slices on each other, or they will lose their crispness and flavor.

Toast of good quality can be made only from sweet, light, well-baked bread; and no amount of toasting will convert inferior bread, or bread that is sour, heavy, and half-baked, into toast that is digestible or fit to be eaten.

GRIDDLE BROILING.

It goes without saying that a griddle cannot supersede or fill the place of a broiler. But when the fire is not in proper condition for a broiler to be used advantageously, a hot griddle can be made to serve as a very acceptable substitute. And steaks, chops, etc., cooked on a hot griddle—if properly done—are just as much broiled as if they had been cooked in a broiler over hot coals. For the outer surfaces can be seared as thoroughly, and the juices retained as perfectly, by the latter as by the former method. Food broiled on a griddle differs somewhat in flavor from food broiled on a gridiron or broiler; but when one has to choose between the use of a wire broiler over a slow fire, and the use of a hot griddle over a quick fire, there should be no hesitancy about deciding in favor of using the griddle.

To Broil Steak or Chops on a Griddle.—Use a cast-iron or steel griddle. Have it smoking hot. Lay upon it the steak or chops to be cooked, and press the meat close to the griddle. When the side next the griddle is brown, turn and let the other side brown, and so turn and let brown as often as is necessary to keep the surface seared and the juices within the meat. If left too long upon the same side the heat of the griddle will force the juices through the upper surface of the meat, but if the article being cooked is turned frequently enough the juices may be retained within, as perfectly as when the broiling is done in a broiler over the coals.

For broiling steak or chops on a griddle most successfully it is better to have them only of medium thickness, and it may frequently be desirable to remove the bone before placing upon the griddle. It is certainly always best to do so when the bone projects enough to prevent the surface of the meat adhering to the griddle. A thick steak, after both sides have been seared on the griddle, may without removal therefrom be thoroughly cooked by being put into a very hot oven for eight or ten minutes. If the broiling has been skilfully done, when the steak or chop is lifted to the platter a small piece of butter can be put on the griddle, which should stand in a cool place, and with a spoon or knife the brown juices of the meat that adhere thereto can be removed, mingled with the melted butter, and poured over the steak or chop.

To Broil Oysters on a Griddle.—Drain the oysters in a colander or sieve, dip each oyster in melted butter that has been clarified, and lay upon a plate for convenient handling. Have a griddle clean, smoking hot, and perfectly dry. Fill it quickly with the drained oysters, laying them closely together upon it. By the time the griddle is filled, if the fire is sufficiently hot, the oysters first laid upon it will be browned and broiled. With a limber knife and a fork turn the oysters upon the griddle, in the order in which they were laid upon it. As soon as they are turned begin removing those first put upon the griddle, and so proceed until they are all lifted upon a warm platter on which salt, pepper, and butter have been placed. Or they can be laid upon thin slices of toast and seasoned with salt, pepper, and melted butter.

OVEN BROILING.

Experiments prove that many articles of food can be broiled perfectly in the oven of an ordinary range, by the application of hot air. And although there are many that cannot be so broiled, notably all meats with cut surfaces, no reason exists why the things that can be broiled better and more conveniently in an oven than over coals should not be so broiled, and this method of cooking be known as oven broiling—which it actually is—rather than baking or roasting.

The temperature of an oven for successful broiling

should be at least five hundred degrees—considerably higher than for baking bread or roasting meats—and should remain so until the article to be broiled has begun to brown nicely, when the heat can be lessened and the cooking finished at a lower temperature.

To Broil a Chicken in the Oven.—After the chicken has been split down the back and properly prepared, lay it inside down upon a meat-board and press the joints and breast-bone close to the board with a rolling-pin—crushing them down until the chicken is quite flat—then wipe off all moisture with a dry towel, and lay the flattened chicken inside down upon a smoking hot roasting pan. Put a weight upon it to keep it pressed close to the pan until well seared and lightly browned. After the searing and browning have been accomplished remove the weight, and put the chicken, without taking it from the pan, into a very hot oven. Place it on the upper grate so the greatest heat may be from above. Close the oven door and leave the chicken undisturbed for twenty minutes. At the end of that time it will be evenly browned on the outside, and, if young and not large, will be perfectly cooked all through. If full grown or very large it will have to be cooked from forty to sixty minutes. When cooked, lay upon a platter, season with salt, pepper, and melted butter, and serve.

To Broil Quail in the Oven.—Plunge the prepared birds in deep fat at frying temperature for half a minute, then place them as close together as possible on a roasting pan, and put them in a very hot oven for fifteen minutes, or until nicely browned all over. Or dip them in melted butter, instead of immersing in hot fat, lay in the roasting pan, put in the oven, and broil.

Small birds of any kind may be broiled in the same manner as quail, and served on thin slices of either dry or buttered toast.

To Broil a Rabbit in the Oven.—Spread the prepared rabbit open, flatten with a rolling-pin or mallet, lay inside down in a roasting pan, and broil in a hot oven like a chicken. When the rabbit is thoroughly cooked pour into the roasting pan two or three tablespoonfuls of hot water, add two of melted butter and one of minced parsley, let simmer a few minutes, season to taste with pepper and salt, pour over the rabbit, and serve.

To Broil a Squirrel in the Oven.—A squirrel may be prepared, cooked, and served in the same manner as a rabbit. The flavor of parsley is so admirably adapted to that of rabbit or squirrel that it can always be appropriately used with either.

To Broil a Fish in the Oven.—Open the fish down the front, lay it, skin side down, on a fish rack, or on oiled paper, in a roasting pan, season with salt, pepper, and melted butter, and dust with flour. Put to cook on the upper grate of a hot oven, and, when nicely browned, place on a warm platter, season with plain or parsley butter, and serve. A fish weighing three or four pounds will broil in an oven at the right temperature in about half an hour, and one of larger size in a proportionately greater length of time.

CHAPTER VI.

BAKING.

ROASTING used to be done before an open fire, and before the invention of cook-stoves and ranges was a very important branch of the culinary art. The operation was performed by placing the fish, fowl, or piece of meat to be roasted before an open fire, at the proper distance therefrom, on what was called a "spit," which was turned frequently while the article being roasted was vigorously basted with water or gravy, to keep it from burning. To our ancestors who roasted in this manner, and baked in a clay or brick oven, built especially for the purpose, or, as was generally the case, baked in an iron bake kettle, or "Dutch oven," by placing coals beneath it and coals on the lid, the words roasting and baking had different meanings.

In her book on "Practical Cookery" Mrs. Henderson says: "Beef, mutton, turkeys, ducks, or birds, in fact, every kind of meat, is tenfold better roasted than baked," and old people who were in early life accustomed to the open-fire method of roasting, stoutly contend that all articles so cooked are far tenderer, juicier, and sweeter than those cooked in the closed oven of a stove or range. But since there is no probability of the practical cook-stove and range of the present day being discarded for the poetic brick oven and open fireplace of the past, it is useless to advance arguments either for or against the old-time methods of roasting and baking. The cook-stove and range have come to stay, and roasting and baking are processes so similar nowadays that the distinction between the two processes is, for practical purposes, a "distinction without a difference." Moreover, people have got so in the habit of using the terms baking and roasting indiscriminately when speaking of the cooking of fish, fowl, meats, vegetables, fruit, etc., in ovens of stoves and ranges, that no misapprehension arises from such use of the words; and, as there is essentially no difference in the results, it matters very little whether we call this process of cooking food in the oven roasting or baking.

It is quite as important to know how to bake properly as it is to know how to prepare properly, or make ready for baking, the different articles of food that must undergo the process of baking in their preparation for the table; and the anticipated results that should legitimately follow the careful mixing and seasoning of dishes are often defeated by ignorant or careless baking. Many a good thing is spoiled in the oven, and probably as much food is ruined by being improperly baked as by being improperly prepared.

To become skilful in baking one must know the temperature required for baking different articles of food, and also the method of applying the heat. For example: the temperature for baking bread should be at least 375 degrees; for roasting beef, lamb, mutton, veal, and other meats that have had their cut surfaces seared, it should be about the same; for roasting poultry and meats that have not had their cut surfaces previously seared it should be 50 or 75 degrees higher; while for broiling chickens, etc., it should be at least 150, probably 200, degrees higher than for bread. And as an oven thermometer is readily obtainable, which, when set in the door of a cook-stove or range, indicates on the outside the temperature of the inside of the oven, it ought to be an easy matter for any one to become an expert in the use of an oven.

It is generally supposed that the temperature should be higher for roasting meats than for baking bread, but such is not the fact, unless the meat has not previously had its cut surfaces seared; and in such case an extreme temperature should be maintained only long enough to sear properly the cut surfaces of the roast. When a joint of meat has been properly seared its juices will be richer and its flavor much finer if it is roasted in an oven of the right temperature, than if it is roasted in an oven with the temperature either too high or too low. Bread, rolls, biscuit, and pastry require a higher temperature than cake, buns, and other delicate preparations of dough. Cake baked in thin layers and known as "layer cake" will bear almost as much heat as buns, but loaf cake requires a considerably lower temperature, until it has fully risen. The more delicate the cake the less heat it will bear. White sponge cake or angel food requires less heat than any other kind of cake, and less, perhaps, than anything that is baked, except omelet soufflé and kisses.

Some articles, for perfect baking, require greater heat at the top than at the bottom, some require greater heat at the bottom than at the top, while others require a uniform heat at the top, sides, and bottom. For roasting meats, poultry, fish, bread, etc., the best position is in the middle of the oven where the heat is uniform. For broiling, chicken, fish, etc., should be placed upon the upper grate so as to have sufficient heat to broil and brown them. But for bread, cake, puff paste, and such articles as are expected to grow light and puff after being put in the oven, the greatest heat should be at the bottom.

When a thermometer is not used this is a reliable method of ascertaining the temperature of an oven: Put a spoonful of flour on a piece of paper, slip it in the oven, close the door, and if the flour browns nicely and evenly in two minutes, the temperature is about right for bread, and can, after a little practice, be graded to suit other articles of food quite accurately.

To Roast Beef.—Place the clean cut side of the meat upon a smoking hot pan. Press it close to the pan until seared and slightly brown. Reverse it and let the opposite side become similarly seared and brown, then put it at once into the oven, the heat of which should be the same as for bread, and leave it undisturbed till cooked. If the oven is not too hot the meat will require no basting. When the temperature of the oven is correct and the cooking is going on properly the meat will keep up a gentle sputtering in the pan; but if, upon opening the oven door, this sputtering is not distinctly audible more heat is required, and the temperature of the oven should be increased. If, however, smoke should be discernible in the oven the heat is too intense and should be lessened, as the drippings in the pan will not brown and smoke unless the heat of the oven is too great.

For roasting beef in this manner, after it has been seared, fifteen minutes should be allowed for each inch in thickness the roast may be, without regard to its width or weight. A roast of beef that is three inches in thickness will cook rare in three quarters of an hour, a roast that is six inches in thickness will cook rare in an hour and a half, and so on in about the same ratio with different sized roasts. If a roast is desired medium or well cooked, additional time must be allowed, and it can thus be cooked to suit any taste. A roast that will require more than an hour to cook should be placed upon a rack or rest in the pan after it has been seared, as there will then be no danger of its becoming grease-soaked or burned, and when half done it should be turned over on the rack that both sides may be roasted alike. After the roast has been removed from the pan, if the greater portion of the drippings is carefully poured off, a delicious gravy can be made from the brown jelly or glaze adhering to the bottom of the pan.

In a little cook-book entitled "Just How" the author, Mrs. Whitney, says:

"In roasting meat do not put it at first in a very hot oven, but have a good fire growing hotter that will make the heat brisk and sustain it after the meat is heated through. Let it heat gradually, and yield some portion of the juice for gravy, before you seal up the surface by browning. A joint of meat after being well washed and trimmed should be rubbed evenly with fine salt before being put to roast. Put in at first a pint of water with a teaspoonful of salt for the basting. If you follow this method carefully there will be no trouble with the gravy."

It is to be hoped not. But how about the meat? The method of roasting recommended by Mrs. Whitney is in all probability an excellent one for producing good gravy, and if the production of gravy was the object in view might pass unchallenged as a model method for making it. But is it altogether just to the roast to sacrifice it for the sake of the gravy, when good gravy material is so easily obtained from odds and ends and tough pieces of meat? And is it not a little unfair to scientific cookery to call such a method of cooking meat roasting?

For roasting meats the method adopted should be the one that preserves the juices within the meat in the most perfect manner, thus rendering it sweet, juicy, and tender. Salt and water have a tendency to extract the juices of meat and toughen it, and basting is a troublesome, as well as a damaging, process. Why, then, should beef and mutton and lamb and such meats as are injured by salting and basting have the delicate flavor, and much of the nutrition, tortured out of them by being subjected to the operation? Searing almost instantly coats the cut sides of a piece of meat, and prevents the escape of the juices in the process of roasting, while a firm, steady heat gently but thoroughly cooks it, thus preserving both juices and flavor.

To Roast Mutton.—A saddle or joint of mutton should be prepared by carefully removing the outer skin, searing the cut surfaces, and roasting in the same manner that beef is roasted. Mutton requires a longer time than beef to roast. Currant or other acid jelly should be served with roast mutton.

To Roast Lamb.—Prepare and roast the same as mutton. Serve with either jelly or mint sauce.

To Roast a Leg of Lamb or Mutton.—Remove the outer skin carefully and sear the cut end. Roast lamb an hour and a quarter, mutton an hour and three quarters. A leg of lamb or mutton, because it is less fat and more juicy, is preferred by many to the loin.

Venison should be roasted like mutton and served with jelly.

To Roast Veal.—Veal is a meat that lacks flavor and richness, and is greatly improved by seasoning with salt, sugar, and pepper before it is cooked. Veal will bear more salt than beef, mutton, or poultry, and about half as much sugar as salt should be used in seasoning it. Shake the sugar from a dredging box directly upon the meat, then add the salt and pepper. If it is to be stuffed, prepare a stuffing as directed on page 27 and fill all available spaces with it. Make pockets under the skin and fill them with it, or pack it upon the inside of the roast, roll up tightly, pin with skewers, tie securely with twine, place upon a rack in the roasting pan, and put in the oven. As soon as it is a light brown color baste with a thin gravy, and renew the operation every fifteen minutes until the roast is thoroughly cooked. It requires fully twice as long a time to roast veal as it does to roast beef or mutton, and as the frequent bastings keep it from becoming hardened, a piece of veal weighing not more than three or four pounds can be roasted with advantage two or two and a half hours.

To Roast Fresh Pork.—Season, like veal, with salt, sugar, and pepper. A little powdered sage may also be added, if liked. Roast the same as veal and baste, every fifteen minutes after the pork has begun to brown, with hot water seasoned with salt and pepper. Pork requires very thorough cooking to render it wholesome or palatable, and should be roasted a greater length of time even than veal.

To Roast a Leg of Young Pork.—Remove the bone, fill the cavity with highly seasoned bread crumbs, prepared as for veal, with the addition of a little powdered sage, if liked, and roast as directed for pork.

Roast Turkey.—"With much experience in hotel life," writes Mrs. Henderson in a book on cookery, "I have never seen a piece of turkey on a hotel table that was fit to eat. Besides being tasteless they are almost invariably under-cooked. A small turkey of seven or eight pounds should be roasted or baked three hours at least. A very large turkey should not be cooked a minute less than four hours—an extra hour is preferable to a minute less." Mrs. Henderson, who generally writes intelligently on culinary subjects, has suffered so acutely in her hotel experiences in being forced to eat under-done turkey that she inclines a little to the other extreme, and by strictly following her directions one can scarcely fail to have over-cooked turkey. If the heat of the oven is as great as the turkey, with frequent bastings, will bear, without becoming too brown, and is kept firm and steady, a seven-pound turkey will cook just right in two hours; and with the oven at the proper temperature, twenty minutes to the pound is as much cooking as any turkey will bear. Turkey, when properly roasted, is juicy, tender, and high-flavored; when over-done it is dry and tasteless; but when under-done it is nauseating and unfit to be eaten.

To Roast a Turkey.—Place the turkey, after it has been properly cleaned, in a large bowl, tail downward, put the prepared crumbs, for which see page 27, in at the neck until the breast becomes plump, then draw the skin together, and fasten over on the back. Reverse the position of the turkey in the bowl, put the remaining crumbs in the body, at the opening through which the entrails were removed, and sew it up with strong thread. Press the wings and legs as close to the body as possible, and secure them firmly in position with strings or skewers. Lay the turkey, breast downward, on a rack in the roasting pan, and let it remain in that position until the back is a light brown color, then turn it over, and let the breast and sides brown in a similar manner. Do not put any water in the pan during this process. When the entire turkey is nicely browned begin basting with a thin gravy. As this basting gravy evaporates, add a little boiling water to keep it from burning in the pan, and baste as often as the skin of the turkey becomes dry, until the roasting is completed.

To Roast a Chicken.—The method of preparing and roasting a chicken is the same as for preparing and roasting a turkey. The time required for roasting a chicken varies, according to its size and age. But an hour and a half is sufficient time to allow for a large, full-grown chicken not over a year old. Fowls more than a year old should be steamed a longer or shorter time, according to age, before being roasted, or they will be tough and dry. But boiling and stewing are such admirable methods of cooking tough fowls that it is advisable never to roast a chicken unless it is young and tender.

To Roast Wild Duck.—After wild ducks have been prepared for roasting, rub them inside with salt and pepper, put in each duck a small piece of butter and a little currant or cranberry jelly, and roast twenty-five or thirty minutes; or fill them with bread moistened with currant or cranberry juice and seasoned with salt, pepper, and butter. A wild duck that has a fishy flavor will be improved by parboiling, before roasting, in water with a medium-sized onion.

To Roast Quails.—Stuff, place on their backs close together in a roasting pan, and put in a very hot oven. As soon as they are nicely browned, baste with mushroom, celery, or some simple sauce. Quail will roast in about thirty minutes.

To Roast Sweetbreads.—Sweetbreads, after they have been soaked in salt water and properly trimmed, should be rolled in flour, then in melted butter, placed close together in a roasting pan, put in a hot oven, and, when brown, basted with any sauce preferred.

To Bake a Heart and Liver.—Soak the liver an hour in cold water that has been well salted. Boil the heart in salted water until tender. Then put them in the baking pan together, and dredge with flour. Add a spoonful of butter and a sprinkle of pepper to the water in which the heart boiled, and pour into the pan with the heart and liver. Baste frequently and bake an hour.

A calf or beef tongue can be boiled and baked in the same manner as a heart. The skin must be removed from the tongue when boiled, before it is prepared for baking.

To Bake a Fish.—Fill the fish lightly with stuffing prepared as directed on page 28, and truss it in this manner: Make a large knot on the end of a strong piece of twine, or tie the end of the twine around a short wire skewer. With a trussing needle draw the twine through the fish, close to the head, then slightly below the middle, and again close to the tail. Draw the cord or twine tight enough to hold the fish in a position resembling the letter S, and fasten it. Place the fish on its belly in a roasting pan and bake until cooked and nicely browned, basting occasionally while it is baking with hot water and butter, or with a thin gravy, if preferred. When cooked, remove the cord and serve the fish in the same curved position in which it was baked, on a warm platter, garnished with parsley, cress, or celery; or bake, without stuffing, in this manner: Make gashes across the fish, on each side, about two inches apart. Put slices of salt pork or breakfast bacon in the baking pan, and lay the fish on them. Cover the gashes on the upper side in a similar manner with slices of pork or bacon, then set in the oven, and close the door until the fish is cooked. If the oven is at the proper temperature the fish will require no attention until ready to serve. The length of time required to bake a fish depends upon its size, but when sufficiently cooked the flesh will flake and separate easily. A medium-sized fish will roast in three quarters of an hour. A quick heat is necessary to develop the finest flavors of fish; and to bake a fish properly it should be given all the heat it will bear without burning.

To Scollop Oysters.—Drain a quart of oysters. To a pint of Bread Crumbs No. 2 add salt and pepper sufficient to season the oysters properly. Mix the seasoning uniformly through the crumbs with a fork. Then enrich them by sprinkling through, and mixing with them, half a cup of melted butter. Take a fire-proof dish or baking pan not more than two inches deep, in which to cook the oysters. Scatter a thin layer of the seasoned crumbs over the bottom of the dish. Cover the crumbs with oysters, laying the oysters close together, but not overlapping each other. Sprinkle with the crumbs until nearly hidden from view, then add another layer of oysters and again sprinkle with crumbs. The top layer of crumbs should be heavier than either of the other layers—should contain fully one half the quantity of crumbs used—and but two layers of oysters should be put in the dish. Do not pour oyster juice, water, or liquid of any kind over the oysters after they are put in the dish. Bake in an oven, at the same temperature as for beef, for fifteen or twenty minutes, or until the crumbs on top are a rich chestnut brown. Remove from the oven as soon as cooked and serve at once, and the oysters will be plump, juicy, hot to the center, and surrounded by a delicious, moist coating of crumbs.

To Scollop Oysters, No. 2.—Drain a quart of oysters.

Scald and skim the juice drained from them. Butter a baking dish and lay three or four thin slices of buttered toast upon the bottom of the dish. Put half the oysters upon the toast. Cover them with thin slices of buttered toast, and put the balance of the oysters upon the toast. Add hot, sweet cream to the liquor drained from the oysters until there is a pint in all, then season to taste with salt and pepper, and pour it over the oysters in the dish. Bake fifteen or twenty minutes in an oven at the temperature for roasting meats. Serve at once.

If oysters are cooked a long time in a deep mass the juices are drawn from them, and they become tough and indigestible; and if cracker crumbs are used in scolloping oysters they give the oysters a peculiar, unpleasant flavor.

To Bake Potatoes.—The potato furnishes an excellent illustration of right and wrong methods of baking. There is, of course, but one right method of baking potatoes; but they are baked by three different methods, and it is only by accident, and not oftener than once in ten times that the average cook in baking potatoes pursues the proper method. Following one method, the potato is placed in a very hot oven, and before it is half cooked a thick crust is formed which is sure to be charred and burned by the time the potato is thoroughly baked. Following another method, the potato is placed in an oven at a low temperature and the oven is allowed to remain at the same temperature until the baking is completed, in which case the result is a soft, flabby, limp production devoid of character and almost flavorless. Following another method, which is the correct one, the potato is placed in an oven of moderate temperature and subjected to a gradually increasing heat, until the inside is thoroughly cooked, the skin has assumed a light brown color and a firm consistency, and the atmosphere is filled with the delicious aroma of a perfectly baked potato.

An excellent method of baking potatoes, and one that will be found convenient when it is necessary to bake them in less time than is required to do it in the oven, is this: Put the potatoes into boiling water and let them boil rapidly for ten or fifteen minutes, then bake in a hot oven until they are well cooked and have a rich brown skin. Parboiling potatoes in this manner heats them all through so quickly and thoroughly that the time required to bake them afterward is reduced at least one half. When baked potatoes are taken from the oven a gash about an inch in length should be made lengthwise in each potato, and the ends should then be pressed, to widen the gash and permit the steam to escape. Baked potatoes should be served in a deep dish or tureen, lined with a napkin that can be lightly folded over so as to protect them from the cold air. Served in this manner they will remain hot and mealy for a considerable length of time.

To Bake Sweet Potatoes.—Sweet potatoes may be baked like white potatoes; or they may be cooked in this manner: Boil in a liberal quantity of water until they can be easily punctured with a fork, then drain, remove the skin, divide into halves lengthwise, dust with salt and sugar, roll in melted butter, place in a dripping pan, and bake in a hot oven until a rich brown crust is formed. After sweet potatoes have been parboiled and peeled they may be put in the roasting pan with turkey, chicken, beef, veal, or other meats, and thus baked. White potatoes can be treated in a similar manner. Sweet potatoes are improved in flavor by being very thoroughly cooked.

To Bake Tomatoes.—Select perfect tomatoes of medium size, wash, wipe, and place together, with the stem side down, in a shallow earthen or porcelain-lined baking dish that has been well greased with butter. Bake in a hot oven an hour, or until the skins are brown and the tomatoes cooked all through. Serve with salt, pepper, butter, and a sprinkle of sugar, if liked.

Or wash and wipe medium-sized tomatoes, cut them in halves, and place, skin side down, in a baking dish. Then season with salt, pepper, and sugar, if liked, cover with prepared Bread Crumbs No. 2, and bake until the crumbs are nicely browned and the tomatoes well cooked.

Another method of baking tomatoes is to lay the tomatoes, after they have been peeled, in a buttered baking dish, season with salt, pepper, and sugar, baste with melted butter, and bake till nicely browned.

Still another method is to cover the bottom of a buttered baking dish with prepared bread crumbs, fill with tomatoes that have been peeled and sliced, sprinkle a layer of bread crumbs on the tomatoes, and bake.

A little finely minced onion—about a tablespoonful to each quart of tomatoes—may be added to tomatoes that are to be baked, either by sprinkling on the bottom or top of the dish.

To Bake Onions.—Peel the onions, put them in a buttered baking dish, season with salt and pepper, and baste with butter. Then cover the dish and bake until the onions are tender. Serve in this condition; or remove the cover and let the surface of the onions brown before serving. Or the butter may be omitted, and as soon as the onions are tender a tablespoonful of cream for each onion may be added, and the cooking continued for ten or fifteen minutes longer.

Another method of baking onions is to peel, boil in salted water ten minutes, drain, put in a buttered baking pan, season with salt and pepper, add a little butter and milk, and cook slowly until done; or omit the butter and milk, and add a tablespoonful of soup stock for each onion.

To Bake Squash, No. 1.—Select a solid Hubbard, or other good squash. Wash, wipe, and cut in pieces a suitable size for serving. Lay the pieces close together, skin side down, in a shallow baking pan, and bake in a moderate oven an hour, or until thoroughly cooked.

To Bake Squash, No. 2.—Pare and cut in pieces, put in a crock, cover closely, and bake two hours, then mash smooth, and season to taste with salt, pepper, and butter.

To Bake Corn, No. 1.—Turn back the husk on each ear of corn and carefully remove the silk, then replace the husk and tie at the small end. Lay the ears thus prepared in a baking pan and bake in a hot oven half an hour, or until thoroughly cooked.

To Bake Corn, No. 2.—Cut the corn from the cob, and scrape off the milk and eyes of the grains. To each pint of corn thus prepared add a quarter of a pint of sweet cream, milk, or water, season to taste with salt, pepper, and butter, pour into a buttered pudding dish, and bake half an hour, or until cooked.

To Bake Beans.—Soak a quart of white beans in cold water over night, or for eight or ten hours, then drain and put to cook in sufficient cold water to cover them. Add a teaspoonful of salt and half a teaspoonful of soda, and as soon as the water boils drain it off. Put in the pot in which the beans are to be baked half a pound of salt pork or corned beef and a tablespoonful of white sugar, or twice as much New Orleans molasses. Pour in the beans, fill the pot to within an inch of the top with boiling water, cover with a close-fitting lid, and bake in a very moderate oven from twelve to eighteen hours. As the water evaporates replace it with sufficient boiling water to keep the beans covered during the entire time they are in the oven. If the beans are liked browned they can be poured into a shallow baking pan and put in a hot oven until they are the color desired.

To Bake Apples, No. 1.—Select apples of a uniform size, remove the center of the blossom end and specks that may be in the fruit, wash and rinse in clean water, place, stems upward, in an earthen or granite-ware baking dish, pierce in several places with a fork, and put in an oven at the temperature required for bread. When perfectly baked the skins will be brown, and the flesh soft and rich in flavor.

To Bake Apples, No. 2.—Pare and core the apples, leaving them whole, rinse in cold water, and place close together in a baking dish, the bottom of which has been well greased with butter and lightly sprinkled with granulated sugar. Sprinkle sugar over the apples and bake in a hot oven until they are a rich brown color. Unless the apples are very tart and juicy they should, when put to bake, be covered for about ten minutes. Apples baked in this manner are delicious served with the meat course at dinner. If they are to be served with cream for dessert, a little water and more sugar may be added when put to bake, and they may also be flavored with orange, lemon, or other fruit flavoring. But if the seeds are removed from the cores and put in the baking dish with the apples they will give them a finer flavor than any foreign flavoring substance that can be added.

Sweet apples may be baked in the same manner as sour apples, but when pared, they should be basted with thin syrup, or with New Orleans molasses and water mixed in equal proportions.

Pears are baked in all respects like apples.

To Bake Bananas.—Peel the bananas, roll in melted butter and granulated sugar, lay a little distance apart in a roasting pan, and brown in a hot oven. Shake the pan occasionally while the bananas are baking.

To Bake Almonds.—To blanch or skin almonds pour hot water over them and let them remain in the water until the skins can be slipped off readily. After they are blanched mix a teaspoonful of olive oil or melted butter with each quart of almonds, put them in a roasting pan, and cook till a light brown, in an oven of the temperature required for bread. Dust with fine salt as soon as taken from the oven.

To Bake Rice Pudding.—Stir together one cup of rice, one cup of granulated sugar, nine cups of cold, sweet milk, and salt to taste. Pour into a baking dish and put in an oven, the temperature of which is so low that it will require about half an hour to bring the mixture to boiling heat. As soon as the surface of the milk thickens and becomes wrinkled it should be stirred well, and every time the scum forms the stirring should be repeated, until the rice is tender. As soon as the rice is tender the stirring should cease, but the heat of the oven should be increased until the surface of the pudding assumes a light brown color. It is then sufficiently baked and should be removed from the oven. If easier or more convenient, the pudding may be cooked on the top of the range where the heat is gentle, until it is ready to bake and brown in the oven. This slow, gradual cooking condenses the milk and swells and cooks the rice, thus giving without the addition of cream, butter, or eggs, a rich pudding that is finer in flavor and more digestible because of the absence of these ingredients.

To Bake Custards.—Custards and all soufflé puddings—puddings composed largely of eggs—should be baked at a low, uniform temperature. For this reason it is advisable to bake by setting the dish containing the custard or pudding in a pan of hot water, in the oven. A custard pudding is cooked sufficiently as soon as it becomes stiffened at the center, and when it reaches that condition should be immediately removed from the oven. If allowed to remain longer the eggs harden, whey appears, and the delicacy of the pudding is destroyed.

CHAPTER VII.

BOILING.

THE chimney-bar, and the crane on which half-a-dozen pots and kettles of various sizes dangled, have so effectually passed into oblivion, that, to people of the present generation, the names of these articles, so indispensable to every kitchen only half a century ago, have no significance whatever. Indeed, the open fireplace is so completely superseded by the cook-stove and range, that the statement of their ever having been in general use for cooking purposes sounds more like a poetic fiction than a prosy fact. Even on the outer verge of civilization houses are now usually built without fireplaces; and the cook-stove is in such general use that it is often set up under a tree, or in a temporary tent, and there brought into requisition for culinary purposes, while the future house of the pioneer is in process of erection. In the mode of boiling now generally pursued on stoves and ranges, there is, however, no material change from that which was in vogue when the pot hung on the bar or crane in the huge fireplace, and its steam went puffing up the wide-mouthed chimney.

Boiling is the term applied to the cooking of articles in water after it has reached the boiling point. When the density of the water is increased by the addition of salt or sugar, or some other substances, it retains heat longer, and requires a higher temperature to make it boil; but on mountains, or where the pressure of the atmosphere is lessened by any cause, it boils at a lower temperature. The thermometer shows that under ordinary conditions, at the level of the sea, water boils at 212 degrees, and that after it has reached the boiling point and begins to escape in steam, it is only a waste of fuel to increase the heat of the fire. The water will evaporate or pass off in steam more rapidly by the addition of more heat, but it will grow no hotter, and articles immersed in it will cook no sooner by being rapidly boiled.

Hard and Soft Water.—The solvent power of soft water is much greater than that of hard water. Consequently soft water, or water that is free from mineral matter, makes its way into organized tissue much more readily than hard water, and is, on that account, preferable for such culinary purposes as making soups, tea, coffee, and all infusions where the object is to extract the valuable properties of the animal and vegetable matter subjected to the process of boiling or steeping. The solvent action of soft water upon some green vegetables is powerful enough, however, to destroy the firmness essential to the preservation of their juices and their peculiarly distinctive flavors, and to guard against this dissolving action, and prevent the vegetables from becoming too tender, it is advisable to salt quite freely the water in which they are to be boiled, so as to harden it sufficiently to preserve the form of the vegetables and hinder the evaporation of their flavoring principles.

How to Boil.—Fish, meats, and poultry that are to be boiled should be immersed in boiling water, and boiled rapidly for from two to ten minutes—the length of time depending upon the article to be cooked—and should then be permitted to fall to simmering temperature, at which temperature the water should be held as uniformly as possible until the process of cooking is finished. The reason for such mode of procedure is simply this: When a piece of meat is plunged into boiling water the outer part contracts, the albumen, which is nearer the surface, coagulates, and the internal juices are kept from escaping into the water by which it is surrounded, or from being diluted and weakened by the absorption of water through the pores of the flesh. And the very reason that should induce us to place meats in boiling water and boil them rapidly for a few minutes should deter us, if we gave the matter any thought, from continuing the rapid boiling. The coagulating and hardening process, which is desirable for the outside of the meat, any one can see at a glance, is undesirable when it is no longer necessary to form a coating or barrier for the preservation of its juices and flavors. Therefore, after meat has been boiled rapidly for a short time the remainder of the cooking should be done gently, by simmering, so that it can go on gradually through the agency of the natural moisture of the flesh being converted into steam or vapor by the heat. For meat when properly cooked—whether on a spit, in an oven, or submerged in boiling liquid—is cooked mainly by its own steam. And the skill of a cook consists to a great extent in knowing how to regulate and temper the heat.

To subject a medium-sized fish to rapid boiling for two minutes effects as much in the way of hardening the surface and preventing the escape of juices and the loss of flavors as ten minutes does for a leg of mutton; and for an ordinary sized piece of meat of any kind ten minutes is about the longest time required for this purpose. Salted meats before being put to boil should always be soaked for several hours in cold water.

The difference between the right and wrong method of boiling is perhaps as apparent in boiled chicken as in any other article. A chicken immersed in a large quantity of water and boiled rapidly until ragged becomes a tasteless object, only a trifle more nutritious than soup meat; but boiled properly in a small quantity of liquid, the skin remains unbroken, the flesh becomes tender, and all the juices and flavors are retained in the fowl. A properly boiled chicken is a very appetizing dish, and is occasionally a desirable change from the almost invariable roast chicken.

To Boil a Chicken.—Stuff the chicken, after it has been properly dressed, with Bread Crumbs No. 1, seasoned sharply with salt and pepper, and moistened until sufficiently rich with melted butter. Truss the legs and wings close to the body. Wrap and fasten securely in a cloth that has been dipped in hot water and dredged with flour. Put into a kettle of boiling, salted water—being careful to have enough water to completely submerge the chicken—and cook until the skin assumes a gelatinous appearance and the fowl becomes tender. When done take out, carefully remove all the trussing strings and skewers, and lay on a platter.

Serve, with egg, parsley, oyster, celery, or caper sauce.

A turkey, or any other fowl, can be boiled in the same manner.

To Boil a Leg of Lamb.—Wipe, trim off the fat, wrap and fasten securely in a wet cloth dredged with flour, put in a kettle of boiling water, slightly salted, and cook until tender. When sufficiently done take from the kettle, dip an instant in cold water, remove the cloth, and place the boiled joint on a platter. Serve with drawn butter, or with egg, parsley, or caper sauce.

Mutton can be boiled and served in the same way.

To Boil a Fish.—Dredge the prepared fish lightly with flour, wrap and secure firmly in a cloth, put in a kettle, and cook in slightly salted boiling water. A medium-sized fish will boil in about half an hour, and when it is sufficiently cooked the flesh will flake and separate easily. As soon as done take from the kettle, remove the cloth in which it was boiled, drain well, lay in a folded napkin on a hot platter, garnish with lemon points and sprigs of parsley, and serve with drawn butter or fish sauce.

To Boil a Ham.—Put the prepared ham to cook in boiling water, with the skin side down, and keep it simmering uninterruptedly until sufficiently tender. Allow about twenty minutes' cooking to each pound, and if at the end of that time the ham is not thoroughly done continue the boiling until it can be pierced easily with a fork. If to be eaten cold, let it remain in the water in which it was cooked until cold, then skin and serve as desired; or, after the skin has been removed, cover with fine bread crumbs, moisten with sugar and vinegar, and brown in the oven. If to be eaten warm, take from the vessel in which it was cooked as soon as sufficiently tender, remove the skin, lay on a platter, and serve.

To Boil Corned Beef.—If the beef is too salt soak in cold water until sufficiently freshened, then put to cook in boiling water enough to just cover it and cook until very tender. Cabbage, cauliflower, turnips, spinach, beans, or carrots can be appropriately served with corned beef.

To Boil Spiced Beef.—Select the rump, round, or flank, and if very lean lard with salt pork, or beef suet. Put in a kettle with a medium-sized onion, carrot, and turnip, two or three sprigs of parsley, some trimmings of celery, six cloves, six pepper corns, and a tablespoonful of salt. Cover with boiling water and cook very gently from four to six hours, according to the age and condition of the meat. When the meat is perfectly cooked lift it on to a platter, strain the broth, remove the grease from it, thicken with butter and flour cooked together until brown (see Brown Sauce No. 1), and serve the sauce with the meat.

To Boil an Egg.—Pour a pint of boiling water into a small sauce-pan or other vessel, put the egg in it, cover closely, place it where it will keep hot, and let stand for about six minutes. An egg so cooked will be evenly done all through without being hard, semi-raw, or slimy, and will be tender, delicate, and delicious. To cook eggs properly in this manner a pint of water should be allowed for each egg. And if many eggs are to be cooked at one time the inconvenience of using a large quantity of water can be avoided by pouring boiling water upon the eggs, letting it stand a minute, then pouring it off and replacing with more boiling water.

To hard-boil an egg put it in a pint of boiling water and let it remain there twenty minutes. This will render the yolk dry and mealy. Or put the egg in cold water, bring the water to the boiling point, and let the egg remain in it for fifteen minutes.

To Boil Vegetables.—The general rule in regard to vegetables is: Put them to cook in slightly salted boiling water and keep them simmering until done.

To Boil Potatoes.—Boiling is the most common method of cooking potatoes, yet comparatively few people know how to boil a potato so that it will be dry, mealy, and fine-flavored. To boil either pared or unpared potatoes, put them in a liberal allowance of slightly salted boiling water, and keep them cooking gently until tender enough to be pierced easily with a fork, then drain off the water, sprinkle a little salt over the potatoes, cover them with a towel or napkin, and set the kettle containing them back on the range where they will dry off and keep warm. A medium-sized potato will boil in twenty-five minutes. Some prefer to have potatoes pared before they are put to cook, others prefer to have them boiled in their skins and the skins removed before the potatoes are sent to table, while others again prefer to have them boiled and served in their skins. But as there is no positive evidence that they are more nutritious or digestible when cooked pared, than they are when cooked unpared, it may be safely left to individual taste or fancy to determine whether potatoes shall be boiled with or without their skins.

To Boil Macaroni.—Macaroni is composed of wheat flour and water, and is simply paste of the proper consistency formed into certain shapes and dried. But it occupies the anomalous position of being classed among vegetables, and this is the best method of cooking it: Break the macaroni in pieces any length desired, put into well-salted boiling water, cook an hour, or until tender enough to be easily mashed with the fingers, then drain in a colander. Macaroni is inexpensive, is easily prepared for the table, and when properly cooked makes a very palatable and nutritious dish. Boiled macaroni should be served with drawn butter, or with white, brown, tomato, or other sauce, or with grated cheese.

To Boil Asparagus.—Wash the asparagus, tie it in small bundles, cook till tender, and serve on toast, with melted butter, white sauce, or sauce Hollandaise.

To Boil String Beans.—Put the prepared beans in boiling water slightly salted, boil gently fifteen minutes, drain, add just enough boiling water to cover the beans, simmer gently till tender, serve with melted butter or white sauce; or let the water evaporate, as the beans become sufficiently cooked, add sweet cream, and season with salt and pepper.

To Boil Cauliflower.—Trim, wash, boil gently until tender, drain carefully, put in a vegetable dish, and dress with drawn butter or white sauce. The white sauce may be flavored with grated cheese.

To Boil Corn.—Remove the husk and silk from the ears of corn, boil ten minutes, or until cooked, cut the corn from the cob, season with salt, pepper, and butter, and serve in a heated dish ; or lay the ears on a platter and serve.

To Boil Carrots.—Wash, scrape, boil till tender, drain, season with butter, salt, and pepper ; or slice and serve with white sauce.

To Boil Beets.—Wash the beets, boil them till tender, rub off the skin, cut in slices, and season with salt, pepper, and melted butter.

To Boil Cabbage.—Trim, wash, and divide each head of cabbage in quarters or eighths, boil till tender, drain, press out the water, and serve with white sauce or drawn butter.

To Boil Turnips.—Wash and pare the turnips, boil till tender, drain in a colander, press out the water, mash fine, and season with salt, pepper, and butter. Or after they are drained cut in slices and serve with cream, or with drawn butter to which vinegar or lemon juice has been added until it is slightly acid.

To Boil Parsnips.—Wash, boil till tender, drain, cut in slices, serve with drawn butter, or with a white sauce to which a little vinegar or lemon juice may be added.

To Boil Sweet Potatoes.—Wash, boil till tender, drain, and dry off the same as white potatoes. Sweet potatoes are much dryer and nicer steamed than boiled.

To Boil Spinach.—Put the prepared spinach in a small quantity of boiling water, cover closely, boil ten minutes, or till tender, drain in a colander, press out the water, season with salt, pepper, and butter, and serve with poached eggs, or with hard-boiled eggs cut in slices. Or after it is cooked and drained, chop fine, put in a stew-pan with a lump of butter, add a little sweet cream, season with salt and pepper, stir till well heated, and serve with, or without, poached or hard-boiled eggs.

To Boil Rice.—Put a cup of prepared rice into two quarts of boiling water and boil rapidly for fifteen or twenty minutes, drain in a sieve or colander, return to the vessel in which it was cooked, and set on the back of the range to dry off. Rice cooked and drained in this manner is very good, but is dry and tasteless in comparison with rice cooked according to the following method : Put a cup of rice into three cups of cold water slightly salted. Place it over a moderately brisk fire. Stir from the bottom occasionally with a wooden spoon, while the rice is swelling. After the water begins to boil briskly, and the rice to hop about, let it cook without stirring until it becomes so tender that the grains can be crushed between the fingers, then remove to a cooler part of the range and let simmer gently for a few minutes. During the time it is simmering lift the rice lightly from the bottom of the vessel by inserting a fork at the side of, and underneath, the rice. This lifting with the fork is quite important, as it aids the drying off, and, when skilfully done, leaves the grains distinct and separate.

CEREALS.

Preparations of the different varieties of grain are growing into popular favor so rapidly that every one should be acquainted with the best method of preparing them. Oatmeal, rolled wheat, hominy, and other cereals, when sent to table, as they generally are, in a half-raw, sloppy, or slimy condition, are not inviting articles of diet, and if eaten at all are eaten under protest and without relish. Yet when properly cooked and served, any one of them will make as delicious a breakfast or supper dish as can be desired.

To Cook Cereals.—Pearled wheat, pearled barley, cracked wheat, crushed wheat, rolled wheat, rolled barley, rolled oats, oatmeal, avena, coarse hominy, fine hominy, farina, farinose, and numerous other grain products that belong in the category of cereals can be cooked very nicely in an ordinary agate ware or porcelain-lined stew-pan, if carefully watched and frequently stirred. But as much stirring, while cooking, renders cereals starchy and robs them of some of their finest flavors it is better, as well as more convenient, to cook them in a double boiler or farina kettle. Fill the outside boiler about two thirds full of boiling water, set the inside boiler or kettle in it, put the proper quantity of boiling liquid in the inside kettle, add the requisite amount of salt, and sprinkle in the grain or meal, stirring slowly until it swells or thickens enough to keep it from settling on the bottom of the kettle, then cease stirring, cover closely, and let it simmer until thoroughly cooked. All mushes thicken in cooling, and in preparing any of the cereals to be eaten cold, the proportion of liquid used should be increased about one third. Water alone can be used for cooking any of the grains or grain products; but some of them are richer and finer flavored when the liquid used in their preparation is milk and water mixed in about equal proportions. This is more especially the case with barley, rice, hominy, farina, and farinose. The quantity of salt that should be used in cooking cereals depends considerably upon individual taste, but care should be taken not to use too much, and a safe general rule is to add half a teaspoonful of salt to each pint of liquid.

The general idea is that the cereals—grains and grain products of all kinds—can be cooked in from ten to thirty minutes, and most of them are served after they have been cooked about that length of time. All cereals, however, are much finer flavored and more digestible when thoroughly cooked—in fact, thorough cooking is the main point to be observed in the preparation of cereals for the table—and this necessitates cooking them slowly, in a proper quantity of liquid, for a considerable length of time. If liquid has to be added during the process of cooking, or has to be drained off, after the grain is thoroughly cooked, some of the fine flavor is lost, and the result of such improper methods is generally an insipid mess, instead of a savory and appetizing dish. It is, therefore, very important that the same cup or vessel used for measuring the grain should be used for measuring the liquid in which the grain is to be cooked, so that the quantity of liquid be just sufficient to make the mush or porridge the proper consistency, and to perfectly develop the flavor of the cereal.

The amount of liquid necessary, and the length of time required for cooking cereals properly, depend greatly on the nature of the cereals and the manner in which they have been milled or prepared, and cannot be given with accuracy without knowing the special brand of the cereal to be cooked. The following will, however, be found approximately correct as regards the proportions of grain and liquid to be used, and the length of time required to cook the grain and grain products mentioned :

Farina.—Six cups of liquid to each cup of farina. Cook half an hour.

Coarse hominy.—Six cups of liquid to each cup of hominy. Cook from six to ten hours.

Cracked wheat.—Five cups of liquid to each cup of wheat. Cook from three to six hours.

Fine hominy.—Four cups of liquid to each cup of hominy. Cook from three to six hours.

Coarse oatmeal.—Four cups of liquid to each cup of oatmeal. Cook from three to six hours.

Rolled wheat, barley, or oats.—Three cups of liquid to each cup of grain. Cook an hour.

BEVERAGES.

To Make Coffee, No. 1.—Any variety of coffee preferred may be used for making the beverage, but a mixture of one third Mocha and two thirds Java and two tablespoonfuls, or about an ounce, of ground coffee to each pint of water makes coffee that suits the average taste. It may be made stronger or weaker if desired, but it is always better to make coffee too strong than too weak. If it is made too strong it is easy to weaken it by the addition of water or milk, but if made too weak it is a difficult matter to strengthen it.

When a pot with a cloth bag or other strainer is used in making coffee it is only necessary to put the desired quantity of finely ground coffee into the strainer, pour slowly over it one third the quantity of boiling water to be used in making the coffee, cover the pot closely, and let stand until the water has trickled through the strainer, then pour on another third, and when that has trickled through add the remaining third, and in a minute the coffee will be ready to serve.

It is not advisable to pour on all the water at once, as rinsing the coffee several times extracts the strength more perfectly. And to pour on all the water at once and pour the dripped coffee back into the strainer exposes it to loss of both strength and flavor. The water should be boiling hot when poured over the coffee, and should at first be poured around the outer edge of the coffee close to the sides of the pot and gradually toward the center. If poured into the center at first the coffee will be forced against the sides of the strainer without being moistened enough to extract its strength. Coffee should be ground quite fine for making it in this manner, but should not be crushed or pulverized.

To Make Coffee, No. 2.—Mix the ground coffee with the white of an egg and a little cold water, stir well together, add half the amount of boiling water to be used in making the coffee, and set the pot on the stove until it boils. Let it simmer five minutes after it reaches the boiling point, add the balance of the boiling water, pour out a cup of the coffee and pour back into the pot, add a tablespoonful of cold water, and the coffee is ready to serve.

To Make Coffee, No. 3.—Mix the coffee and egg, add one third the quantity of water to be used, cold, set the pot on the stove until it boils, add another third of the cold water, and as soon as it boils add the balance of the cold water. When it again boils pour in a spoonful of cold water and it will be ready to serve.

Coffee should not be ground very fine when used in a pot without a strainer. If pulverized or ground very fine it renders the coffee troublesome to settle.

Sugar caramel, used to sweeten coffee, improves it for many tastes, and coffee that is poor and flavorless can be greatly improved by the addition of sugar caramel.

To Make Hygienic Coffee.—Pour a pint of New Orleans molasses over four quarts of clean, coarse, wheat bran and rub lightly between the hands until thoroughly mixed. Put the moist bran in a roasting pan and roast in the oven like coffee, stirring every few minutes, until it assumes a rich brown color. Make the same as Coffee No. 2, using about twice the quantity, or mix, in equal proportions, with any variety of ground coffee, and make in the same manner.

To Make Green Tea.—The proper quantity of tea to use is one teaspoonful to each pint of water. Heat the teapot by rinsing it well with boiling water. Put the tea in the pot, pour on enough boiling water to thoroughly saturate it. Set the pot back on the stove where it will keep hot, but not boil, and let the tea steep from five to ten minutes, then pour on the quantity of water needed, and the tea will be ready for use; or pour on all the water at once, when the tea is put in the pot, and let it steep.

To Make Black or Oolong Tea.—Use two teaspoonfuls of tea to each pint of water and make the same as green tea.

To Make Ceylon or English Breakfast Tea.—These varieties of tea should be steeped at table, as they lose immensely in flavor by standing even a few minutes.

They are frequently steeped in individual cups, but are finer flavored when made in a pot. Have the pot well heated. Put in two or three teaspoonfuls of tea to each pint of water—the exact quantity can be determined only by the special kind of tea—add the boiling water, and the tea will be ready for use at once.

The gases that are in water and give it an agreeable flavor, are driven off by boiling, and water that has boiled for any length of time, or that has stood in the kettle and been reboiled, will not make good tea, neither will water that has not quite reached the boiling point. Therefore only freshly boiled boiling water should be used for making tea.

To Make Chocolate or Cocoa.—Excellent chocolate and cocoa can be prepared by following the formula that accompanies each package of those respective articles.

To Make Koumiss.—Dissolve about half of a half-ounce cake of compressed yeast and two tablespoonfuls of granulated sugar in a quart of new milk. Pour into a bottle, leaving an inch space at the top, cork tightly, fasten the cork securely, and shake well. Let the bottle stand at a temperature of not less than sixty degrees from six to ten hours, then lay it on its side in an ice-box or other cold place from four to six hours more, and it will be ready for use. Bottles that have self-fastening stoppers are the most convenient to use in making koumiss. If it is preferred more acid let the bottle remain in the ice-box a greater length of time.

CHAPTER VIII.

STEAMING.

STEAMING is a modified form of boiling, in which food is cooked by exposure to hot steam instead of by immersion in boiling water. And a large proportion of the puddings that are usually boiled, fish of a delicate flavor, potatoes that fall to pieces easily in being boiled, corn on the cob, rice when the starch is to be preserved, Hubbard and other hard-shell squashes, and a variety of other articles are better steamed than boiled.

To Steam a Fish.—Dust a prepared fish, inside and outside, with salt. Dredge the outside lightly with flour, wrap in a cloth, and place in a steamer over boiling water. Cover the steamer closely, and cook until the fish will flake easily. A five-pound fish will steam in half an hour. Serve on a hot platter in a napkin. Serve with it, in a tureen, drawn butter, parsley sauce, egg sauce, or sauce Hollandaise. Boiled potatoes or boiled carrots should be served with steamed fish, and if a relish is desired, sliced cucumbers, sliced tomatoes, cresses, or pickles are appropriate. Either catsup or fish sauce is also permissible.

To Steam Oysters.—Wash the unopened shells containing the oysters and place them in a steamer over boiling water. Cover closely and cook five minutes. Serve the oysters in their shells, and serve with them, in a sauce tureen, hot lemon butter.

Clams should be steamed in the same manner as oysters.

To Steam Potatoes.—Place the potatoes, either pared or unpared, in a steamer over boiling water. Cover closely and cook forty-five minutes, or until the potatoes are done, which can be ascertained by testing them with a fork. Serve in a napkin in a heated dish, and fold the corners of the napkin over the potatoes.

Sweet potatoes can be steamed in the same manner.

To Steam Corn.—Remove the outside husks and silk from each ear of corn. Fold back the inner husks and pick off worms, dirt, or defective grains, then twist the husks together at the small end of the cob, and lay the ears in a steamer over boiling water. Cook fifteen minutes and serve, without removing the husk, in a napkin, on a platter.

To Steam Rice.—Pick over and wash the rice. Put it in the dish in which it is to be served and add a level teaspoonful of salt and three cups of boiling water to each cup of rice. Set in a steamer over boiling water, and cook half an hour, or until the rice is tender. Milk may be mixed with the water in any proportion desired; or, if preferred, milk alone may be used instead of water.

To Steam Squash.—Wash the squash, saw it in half crosswise, and with a stiff metal spoon remove the seeds and stringy portions. Lay the prepared pieces, inside down, in a steamer, over boiling water, and cook an hour, or until done, then take from the steamer and scrape the cooked squash clean from the shells. Put it in a heated bowl or sauce-pan, season to taste with butter, salt, and pepper, mash smooth, and serve in a heated tureen or vegetable dish.

If the squash should be watery, dry off in a saucepan on the back of the range; if very dry, add a little sweet cream or milk in seasoning; and if lacking in sweetness, add a small quantity of sugar.

To Steam a Roly-Poly.—Wring a towel out of hot water, dredge with flour, lay the pudding on it, and fold the towel over the pudding. Place in a steamer over boiling water, cook half an hour or longer—according to the size or material of the pudding—and when done, lift from the steamer, in the towel in which it cooked, fold back the top covering, and roll the pudding upon a hot platter.

To Steam a Batter Pudding.—Put the pudding in a buttered mold, fasten on the lid, and place the mold in a steamer over boiling water. Cover closely, and cook from one to four hours, according to the special kind of pudding. When the pudding is done submerge the mold in cold water an instant, and the pudding will turn out without difficulty.

To Steam Small Puddings.—Fill individual molds, or cups, with the pudding batter or mixture, place in a steamer over boiling water, cover closely, and cook fifteen minutes, or longer, according to the special kind of pudding.

To Steam Eggs.—Break the eggs into a shallow dish, season to taste, and steam from three to five minutes.

CHAPTER IX.

STEWING.

STEWING, like steaming, is merely a modified form of boiling, differing from it mainly in these two respects: In boiling, most articles are cooked whole and in considerable water; whereas, in stewing, they are usually cut in pieces and cooked in a limited quantity of water. For instance, a fowl, or joint of meat, may be boiled in water enough to make a limited amount of soup, in addition to the sauce or gravy for the fowl or joint of meat; but neither should be stewed in a greater quantity of liquid than is sufficient to cook it and make the sauce with which it is served. There are exceptions to these rules, as carrots, parsnips, onions, turnips, pie-plant, and some other high-flavored vegetables, are improved by parboiling and draining before being stewed; but in the main they hold good and are applicable to the boiling and stewing of most articles of food.

To Stew a Chicken.—Cut the prepared chicken in pieces suitable for serving. Separate the thigh, leg, and wing joints, divide the breast into four or more compact pieces, and separate the neck, back, etc. Put the gizzard, heart, wings, and legs in the bottom of the kettle, then put in the neck, back, and bony pieces, reserving the second joints and breast for the top. Add a pint of boiling water for each full-grown fowl, cover the kettle closely, and after it has stewed a few minutes, add a tablespoonful each of butter and flour stirred to a smooth paste. Let it cook slowly, but unceasingly, until the fowl is tender, which can be ascertained by examining the pieces on top. If the top pieces are found to be sufficiently cooked, those beneath will be also, as in placing the pieces in the kettle, those requiring the most cooking were put at the bottom so as to be subjected to the greatest heat. A one-year-old fowl will stew in about an hour and a half, and each added year in age necessitates an additional hour's cooking. When the fowl has stewed until perfectly tender, drain into a bowl all the liquid or broth, and set the kettle, with the pieces undisturbed in it, upon the back of the stove. If the broth is too oily, skim from it as much grease as you wish, then add to it a spoonful of flour stirred to a smooth paste with half a spoonful of butter, and season highly with salt and pepper, as this broth or gravy must season the entire fowl. After the gravy has been seasoned, pour it over the fowl in the kettle, let it simmer gently for about ten minutes, then serve fowl and gravy together in the same platter.

Meats stewed in a closely covered vessel need not be entirely covered with liquid, and a fowl, by occasionally turning, can be cooked whole in a quantity barely sufficient for gravy or sauce.

Celery is always a suitable flavoring for stewed chicken, and several roots or stalks of celery can be added when the chicken is put to cook, and after being stewed with it can be removed when the chicken is served. Parsley may be used for flavoring whenever desired, and the flavor of stewed chicken may be varied occasionally by cooking with the chicken a small onion and a small blade of mace.

Stewed Chicken with Mushrooms.—After the broth has been drained from stewed chicken as directed above, add a pint of mushrooms to the chicken in the kettle before pouring the gravy over it. If canned mushrooms are used, add the water in the can to the broth, and make into sauce.

Stewed Chicken with Truffles.—Two medium-sized truffles are sufficient to flavor a full-grown fowl. Cut the truffles in small pieces, put them in the kettle with the chicken when put to cook, and stew and serve with it.

To Stew Veal.—The ribs, breast, and thin pieces containing a good deal of fat are the most desirable portions of veal for stewing. Remove the outer skin, cut the meat in pieces suitable for serving, and stew and serve like chicken.

To Stew Beef.—Select the same portions of beef as of veal. Remove the outer skin, cut the meat in pieces suitable for serving, put in a stew-pan or kettle with a teaspoonful of salt and just sufficient hot water to cover it, cover closely, and let cook until tender. Beef, if young, will stew in three hours, but if old and tough five or six hours' stewing may be required to cook it perfectly. It is always best, however, in stewing meats to allow sufficient time, as the stew when done can generally be kept warm for several hours without detriment. When the beef is cooked drain the broth from it, remove the grease from the broth, add the necessary quantity of flour and butter stirred to a smooth paste, and, as soon as the flour is uniformly mixed with the broth, season to taste with salt and pepper, pour over the meat, simmer ten minutes, and serve. For flavoring stewed beef an onion, a tomato, a teaspoonful of sugar, and two or three cloves, put to cook with the meat, form a good combination. Another good combination is formed by the addition of an onion, a carrot, and a tomato, or an onion, a sweet turnip, and a tomato. Celery roots and trimmings may be added to any of these combinations, and always improve them. The vegetables forming the flavoring combinations may be removed from the stew before it is served, or may be served with it.

To Stew Mutton.—Select thin portions of mutton in which the lean and fat are about equally combined. Remove the outer skin, cut the meat in pieces suitable for serving, put it in a sauce-pan, add a teaspoonful of salt and hot water enough to barely cover the meat. Cover the sauce-pan closely, and let the meat cook slowly for three or four hours, or until tender, then drain the broth from it, remove the grease from the broth, add to the broth a tablespoonful of butter and two tablespoonfuls of flour stirred to a smooth paste, and stir until the butter melts and the flour mingles uniformly with the broth. Then season to taste, pour over the mutton, add a tablespoonful of minced parsley or capers, let simmer five minutes, and serve.

No better flavoring material can be used for either boiled or stewed mutton than parsley or capers. But, if desired, **a mixture of such** vegetables as are appropriately used with stewed beef may be used with stewed mutton.

To Stew Lamb.—Lamb should be prepared and stewed like mutton. It, however, requires only an hour and a half or two hours' stewing. Parsley or capers make the best flavoring for stewed lamb.

To Stew Rabbit or Squirrel.—Rabbits and squirrels are prepared and stewed in the same manner as fowls, with the addition of a tablespoonful of minced parsley to each rabbit or squirrel, when put to cook. Parsley seems better adapted for seasoning rabbits or squirrels than any other herb or flavoring principle; but for an occasional change any flavoring that is permissible with chicken or veal may be used with either rabbit or squirrel.

FRICASSEEING.

Stews are often, but very incorrectly, termed fricassees. A fricassee is a combination of a sauté and a stew, and the meat for a fricassee should always be sautéd or browned before it is put to stew. This sautéing or browning is best done in a small quantity of clarified butter, although drippings of beef or veal may be used, if preferred.

A brown stew can be made by adding the butter designed for the gravy to the fowl or meat after it has been stewed and the broth drained from it, and letting it brown in the kettle or sauce-pan, then mixing the flour for the gravy, with cold water, and adding to the broth before it is poured over the browned meat. A stew made in this manner resembles a fricassee somewhat, but is in many respects inferior to it.

To Fricassee a Chicken.—Prepare a chicken as for stewing. Season the pieces with salt and pepper, roll in flour, fry or sauté until light brown in color, then place in the stewing kettle. Put a pint of water in the pan in which the chicken was browned and after it has simmered five minutes pour it over the chicken. Cover the kettle closely and let the chicken simmer gently until cooked. Lift into a platter when done, and if there is not sufficient sauce add more water, and more flour, if required, to that in the kettle, cook five minutes, and strain over the chicken. A spoonful of sweet cream added to the sauce improves it for chicken or veal.

Lamb, mutton, and veal are prepared and fricasseed in the same manner as chicken.

BRAISING.

Braising, like fricasseeing, is a combination of frying or sautéing and stewing. It is usually done, however, in an oven, in a braising pan having a close-fitting cover. The advantages of braising over stewing, for certain articles, are that a more uniform temperature can be obtained and the flavors of the food be better preserved on account of there being less evaporation. Braising is an excellent mode of cooking tough meats and poultry.

To Braise Poultry or Meats.—Prepare as for stewing. Cut in pieces suitable for serving, season lightly with salt and pepper, roll in flour, brown in clarified butter or drippings in a frying pan or spider, then put in a braising kettle with such vegetables, herbs, and spices as are to be used for flavoring, add half as much water as for stewing, cover closely, set in a moderate oven, and let cook slowly for several hours. Simple veal or beef broth may be used in place of water.

To Braise a Calf's Heart.—After the heart has soaked an hour in cold salt water remove the cartilage, fill the opening left by its removal with seasoned bread crumbs or sausage meat, tie up and sauté until brown, in clarified butter or drippings, place in a braising pan, add such flavorings as may be desired, and half as much hot water or broth as would be used for stewing, cover closely, put in a moderate oven, and let cook slowly for four or five hours.

TO STEW VEGETABLES.

Much less water is required for stewing than for boiling articles of food. With this exception, the general rule in regard to boiling vegetables is the same as in regard to stewing them, viz.: Put to cook in slightly salted boiling water and keep simmering gently until done. The length of time necessary for boiling or stewing vegetables depends so much upon the age and condition of the vegetables, and varies so greatly, that it is impossible to give it with any degree of accuracy. All vegetables, however, cook tender in a much shorter length of time when young and fresh than they do when old and stale.

To Stew Beets.—Wash, parboil an hour, rub off the skin, cut in slices, put in a stew-pan, cover with broth or water, add a lump of butter rolled in flour, simmer till tender, and season with salt and pepper.

To Stew Green Shelled Beans.—Put the beans in

just sufficient water to cover them, stew gently half an hour, or till tender, add a little sweet cream, and season with salt and pepper; or omit the cream, add a little butter, and season with salt and pepper.

To Stew Dried Beans.—Wash and soak well. Put to cook in a liberal supply of cold water, to which a pinch of soda has been added. Pour off this water as soon as it boils, and add enough cold water to barely cover the beans. Salt lightly, cook gently four hours, or until very tender, then season with salt, pepper, and butter; or serve with white or brown sauce.

To Stew Carrots.—Wash, pare, parboil an hour, drain, slice, put in a stew-pan with a little broth or water, and simmer till tender. Season with salt, pepper, and minced parsley.

To Stew Corn.—Cut the corn from the cob, scrape off the pulp and eyes. Put in a sauce-pan with a half pint of water to each pint of corn. Cover closely, stir occasionally to keep the corn from sticking to the sauce-pan and burning, and stew ten minutes, or till cooked. Season to taste with salt, pepper, and a little cream or butter, and serve.

To Stew Cucumbers.—Pare, split in pieces lengthwise, scrape out the seeds, cover with water, simmer until tender, thicken with flour and butter, and season with salt and pepper.

To Stew Mushrooms.—Put the mushrooms in a stew-pan with a lump of butter, salt and pepper to taste, and a tablespoonful of lemon juice to each pint of mushrooms. Cover closely, stew two minutes, or until tender, then thicken with a teaspoonful of flour, and serve.

The liquor of canned mushrooms should always be used in mushroom sauce or stewed mushrooms.

To Stew Okra.—Wash and slice the pods, simmer in a little water or broth till tender, then season with salt, pepper, and butter, and serve.

To Stew Onions.—Peel, boil half an hour, drain, cover with milk, stew until tender, drain, mash or chop, add a little cream, stir over the fire until thoroughly heated, then season with salt and pepper; or when cooked tender dress with salt, pepper, and butter, and serve whole.

Asparagus Peas.—Wash asparagus, cut it in small pieces, simmer fifteen minutes, or till tender, in just enough water to cover it, thicken slightly with flour and butter stirred together, add a little sweet cream, and season with salt and pepper.

To Stew Cabbage.—Slice or chop cabbage fine, stew in a small quantity of water till tender, season with salt, pepper, and butter, add a little sweet cream or vinegar, and serve. Stewed cabbage is usually called hot slaw, if it contains vinegar.

To Stew Celery.—Cut the stalks of celery into pieces an inch or two inches in length, simmer fifteen minutes, or until tender, in a little water, add sweet cream, season to taste with salt and pepper, and serve; or season, pour over slices of toasted bread, and serve.

To Stew Salsify.—Pare, cut in pieces half an inch in length, stew half an hour, or till tender, drain, and serve with drawn butter or white sauce; or mash fine, when drained, season with salt and pepper, add a little cream, and serve. Salsify should be laid in cold water as soon as pared, to keep it from becoming discolored.

To Stew Tomatoes.—Peel and slice the tomatoes, stew until thoroughly cooked, then season with salt, pepper, and butter. Or cream may be used in place of butter, and, if liked, a delicate flavoring of mace or nutmeg may be added. Simple broth or stock of any kind may be used for stewing tomatoes, and a small quantity of onion or a few cloves may be added. The stew may be thickened, if desired, by the addition of bread crumbs, flour, cornstarch, or boiled rice.

To Stew Parsnips.—Wash, pare, cut in pieces, stew an hour, or till tender, drain, press out the water, mash fine, season with salt and pepper, add a little cream or milk, and stir over the fire about five minutes.

To Stew Peas.—Shell, put in a small quantity of water, cover closely, and stew half an hour, or until tender. Add sweet cream, a lump of butter rolled in flour, and season with salt and pepper.

To Stew Potatoes.—Cut pared potatoes in slices about an eighth of an inch in thickness, stew gently till tender, drain, add a little cream or milk, season with salt and pepper, add a little minced parsley if desired, simmer a few minutes, and serve; or when drained serve with white or other sauce.

To Stew Winter Squash.—Split the squash in halves, remove the seeds and stringy portions, cut in pieces suitable for serving, pare, put in a kettle or stew-pan with a small quantity of boiling water, cover closely, and simmer gently until cooked. Serve with melted butter or with white or brown sauce. Or remove the lid from the stew-pan as soon as the squash is tender, let it dry off, then mash fine and season with salt, pepper, and butter.

To Stew Summer Squash.—Cut the squashes in pieces, put them to cook in a little water, and when tender, drain, mash fine, and season with salt, pepper, butter, and sweet cream.

TO COOK FRESH FRUITS.

Fresh fruits and berries of all kinds are usually cooked by stewing, and should always be cooked in earthen, granite, aluminum, or porcelain-lined vessels, and stirred only with a wooden spoon. The use of tin or iron utensils for either cooking or stirring acid fruit affects both the color and flavor deleteriously. A little salt develops and emphasizes the flavor of cooked fruits or berries, and a slight pinch should be added to them while cooking, or when hot. Care should be taken, however, not to use too much. Sugar cooked for a few minutes with acid fruit is converted into glucose and loses its sweetening qualities to such an extent that two pounds of sugar added to acid fruit while cooking will sweeten it but little more than one pound will, if added to the fruit after it is cooked. Consequently it is not advisable in sweetening stewed fruit to add the sugar to the fruit and cook it with it any length of time.

Jellies, jams, and marmalades are generally much finer in quality when made by gently simmering the fruit juices, or the crushed fruit used in their preparation, until sufficiently cooked, before adding the sugar, so that after it is added the cooking need be continued only long enough to dissolve it thoroughly and perfectly combine it with the juice or fruit. So also are nearly all manner of fruit preserves. The strawberry is a notable exception, as both color and flavor seem to be better retained when the sugar is cooked with the fruit.

Apples should be stewed as rapidly as possible in order to preserve the flavor of the fruit. At the beginning of the process, a little water—as little as will serve the purpose—should be added to the prepared fruit in the kettle, which should be kept closely covered while it is cooking. The quantity of water depends in a great measure upon the dryness or juiciness of the apples. If they are juicy a tablespoonful to each pint will be sufficient; whereas, if they are dry, a teacupful may not be too much. The flavor of the apple is usually delicate and easily destroyed, therefore only the quantity of water requisite for thorough cooking should be used. For the same reason all unnecessary stirring, during or after cooking, should be avoided.

Apples, and stewed fruits generally, are finer flavored, and agree with most people better, if eaten while warm than when cold.

To Stew Apples.—Pare, quarter, core, and wash the apples. Place the prepared quarters in a sauce-pan with a small quantity of hot water, cover closely, and stew rapidly for five minutes. Upon removing the cover, the apples, if done, will be broken and so tender as to fall apart readily. If not done, replace the cover and cook a few minutes longer. Put in a bowl or dish half the quantity of sugar required, pour the cooked apples into the dish, sprinkle the other half of the sugar over them, **cover closely, and serve** hot or warm.

To Stew Cranberries, No. 1.—To a quart of cranberries picked and washed add three fourths of a pint of boiling water, cover closely, and cook five minutes over a quick fire. Mash with a wooden spoon such of the berries as have not burst, and rub through a colander or pumpkin strainer into an earthen dish or bowl. Put the pulp into the sauce-pan in which the berries were cooked, add three fourths of a pint of granulated sugar, simmer five minutes, and serve hot or cold. When cold the sauce will be jellied.

To Stew Cranberries, No. 2.—Stew and mash the cranberries as described above, then add the sugar, cook five minutes, and serve.

To Make Cranberry Jelly.—Cook and mash the cranberries as above described, then pour into a jelly bag and let the juice drip through. To each cupful of juice add a cupful of granulated sugar, put into a sauce-pan, simmer five minutes, and pour into molds or cups.

To Stew Pie-Plant.—Wash, but do not skin, the pie-plant, cut it in pieces an inch in length, cover with cold water, and heat to boiling point. Then drain off all the water, add a cup and a half of sugar to each quart of pie-plant, simmer five minutes, and serve warm.

To Stew Green Gooseberries.—Pick over, stem, and wash the gooseberries. Cook and serve like pie-plant. Gooseberries and pie-plant require about an equal amount of sugar to sweeten them.

To Stew Pears.—Wash the pears and remove blemishes, or pare, if preferred. Leave the pears whole. To each quart add a cup of New Orleans molasses, a cup of hot water, and six cloves. Cover closely and cook gently until very tender.

To Stew Peaches.—Prepare peaches the same as pears. To each quart of peaches add a cup of hot water and three quarters of a cup of sugar. Cover closely and stew gently until cooked.

To Stew Plums.—Pick over and wash the plums, and to each quart of fruit add a cup of hot water. Cover closely and stew until cooked, then add sugar to taste, and let simmer five minutes, or until the sugar is perfectly dissolved and mixed with the fruit. Serve hot or cold.

Very acid plums require a pint of sugar to each quart of plums, while sweet ones do not require more than a quarter that amount. If the sugar is added when the plums are put to cook it will toughen their skins and injure their flavor.

To Make Cider Apple Sauce.—Boil sweet cider until it is reduced one half, then add sweet apples that have been pared, quartered, and cored, and cook slowly until the apples are dark and transparent. The apples should be covered by the cider while cooking. If canned while hot, cider apple sauce will keep almost indefinitely, but if put in jars in a cool place it will keep several weeks without being canned.

TO COOK DRIED FRUITS.

Apples, plums, peaches, and all kinds of dried fruits are usually cooked without being properly soaked, and are often sent to table with a wrinkled and uncomely appearance, and frequently with an accumulation of dust and grit about them that in no way adds to their attractiveness or flavors.

Dried fruit of every kind, after being thoroughly cleansed by washing in warm water, should be soaked in cold water until it loses its dried and wrinkled appearance, should be put to cook in the same water, and be simmered or stewed slowly and continuously for several hours, or until it becomes soft, when it should be sweetened and removed from the fire.

Many dried fruits have their respective flavors modified and improved when two or more varieties are stewed together, or cooked in conjunction with each other. Especially is this the case with such as are very sweet or very acid.

To Stew Dried Prunes.—Wash the prunes and soak them over night, or for six or eight hours, in cold water, then put to cook in the water in which they were soaked, and let them simmer gently for two hours. Sweeten to taste and simmer five minutes. Serve hot or cold.

Most prunes are improved by having an equal quantity of dried apricots stewed with them. In such case cook the prunes an hour, then add the soaked apricots and cook the two together another hour.

The quantity of water necessary in stewing prunes, or other dried fruits, is just sufficient to cover the fruit thoroughly in the sauce-pan.

To Stew Dried Apricots.—Wash the apricots, let them soak several hours in cold water, put them to cook in the water in which they soaked, let simmer gently an hour, then sweeten to taste, simmer five minutes more, and serve.

To Stew Dried Plums.—Soak and stew the same as prunes. If the plums are very sour they will be improved by mixing with them an equal quantity of prunes or seedless raisins.

To Stew Prunellas.—Wash, soak, and stew like apricots. Both apricots and prunellas make delicious sauce when cooked in combination with equal quantities of either prunes or seedless raisins.

To Stew Dried Apples or Peaches.—Both dried apples and dried peaches should be washed, soaked, and stewed like other dried fruits. Cook until tender, then sweeten and serve. Sauce made of dried fruits, like that made of fresh fruits, is generally finer flavored and more digestible when eaten warm than when eaten cold.

To Stew Seedless or Sultana Raisins.—Pick over, wash, and soak several hours in cold water, then put to cook in the water in which they soaked. Add an equal quantity of prunellas or apricots that have been washed and soaked. Simmer for an hour, or until cooked, sweeten to taste, and serve.

CHAPTER X.

SOUP-MAKING.

IN PREPARING soup stock any ordinary pot or kettle can be used, but every kitchen should be provided with a stock pot or digester, by the use of which two or three times a week many scraps may be saved and a supply of stock always kept on hand, from which a variety of soups and sauces can be prepared at any time with very little trouble. For there are enough scraps of cooked and uncooked meats, trimmings of roasts, steaks, chops, and cutlets, and odds and ends of vegetables in nearly every house to keep the family supplied with nutritious, palatable soup with very little labor, and scarcely any additional expense. Soup stock is the juice or liquid extract of meat, poultry, game, fish, shell fish, or vegetables, and is used as the foundation of nearly all soups. To make soup stock, put into a kettle or digester, in cold water slightly salted, meat of any kind cut in small pieces, or meat and bones well cut and broken, heat the water gradually until it reaches the boiling point, then keep it simmering continuously until the juices of the meat are all extracted. The albumen of all meats is curdled and hardened by being put into boiling water, but is dissolved and extracted by cold water; and when meat is put into a vessel of cold water and put over the fire and soaked until the water reaches the boiling temperature, and is afterward permitted to simmer gently, all its juices are extracted and mingled with the water so perfectly that the flavor of the stock is much finer than when boiled rapidly. Continuous simmering is very essential in soup-making. To let the stock boil rapidly is objectionable, and to let it stop simmering before the process is finished is also objectionable.

The flavor of soup depends greatly upon the freshness of the meat of which it is made, and the evenness of the temperature at which it is cooked. Tough and coarse pieces of meat make good soups and sauces, and can be converted into stock advantageously, as can also a great many refuse bits and scraps. But it is quite important that all meats of which stock is to made should be cooked before they get stale; and the fresher the meat is, the finer will be the quality of the stock or juice extracted from it, and the better the soup made therefrom. It is quite customary to carefully remove all the scum that rises to the surface when preparing soup stock, but there is no necessity whatever for doing so, as this scum is merely albumen or meat-juice coagulated by the increasing temperature of the water. If permitted to remain after the water reaches the boiling point it will shortly become incorporated with the stock and increase its nutritive value. Its removal is not, therefore, recommended.

When meat and bones are well cut and broken up, all their valuable properties can, by proper cooking, be extracted in four or five hours. After simmering that length of time the kettle should be taken from the fire, the stock strained through a colander into an earthen bowl, and, unless wanted for immediate use, should be set where it will cool as rapidly as possible, as the more rapidly it cools the finer will be its flavor, and the greater the length of time it can be kept. If stock is made of meat alone it will remain in liquid form when cold; but if made of meat and bones in about equal proportions, it will be quite stiff and gelatinous on account of the gelatine extracted from the bones in cooking.

Some soups are made without a special stock having been previously prepared, but stock of some kind is the base of a large majority of soups, and is the fluid foundation with which other materials are mixed and incorporated to form the various soups that in cook-books and bills of fare are designated potages, purées, and consommés.

Soup stock may be classified as:

1. Simple Stock.
2. Compound Stock.
3. Mixed Stock No. 1.
4. Mixed Stock No. 2.

Simple stock is the extract from a single kind of flesh, fish, fowl, or vegetable. Compound stock is the extract of two or more kinds of flesh, fish, fowl, or vegetables. Mixed Stock No. 1 is stock made from scraps and odds and ends of uncooked meats, vegetables, etc. And Mixed Stock No. 2 is stock made from scraps and odds and ends of cooked meats, vegetables, etc.

Simple Stock of Vegetables.—Cut the prepared vegetable of which the stock is to be made into small pieces, put in slightly salted water, and simmer gently until the vegetable is tender, and the stock sufficiently flavored.

Asparagus Stock.—Cut the tender ends or points from a bunch of asparagus and reserve for stewing. Put the remainder into two quarts of slightly salted water, and simmer gently until the water is sufficiently flavored with asparagus, then strain and use for soup stock.

Celery Stock.—Put the roots and coarse outside pieces of half a dozen stalks of celery into three pints of slightly salted water, simmer an hour, strain, and use for stock.

Salsify Stock.—To one pint of sliced salsify add a quart of water and half a teaspoonful of salt, simmer slowly until the salsify is tender, strain, and use for stock. The salsify may be dressed with white sauce and served as a vegetable.

Soup stock may, in a similar manner, be made from green peas, corn, etc., but, as a rule, it is advisable to rub peas, corn, and some other vegetables through a sieve and mingle them with the stock.

Beef Stock.—Select a shin or shank of beef containing as much lean meat as bone. Have the bone sawed in sections not more than two inches in length. Remove the skin from the meat and put the meat and bones to cook in sufficient cold water to cover them an inch in depth. Add a teaspoonful of salt to each gallon of water. Bring slowly to boiling point and let simmer four or five hours, or until the meat falls from the bones, then strain through a colander into an earthen bowl and set in a cold, well-ventilated place till cool.

Prepare stock from mutton, veal, or any meat desired, in a similar manner.

Chicken Stock.—Select a large, fat hen two or three years old and prepare as directed on page 21. Separate the joints and cut the back into several pieces, but reserve the breast whole and covered, as much as possible, with unbroken skin. Put all except the breast into a soup kettle, cover with cold water, add half a teaspoonful of salt, some trimmings of celery, a sprig of parsley, or a small onion and small blade of mace, and set to cook; or, if preferred, omit all flavoring materials from the stock. As soon as the water boils place the breast, skin side up, on the top of the other pieces, cover closely, and let simmer four hours, or until the skin of the breast becomes gelatinous. When perfectly cooked remove the breast to a tureen or bowl, strain the broth over it, and set aside to cool. The breast prepared in this way is in perfect condition for being made into salad, croquettes, or creamed chicken. The best portions of the meat from the back and joints can also be used for croquettes or hash. If the stock or broth is wanted for immediate use skim off the grease, after the cooked chicken has been removed, season, and serve.

Stock can be prepared in a similar manner from any kind of poultry or game.

Compound Stock.—Put together in the soup kettle a beef bone, a knuckle of veal, the back, legs, and wings of a fowl, an onion, a carrot, the roots and trimmings of six stalks of celery, and six cloves. Cover with cold water, add a teaspoonful of salt, let simmer four or five hours, strain, and set aside to cool.

Mixed Stock No. 1.—Take the trimmings of beef, veal, mutton, lamb, or meat of any kind, the shank bone of a ham, the roots and trimmings of celery, the odds and ends of corn, beans, or peas, and an onion, a turnip, and a carrot. Skin, wash, or otherwise prepare them. Put them altogether into a stock pot—putting the bones in first—add salt, six or eight cloves, and a small pepper pod, if at hand, and cover with cold water. Set to cook, let simmer five hours, strain into a bowl, and let cool. When cool remove the grease and the stock will be ready for use.

Mixed Stock No. 2.—Take the skeleton of a turkey, chicken, or other fowl or bird, with any odds and ends of chops or steaks, or bones of roast beef or other meat, and put together in the stock pot with any stewed onion, tomatoes, corn, carrots, celery, or other well-flavored cooked vegetables that may be on hand. Cover with cold water, add a little salt, six cloves, a bay leaf, or other sweet herbs, simmer four or five hours, then strain and let cool. When cool remove the grease and the stock is ready for use.

After the stock has been properly prepared there is comparatively little trouble attending the making of any kind of soup desired ; and it may be proceeded with at once, or may be postponed till another day.

The variety of soups that can be made by varying the combinations of materials used in their preparation is almost illimitable, yet all soups can be legitimately classified under four heads, viz.:

1. Plain Soup.
2. Clear Soup.
3. Vegetable Soup.
4. Mixed Soup.

To one or the other of these classes everything in the nature of soup belongs, and the method of making the hundreds of different soups that are in use is so similar in the main that only a limited number of recipes is necessary to enable one to select from such material as is at hand the articles most appropriate for use in any special soup belonging to either of the four classes of soups.

Two of the most important things to remember in soup-making are these:

To render a soup most attractive and palatable its distinctive flavor and individuality must be preserved. And each kind of soup should be distinct in character from every other kind of soup.

The common stock, or consommé, recommended by most cook-books, and generally used, for the base of soups and sauces is, in most instances, prepared by mingling together beef, veal, chicken, carrots, onions, turnips, celery, parsley, cloves, bay leaf, and other vegetables and herbs; and as the human palate not only craves distinctive flavors, but soon tires of the same flavor or the same combination of flavors, the folly of preparing such stock can be seen at a glance, and the importance of observing the rule in regard to preserving the individuality of soups may be realized in a measure.

CLASS I.—PLAIN SOUP.

Celery Broth.—To four cups of celery stock add one cup of white celery, cut in small pieces, and cooked until tender in one cup of slightly salted boiling water. Cover closely, simmer five minutes, season to taste, and serve.

Asparagus Broth.—To four cups of asparagus stock add the points of one bunch of asparagus cooked fifteen minutes, or until tender, in one cup of boiling water slightly salted. Cover closely, simmer five minutes, season to taste, and serve.

Salsify Broth.—To four cups of salsify stock add one cup of salsify sliced thin and cooked fifteen minutes, or until tender, in one cup of slightly salted boiling water. Cover closely, simmer five minutes, season to taste, and serve. In making vegetable broths the water in which the vegetable is cooked should be added to the stock with the vegetable.

Oyster Broth.—To one quart of oysters freed from bits of shell and rinsed in cold water, add two cups of boiling water, and cook until the thin edges of the oysters wrinkle and separate. Season to taste, and serve with crackers or toasted bread.

For making this broth one cup of water and one cup of milk may be substituted for the water; or all milk or all cream may be used. And, if desired, a tablespoonful of butter may be added to either broth.

Clam Broth No. 1.—To one dozen clams, finely chopped, add two cups of cold water, simmer fifteen minutes, strain out the clams, season the broth to taste, and serve.

Clam Broth No. 2.—To one cup of canned clam juice add two cups of boiling water, simmer five minutes, season to taste, and serve.

Chicken Broth No. 1.—Simmer the required quantity of chicken stock five minutes, season to taste, and serve.

Chicken Broth No. 2.—To four cups of chicken stock add one cup of vermicelli. Simmer five minutes, season to taste, and serve.

Chicken Broth No. 3.—To four cups of chicken broth add one cup of boiled rice and one tablespoonful of minced parsley. Simmer five minutes, season to taste, and serve.

Beef Broth No. 1.—Season to taste the quantity of beef stock required, simmer five minutes, and serve.

Beef Broth No. 2.—To four cups of beef stock add one cup of well-cooked barley, simmer five minutes, season to taste, and serve. Rice or crackers or toasted bread may be served with beef broth, if preferred to barley.

Beef Tea No. 1.—Beef tea is made in a somewhat different manner from soup stock, but can be very properly called plain soup. For making beef tea a cut from the round is preferable on account of its juiciness, and care should be taken to have it as fresh as possible; and in preparing it the skin and fat should be all removed and the meat be cut in small pieces. It should then be put in a kettle or sauce-pan, barely covered with cold water, slightly salted, heated to the boiling point, and strained. It is then ready for use.

Beef tea made according to this formula is very palatable, and is relished by invalids when that extracted at a lower temperature is rejected. If allowed to settle the clear portion is simply a stimulant, but when served with the brown particles in it it is very nutritious.

Beef Tea No. 2.—Prepare the meat as directed in last formula. Put it in a glass can or bottle and close tightly. Place the can or bottle on an open rest in a sauce-pan or kettle of water, cover the sauce-pan, and heat the water gradually until near boiling point. When the juice is extracted from the meat it is ready to season and serve.

Beef Extract.—Broil a thick sirloin steak as directed on page 36. Put it on a hot plate, dust lightly with salt, and, after it has stood a few minutes, pierce freely with a knife, and press out the juice with the back of a hot spoon. Serve in liquid form, or moisten thin slices of toasted bread, baked potato, boiled rice, or vermicelli with it.

Mutton Broth No. 1.—Heat mutton stock, season to taste, and serve.

Mutton Broth No. 2.—To four cups of mutton stock add one cup of boiled rice and one tablespoonful of minced parsley. Simmer five minutes, season to taste, and serve. Toasted bread or cooked barley may be served in the broth, if preferred.

Veal Broth.—To four cups of veal broth add one cup of cooked rice, vermicelli, or noodles with one tablespoonful of minced parsley. Simmer five minutes, season to taste, and serve.

CLASS 2.—CLEAR SOUP.

Clear soup is made from stock clarified and enriched in color and flavor. The clarifying process removes much of the flavor and nutrition from the stock, hence it is necessary to enrich it by the addition of meat juices and flavoring extracts. Clear soup should be served in cups, bowls, or soup-plates, as a clear liquid, with transparent thickening, poached eggs, dainty dumplings, or ornamental vegetables. But nothing should be served in it that will injure its clearness.

Clear Soup.—To four cups of simple or compound stock add one cup of lean raw beef cut in dice or small pieces, one egg beaten with one cup of cold water, and one tablespoonful of meat caramel. Mix all well together in a sauce-pan, bring slowly to boiling point, and simmer half an hour. Strain through several folds of cheese-cloth, season to taste, and serve.

Clear Soup with Curry.—To four cups of clarified stock add a teaspoonful of curry powder, simmer five minutes, season to taste, and serve.

Great care should be taken in the use of curry powder, as it is a combination of various herbs and spices, among which pepper is quite prominent.

Clear Soup with Tapioca.—To four cups of clear soup add one cup of pearled tapioca cooked in salted water until transparent, simmer five minutes, and serve.

Clear Soup with Poached Eggs.—Heat the clarified soup to boiling point. Put a neatly-trimmed poached egg in each soup-plate, and serve a ladleful of soup upon it.

Clear Soup with Dainty Dumplings.—Bring the clarified soup to boiling point and drop the dumplings into it, one at a time, in quick succession. As soon as they rise to the surface they are cooked and the soup should be served at once.

Clear Soup with Sliced Lemon.—Slice a lemon crosswise, in very thin slices, and serve one slice in each plate of soup.

Clear Soup with Mixed Flavoring.—Mix together a tablespoonful of lemon juice, a teaspoonful of sugar, half a teaspoonful of lemon peel, a quarter of a teaspoonful of grated nutmeg, and ten drops extract of ginger. Add to a quart of soup stock before clarifying it.

This flavoring is recommended to those who think wine indispensable in clear soup.

Clear Soup with Fancy Vegetables.—To four cups of clear soup add one cup of fresh vegetables, cooked in salted water—composed of about equal portions of carrot, onion, celery, turnip, and string beans, cut in dice, diamonds, or long thin strips—half a cup of cooked green peas, and a tablespoonful of minced parsley. Simmer five minutes, season to taste, and serve.

Macedoine vegetables are mixed vegetables prepared and canned expressly for use in soups. They are convenient and excellent.

CLASS 3.—VEGETABLE SOUPS.

Vegetable soups are made by adding vegetables to either a plain broth, a clear soup, or a vegetable stock. But when only a single vegetable is used in the preparation of a soup the soup is generally given the name of that vegetable, as corn soup, pea soup, bean soup, etc., and when a variety of vegetables is cooked with, or added to, a stock of any kind the soup is known simply as vegetable soup.

It is well to recognize this distinction, and to remember that some vegetables affiliate or harmonize more perfectly than others with certain meat flavors, so as to be able to select only such as are appropriate in each case. As a general rule vegetables delicate in flavor—such as corn, celery, peas, salsify, cauliflower, and okra—should be served in veal or chicken broth in preference to the broth of beef or mutton, while those more pronounced in flavor—such as carrots, onions, turnips, tomatoes, beans, and cabbage—should be served with broths of the latter in preference to broths of the former meats.

When vegetables of high flavor are used in beef or mutton broth, it is always admissible to use also those of delicate flavor, if desired ; but delicately flavored vegetables should not be served in a high-flavored broth, or mingled with stronger flavored vegetables in the preparation of a soup wherein the delicate flavored vegetables are to predominate. Bean soup, pea soup, tomato soup, and various other vegetable soups where a single vegetable is used in such abundance as to give its name legitimately to the soup, may still have used in the preparation of any of them vegetables, herbs, or spices calculated to stimulate or develop the flavor of the main vegetable, or to modify or counteract some undesirable flavor it may possess. In this way onion, cloves, and meat juices render tomato more palatable when served as a soup, a purée, or a sauce. For a similar reason a cup of sweet corn is a great improvement to a purée of beans, supplying it with sweetness and flavor and thereby enriching the flavor of the beans. And, in like manner, a sprig of mint cooked with dried peas, or with green peas that are so mature as to have lost most of their original taste, will obscure their rankness and frequently give them quite a fresh and spicy flavor ; and a slice of breakfast bacon added judiciously to a soup or purée of peas or beans will impart a very desirable piquancy, and greatly improve the rank or heavy natural flavor of the vegetable.

Corn Soup.—To four cups of veal or chicken broth add one cup of tender sweet corn. Simmer fifteen minutes, or until cooked, season to taste, and serve.

Pea Soup.—Cook one cup of green peas half an hour, or until tender, in water enough to just cover them, then add four cups of veal or chicken broth, heat to boiling point, season to taste, and serve.

Tomato Soup No. 1.—To four cups of beef stock add one cup of fresh tomatoes, peeled and cut in small pieces, one tablespoonful of minced onion, and two cloves. Simmer fifteen minutes, season to taste, and serve.

Okra Soup No. 1.—To four cups of chicken, veal, or beef broth add one cup of okra, cut in small pieces. Simmer until cooked, season to taste, and serve.

Salsify Soup.—To four cups of any simple broth add one cup of thinly sliced salsify. Simmer fifteen minutes, or until cooked, season to taste, and serve.

Rice Soup.—To four cups of chicken, veal, or mutton broth add one cup of boiled rice, heat to boiling point, season, and serve.

Hominy Soup.—To four cups of beef broth add one cup of well-boiled hominy. Heat to boiling point, season, and serve.

Barley Soup.—To four cups of beef, mutton, or mixed soup stock add one cup of well-cooked barley. Simmer five minutes, season to taste, and serve.

Macaroni Soup.—To four cups of chicken, veal, or

beef broth add one cup of cooked macaroni. Simmer five minutes, season, and serve.

Noodle Soup.—To four cups of chicken or veal broth add one cup of noodles that have been boiled for twenty minutes in salted water. Simmer five minutes, season, and serve. Italian paste cut in fancy forms can be used, if preferred.

Vegetable Soup No. 1.—To four cups of chicken or veal stock add one cup of thinly sliced salsify, half a cup of corn, either canned or cut from the cob, and a teaspoonful of minced parsley. Simmer until the vegetables are cooked, then add a cup of sweet cream, season to taste, and serve.

Vegetable Soup No. 2.—Cook half a cup each of carrots, turnips, and onions chopped fine. Add four cups of beef stock, half a cup of tomato, and one tablespoonful of minced parsley. Simmer fifteen minutes, season to taste, and serve.

Vegetable Soup No. 3.—Cook half a cup each of carrots, turnips, celery, and onions. Add four cups of mutton broth or compound stock, half a cup of tomatoes, and one cup of cooked barley. Simmer fifteen minutes, season to taste, and serve.

Vegetable Soup No. 4.—To four cups of chicken, veal, or beef stock add half a cup each of cooked peas, beans, corn, tomatoes, and celery. Simmer fifteen minutes, season to taste, and serve.

Okra Soup No. 2.—To four cups of chicken or veal broth add one cup of sliced or canned okra and half a cup each of lima beans and sweet corn cooked. Simmer fifteen minutes, season, and serve.

Okra Soup No. 3.—To four cups of mixed stock add one cup of okra cut in pieces, and half a cup each of cooked string beans, corn, peas, and tomatoes. Simmer fifteen minutes, season to taste, and serve.

Ox-tail Soup.—Cut an ox-tail in small pieces, also a medium-sized onion. Brown in clarified butter. Put in a sauce-pan, add two cups of water, six cups of either simple or compound stock, and a medium-sized carrot, cut in small pieces. Simmer two hours, or until the ox-tail is cooked. Remove the grease, add a cupful of cooked barley, and half a cupful of cooked tomato. Simmer fifteen minutes, season to taste, and serve.

CLASS 4.—MIXED SOUPS.

White soups are perhaps the most delicate variety of mixed soups. In their preparation a portion of cream or milk is used, and they are known as "Cream of Celery," "Cream of Asparagus," etc. Soups made thick with vegetables rubbed through a sieve, in the preparation of which neither cream nor milk is used, are frequently put down on bills of fare as "creams," but they have no legitimate place among that class of soups—all such mixtures are purées.

Mixed soups, like vegetable soups, may be made in almost endless variety, but comparatively few formulas are needed to enable one to understand the principles that govern their preparation.

Cream of Celery No. 1.—Cook together in a sauce-pan until well mixed one tablespoonful of butter and two tablespoonfuls of flour, add four cups of celery stock, and simmer five minutes. Pour in a cup of sweet cream, heat to boiling point, season to taste, and serve.

Cream of Celery No. 2.—Cook together in a sauce-pan one tablespoonful of butter and two tablespoonfuls of flour. Add two cups of celery stock and two cups of chicken stock, and simmer five minutes. Add a cup of sweet cream, heat to boiling point, season to taste, and serve.

Cream of Asparagus.—Cook together one tablespoonful of butter and two tablespoonfuls of flour. Add four cups of asparagus stock, and simmer five minutes. Pour in a cup of sweet cream, heat to boiling point, season to taste, and serve.

Cream of Salsify.—Cook together in a sauce-pan one tablespoonful of butter and two tablespoonfuls of flour. Add four cups of salsify stock and simmer five minutes. Pour in a cup of sweet cream, season to taste, and serve.

Cream of asparagus and cream of salsify are richer in flavor and nutrition when chicken or veal broth is mixed with the vegetable stock, in equal proportions; and they can be so prepared when desired.

Cream of Corn.—Cook together one tablespoonful of butter and two tablespoonfuls of flour. Add one cup of water and one cup of tender sweet corn. Simmer fifteen minutes, or until the corn is cooked, pour in a cup of sweet cream, heat to boiling point, season to taste, and serve.

Cream of Chicken.—Cook together in a sauce-pan one tablespoonful of butter and two tablespoonfuls of flour. Add two cups of chicken broth and simmer five minutes. Pour in two cups of thin sweet cream, heat to boiling point, season to taste, and serve.

This soup may be varied by the addition of a cup of celery stock or a teaspoonful of minced parsley. Or the flavor of the broth may be varied occasionally by cooking with the chicken an onion and a blade of mace.

Cream of Veal.—Cook together in a sauce-pan one tablespoonful of butter and two tablespoonfuls of flour. Add four cups of veal stock and one tablespoonful of minced parsley, and simmer five minutes. Pour in one cup of sweet cream, heat to boiling point, season to taste, and serve.

Tomato Soup No. 2.—To two cups of celery stock add two cups of tomato and a teaspoonful of sugar. Simmer an hour and rub through a sieve. Cook together one tablespoonful of butter and two tablespoonfuls of flour. Add the strained tomato, simmer five minutes, season to taste, and serve.

Transparent Tomato Soup No. 1.—To two cups of clear soup add two cups of tomato rubbed through a sieve, and, when boiling, add one tablespoonful of arrowroot or cornstarch, wet with two tablespoonfuls of cold water. Simmer five minutes, add a tablespoonful of butter, season to taste, and serve.

Transparent Tomato Soup No. 2.—To two cups of clear soup add two cups of cooked tomato, rubbed through a sieve, and one cup of pearled tapioca cooked until transparent. Simmer five minutes, season to taste, and serve.

Brown Soup No. 1.—Cook together in a sauce-pan, until brown, one tablespoonful of butter and two tablespoonfuls of flour. Add four cups of mixed soup stock, simmer five minutes, season to taste, and serve.

Brown Soup No. 2.—Cook together in a sauce-pan, until brown, one tablespoonful of butter and two tablespoonfuls of flour. Add four cups of any kind of stock, one cup of strained tomato, one teaspoonful of sugar, and half a teaspoonful of curry powder. Simmer ten minutes, season to taste, and serve.

Brown Soup No. 3.—To four cups of mixed soup stock add two cups of black beans, boiled and rubbed through a sieve, one cup of strained tomato, one tablespoonful each of sugar and meat caramel, and one tablespoonful of butter and two tablespoonfuls of flour cooked together until brown. Let simmer till smooth, season to taste, and serve with a thin slice of lemon in each plate.

Gumbo Soup.—Separate the joints of a chicken, cut the breast and back in small pieces, and cook in clarified butter until brown. Lift to a sauce-pan and add to the chicken six cups of water. Add a tablespoonful of flour to the butter in the spider, mix well, pour in two cups of water, and let simmer until all the browning on the spider is mixed with the water, then strain into the sauce-pan containing the chicken. Let simmer an hour, add two cups of okra, half a cup of sweet corn, half a cup of tomatoes, skinned and cut in small pieces, half a cup of string beans cut in dice and parboiled, and one tablespoonful of minced onion. Simmer half an hour, season to taste, and serve.

Mock Turtle Soup.—Put a prepared calf's head, after removing the brains, into a soup kettle, add a teaspoonful of salt, cover with boiling water, simmer twenty minutes, drain, and lay in cold water. Tie the brains in a cloth and cook five minutes in boiling salted water. After the head has lain in cold water five minutes, put it again in the kettle, add three quarts of compound stock, four cloves, ten allspice, and a tablespoonful each of sugar and vinegar. Simmer until the meat becomes very tender, then drain and set the stock aside to cool. Remove the meat from the head, and when perfectly cold cut the best portions into large dice. Cook together in a sauce-pan, until brown, two tablespoonfuls each of butter and flour, add the stock from the head—having first removed the grease—the meat cut in dice, the brains cut in small pieces, the yolks of a dozen hard-boiled eggs, the juice of a lemon, half a teaspoonful of grated lemon peel, a fourth of a teaspoonful of grated nutmeg, ten drops extract of ginger, and a tablespoonful of sugar caramel. Simmer five minutes, season to taste, and serve.

A thin slice of lemon may be served in each plate; and, if desired, force meat balls may be added to the ingredients of the soup. Two pairs of calves' feet may be used in place of a calf's head.

Green Turtle Soup.—Let the turtle bleed several hours with its head hanging downward, then divide the shells, and remove the entrails. Clean the fins and fleshy parts, put them in a sauce-pan, cover with water, and simmer until the shells of the fins detach themselves. Drain, cut in small pieces, put in a sauce-pan with six cups of compound stock, simmer gently three hours, or until cooked, then add three hard-boiled eggs, chopped, two cups of Brown Sauce No. 1, the juice of a lemon, the grated peel of half a lemon, a quarter of a grated nutmeg, and ten drops extract of ginger. Simmer five minutes, season to taste, and serve.

Clam Chowder.—Cut a quarter of a pound of salt pork into thin slices. Divide the slices into strips and sauté in a spider until brown and crisp. Put the browned pork into a sauce-pan and add to it a minced onion and a tablespoonful of butter. Chop two dozen clams tolerably fine. Pare and cut in dice a quart of potatoes. Skin and cut in pieces a pint of tomatoes. Break into pieces three or four pilot biscuit. To the pork and onion add these things in alternate layers. Season to taste with salt and pepper. Cover with hot water. Put a tight-fitting lid on the sauce-pan, and simmer gently for half an hour, or until the potato is cooked. Add two cups of hot cream or milk and serve.

Fish Chowder.—Prepare fresh codfish by removing the skin and bones and cutting the fish in pieces about an inch square. Follow the directions given for making clam chowder, using, in place of the clams, four cups of the prepared codfish. Codfish makes the finest fish chowder, but other fish can be used, if desired.

Worcestershire or other fish sauce may be served with either fish or clam chowder.

BISQUES.

Among soups the bisques hold a place about midway between creams and purées. The creams are smoother than either the bisques or purées. In consistency the bisques are thicker than the creams but thinner than the purées.

Bisque of Tomato.—Prepare a Tomato Soup No. 2,

add a cup of sweet cream and a pinch of soda, and serve immediately.

Bisque of Lobster.—To two cups of boiled lobster, freed from bits of shell, add half a cup of tomato and two cups of compound stock. Simmer fifteen minutes, let cool, pound, if necessary, and rub through a sieve. Cook together one tablespoonful of butter and two tablespoonfuls of flour, add the strained lobster, simmer five minutes, pour in two cups of cream, heat to boiling point, season to taste, and serve.

Bisque of Clams.—Simmer two dozen clams in their own juice about five minutes and drain the liquor from them into a bowl. Chop the clams fine, or pound them in a mortar, mix with the liquor, and rub through a sieve. Cook together in a sauce-pan two tablespoonfuls each of butter and flour, add the strained clams and two cups of milk, and heat to boiling point. Stir the mixture while heating, season to taste, and serve.

Bisque of Oysters.—Bisque of oysters may be prepared like bisque of clams. In either case one tablespoonful of butter may be omitted, and a cup of cream substituted for the cup of milk.

PURÉES.

No matter how much of a vegetable is used for thickening a purée a small quantity of arrow-root, corn-starch, or flour should be used to hold the vegetable in solution and make the soup smooth. And when the vegetable is delicate in flavor it should be cooked in a small quantity of water and all the water be used in making the purée.

Puree of Peas.—Cook together one tablespoonful of butter and two tablespoonfuls of flour, add two cups of peas cooked very tender, in just enough water to cover them, and rubbed through a sieve, also the water in which the peas cooked, and two cups of veal or chicken broth. Let simmer ten minutes, season, and serve.

Puree of Tomato No. 1.—Cook together one tablespoonful of butter and two tablespoonfuls of flour, add two cups of cooked tomato, rubbed through a sieve, and two cups of veal or chicken broth. Let simmer five minutes, pour in a cup of sweet cream, bring to boiling point, season to taste, and serve.

Puree of Tomato No. 2.—To two cups of compound soup stock add two cups of cooked tomato strained through a sieve, one tablespoonful of sugar caramel, and one tablespoonful of arrow-root or cornstarch, mixed with two tablespoonfuls of cold water. Let simmer five minutes, add a tablespoonful of butter, season, and serve.

Puree of Tomato No. 3.—Cook together one tablespoonful of butter and two tablespoonfuls of flour, add three cups of cooked tomato rubbed through a sieve, simmer five minutes, pour in a cup of cream, bring to boiling point, season to taste, add a quarter of a teaspoonful of soda, and serve.

Puree of Potato.—Cook together one tablespoonful of butter and two tablespoonfuls of flour, add two cups of boiled potato and one cup of boiled onion rubbed through a sieve, and two cups of hot milk. Let simmer five minutes, pour in a cup of cream, bring to boiling point, season to taste, and serve.

Onions, if liked, may be used in larger proportion in this purée. A desirable change may also be had by frying the onions in clarified butter until brown, adding a little water, and stewing until very tender, before rubbing through the sieve. And when the onions are fried in this manner, a simple broth of any kind may be used in place of milk or cream, with very satisfactory results.

Puree of Beans No. 1.—Cook together one tablespoonful of butter and two tablespoonfuls of flour, add two cups of any simple stock, and two cups of well-cooked beans, rubbed through a sieve. Simmer five minutes, season, and serve.

Puree of Beans No. 2.—Cook together one tablespoonful of butter and two tablespoonfuls of flour, add one cup of sweet milk and two cups of lima beans stewed and rubbed through a sieve. Simmer five minutes, pour in a cup of sweet cream, bring to boiling point, season to taste, and serve.

Puree of Beans No. 3.—Cut two slices of breakfast bacon in small pieces and sauté in a spider until a light brown, add two tablespoonfuls of flour, and when browned lightly add two cups of water, and simmer, in a covered sauce-pan, fifteen minutes. Strain, add two cups of cooked beans rubbed through a sieve, simmer five minutes, season to taste, and, just before serving, add a tablespoonful of tomato catsup.

Puree of Asparagus.—Cook together a tablespoonful of butter and two tablespoonfuls of flour, add one cup of sweet milk and two cups of tender asparagus, cooked and rubbed through a sieve. Let simmer five minutes, pour in a cup of cream, bring to boiling point, season, and serve.

Any simple broth may be used in place of milk and cream in making this purée.

Puree of Spinach.—Cook together one tablespoonful of butter and two tablespoonfuls of flour, add one cup of sweet milk and two cups of cooked spinach rubbed through a sieve. Let simmer five minutes, pour in a cup of sweet cream, bring to boiling point, season to taste, and serve.

Any simple broth may be used in place of milk and cream in this purée.

Puree of Salsify.—Cook together one tablespoonful of butter and two tablespoonfuls of flour, add one cup of sweet milk and two cups of salsify cooked and rubbed through a sieve. Let simmer five minutes, pour in a cup of sweet cream, bring to boiling point, season to taste, and serve.

Chicken or veal broth may be used in place of milk and cream in this purée.

Purées may be made of carrots, turnips, parsnips, beets, and other vegetables in the same way they are made of salsify, asparagus, etc. In a similar manner they can be made of chicken, game, fish, and shell fish—the meat or fish being cooked tender, then ground or pounded and rubbed through a sieve.

Puree of Chestnuts.—Blanch two cups of hulled chestnuts, put them in two cups of boiling water slightly salted, cook until tender, then rub through a sieve. Put into a sauce-pan with two cups of chicken or veal stock, thicken with one tablespoonful of butter and two tablespoonfuls of flour cooked together, add a teaspoonful of sugar, let simmer five minutes, season to taste, and serve.

Puree of Lentils.—In six cups of cold water cook a quart of lentils, a slice of lean ham, the skeleton of a roast chicken or other fowl, an onion, and half a dozen roots of celery. Strain the broth into a saucepan, rub the lentils through a sieve, add them to the broth, thicken with a tablespoonful of butter and two tablespoonfuls of flour cooked together, let simmer five minutes, season, and serve.

A simpler purée of lentils may be made by cooking the lentils in salted water, rubbing them through a sieve, mixing them with the water in which they were cooked, and then thickening the mixture with butter and flour.

Puree of Sorrel.—Boil a quart of sorrel until tender, then drain and rub through a sieve. Cook together a tablespoonful of butter and two tablespoonfuls of flour, add to it the sorrel and four cups of chicken, veal, or beef broth. Let simmer five minutes, season to taste, and serve.

A cup of sweet cream may be added, if liked, just before the purée is taken from the fire.

CHAPTER XI.

MEAT SAUCES.

The principles involved in making meat sauces are similar to those involved in making many soups; and the relation between the two subjects is so intimate that from quite a number of sauces—when properly prepared—excellent soups can be made by simply adding water and seasoning.

A sauce is a liquid, semi-liquid, or stiff mixture composed of oil, butter, cream, flour, eggs, fish, shell fish, game, poultry, meat, vegetables, and fruits or fruit extracts, flavored and seasoned with herbs, spices, and condiments. The mission of a sauce is to improve or render more appetizing the dish with which it is served; and when needed for such purpose it should be chosen with that object in view. Mixtures, denominated sauces, are too frequently and too indiscriminately served. A sauce that is inaptly chosen, and is unsuitable for the dish with which it is served, detracts from, instead of improving, the flavor of the dish. And a sauce served with a dish when it is not needed is simply an impertinence.

A knowledge of these facts should lead to a strict observance of the following rules: 1st, All foods of delicate flavors when freshly cooked are not, except in rare cases, improved by being served with made sauces; 2d,

Pungent and highly flavored sauces should be served with foods that lack flavor, or with those the flavor of which is obtrusive—so they may supply flavor in the former case and modify it in the latter.

To call sauces, soups, and made dishes by arbitrary names that give no idea of their component parts is confusing and misleading to the average reader. Hence the name given to each sauce in the following list is that which best indicates its constituents and character.

Parsley Butter No. 1.—To one tablespoonful of butter add a teaspoonful of minced parsley and mix well. Season and serve.

Parsley Butter No. 2.—Prepare as above and add a teaspoonful of lemon juice.

Brown Butter No. 1.—Cook in a small sauce-pan, until brown, two tablespoonfuls of butter, add a teaspoonful of lemon juice or vinegar, season, and serve on boiled fish, oysters, tripe, calf's brains, etc.

Brown Butter No. 2.—Make like Brown Butter No. 1, then add a tablespoonful of onion juice or grated onion, a teaspoonful of sugar, and half a teaspoonful of mustard. Season and serve.

Brown Butter No. 3.—Cook in a small sauce-pan two tablespoonfuls of butter until brown, add one tablespoonful each of vinegar and Worcestershire sauce, season, and serve. Tomato catsup may be used in place of Worcestershire sauce.

Drawn Butter.—Cook together until well mixed one tablespoonful each of butter and flour, add one cup of water or broth, simmer five minutes, then add another tablespoonful of butter. Season and serve.

Egg Sauce.—To a cup of drawn butter add a hard-boiled egg sliced or minced, and serve.

Mushroom Sauce.—Cook together, until a light brown color, two tablespoonfuls each of butter and flour, add a can of button mushrooms, with the water it contains, and a cupful of water or broth. Simmer five minutes, stirring meanwhile, season, and serve. The flavor of the mushroom is more distinct and pronounced if the sauce is seasoned only with salt and mixed pepper. If broth is used in the preparation of mushroom sauce instead of water, it should be the broth of such meat as the sauce is to be served with—for instance, chicken broth when to be served with chicken, beef broth when to be served with beef, etc.

Fresh Mushroom Sauce.—Put in a granite-ware or porcelain-lined sauce-pan two tablespoonfuls of butter. When hot add two cups of fresh, prepared mushrooms, cover closely, and cook briskly two or three minutes. Season to taste with salt and pepper, and serve with broiled beefsteak, birds, or sweetbreads.

Brown Sauce No. 1.—Cook together until brown two tablespoonfuls each of butter and flour, add two cups of water from the roasting pan, after it has been strained and skimmed of grease, and simmer five minutes. Serve with roast beef, mutton, veal, pork, turkey, chicken, etc.

Brown Sauce No. 2.—Cook together until brown two tablespoonfuls each of butter and flour, add two cups of soup stock, or water from the roasting pan, half a cup of strained tomato, and a tablespoonful of lemon juice. Simmer five minutes, season with salt and mixed pepper, and serve.

Brown Sauce No. 3.—Sauté, in clarified butter or drippings, a medium-sized onion, carrot, and tomato, until a light brown. Put them in a sauce-pan with three cloves, four allspice, some roots and trimmings of celery, two or three sprigs of parsley, a slice of sweet turnip, a small bay leaf, a bit of mace, and a pinch of thyme or other sweet herb. Add four cups of broth or mixed stock, cover closely, and simmer gently for two hours. Strain out the vegetables and herbs, remove the grease, and add to the broth a tablespoonful each of glaze, or meat extract, sugar caramel, Worcestershire sauce, and walnut catsup, or Chili or Chutney sauce. Thicken with two tablespoonfuls each of butter and flour cooked together until brown, season to taste, and serve.

Sauce Piquant No. 1.—To Brown Butter No. 1 add a tablespoonful of mixed pickle chopped fine, heat, season, and serve.

Sauce Piquant No. 2.—Cook together until brown one tablespoonful each of butter and flour, add half a cup of strained tomato and two cups of soup stock, or water from the roasting pan. Simmer five minutes, add half a cup of mixed pickles, chopped fine, heat to boiling point, season, and serve.

Jelly Sauce No. 1.—Brown two tablespoonfuls of butter, add two tablespoonfuls of currant or other acid jelly, cook till melted and hot, season with salt and mixed pepper, and serve with venison steaks, mutton chops, or broiled birds.

Jelly Sauce No. 2.—To two cups of brown sauce add one cup of currant jelly, heat till dissolved and boiling, season to taste, and serve with roast venison, mutton, or wild ducks.

Jelly Sauce No. 3.—Cook together in a sauce-pan two tablespoonfuls of butter and one tablespoonful of flour until brown, add two tablespoonfuls of currant, cranberry, or other acid jelly, one tablespoonful of lemon juice or vinegar, quarter of a teaspoonful each of mustard flour, and grated lemon peel, half as much mace or nutmeg, a dozen olives, chopped fine, and a cup of broth or water from the roasting pan. Simmer five minutes, season, and serve with roast duck, venison, or mutton—or use in re-warming cold roast duck, venison, or mutton.

Parsley Sauce No. 1.—Cook together a tablespoonful each of butter and flour, add a cup of chicken broth and a teaspoonful of minced parsley. Simmer five minutes, add another tablespoonful of butter, season, and serve with boiled chicken.

Parsley Sauce No. 2.—Make as before directed, and just before serving add a hard-boiled egg chopped fine.

Caper Sauce No. 1.—Cook together a tablespoonful each of butter and flour, add one cup of lamb broth, one tablespoonful of capers, and one hard-boiled egg chopped fine. Simmer five minutes, add another tablespoonful of butter, season, and serve with boiled lamb.

Caper Sauce No. 2.—To the ingredients used in the last formula add a tablespoonful of minced parsley and a tablespoonful of vinegar from the capers. Use mutton instead of lamb broth and serve with boiled mutton.

Fish Sauce.—Cook together a tablespoonful each of butter and flour, add one cup of water and a tablespoonful of minced parsley. Simmer five minutes, add another tablespoonful of butter, a tablespoonful each of minced onion and lemon juice, and, if liked, one of bottled fish sauce. Season and serve with boiled or steamed fish.

Oyster Sauce.—To one cup of drawn butter made with water add a dozen medium-sized oysters and simmer five minutes, or until the thin edges wrinkle and separate. Season and serve with boiled codfish, boiled turkey, capon, or chicken.

Celery Sauce.—To one cup of drawn butter made with celery stock add one cup of white celery, cut in dice, and cooked tender. Simmer five minutes, season, and serve with boiled or roasted turkey, chicken, or veal.

Salsify Sauce.—To one cup of drawn butter made with salsify stock add one cup of salsify, cut in small pieces and cooked until tender. Season and serve in place of oyster sauce.

WHITE SAUCES.

White sauces resemble drawn butter sauces, but differ from them in one particular—they invariably contain milk or cream. White sauces may be made distinctive and unlike each other by the use of different flavorings. But the flavoring should always be suited to the food with which the sauce is to be served, and should not darken the color of the sauce. Milk may be used in place of cream in making white sauces, but in such cases an additional spoonful of butter should be added to give richness to the sauce. White sauces made with milk or cream may be used as a substitute for drawn butter, for egg, oyster, celery, or salsify sauce.

Bread Sauce No. 1.—To one cup of sifted bread crumbs add half a cup of finely minced onion and one cup of sweet milk. Simmer ten minutes, add a cup of sweet cream, bring to boiling point, season, and serve.

Bread Sauce No. 2.—To one cup of sifted bread crumbs add one cup of celery broth, simmer ten minutes, add one cup of cream and one cup of cooked celery, bring to boiling point, season, and serve.

White Sauce No. 1.—Cook together until well mixed one tablespoonful each of butter and flour, add a cup of sweet cream, simmer five minutes, season, and serve.

White Sauce No. 2.—Cook together until well mixed two tablespoonfuls each of butter and flour, add a cup of cream, simmer five minutes, season, and serve.

White Sauce No. 3.—Cook together two tablespoonfuls each of butter and flour, add one cup of white soup stock, simmer five minutes, add one cup of sweet cream, heat to boiling point, season, and serve.

White Sauce No. 4.—Cook together until well mixed one tablespoonful of butter and one teaspoonful of flour, add a cup of sweet cream, simmer five minutes, season, and serve.

Shrimp Sauce.—To one cup of White Sauce No. 1 add two tablespoonfuls of lemon juice and two dozen shrimps that have been cooked and prepared, heat to boiling point, season, and serve.

This sauce may be varied occasionally by adding to it a teaspoonful of anchovy paste.

Lobster Sauce No. 1.—To one cup of White Sauce No. 1 add one cup of cooked lobster, picked into small pieces, two tablespoonfuls of lemon juice, and a salt spoonful of mustard. Heat to boiling point, season, and serve.

The coral of the lobster mashed to a smooth paste with a little butter and added to this sauce improves it.

Lobster Sauce No. 2.—To one cup of White Sauce No. 1 add half a cup of strained cooked tomato and one cup of cooked lobster meat cut in small pieces, or pounded and rubbed through a sieve, heat to boiling point, season, and serve.

Anchovy Sauce.—To one cup of White Sauce No. 1 add a tablespoonful each of lemon juice and anchovy paste, heat to boiling point, season, and serve.

Egg, parsley, caper, lobster, shrimp, and anchovy sauce are all used as sauces for boiled fish, and are all excellent, but the most popular of all fish sauces is:

Sauce Hollandaise No. 1.—To one cup of White Sauce No. 1 add a quarter of a teaspoonful of ground mace, a teaspoonful of onion juice, and a tablespoonful of lemon juice or vinegar. Bring to boiling point, then stir in the yolks of three eggs, well beaten, with a tablespoonful of water. Add the eggs slowly and continue the cooking, after the egg is all in, for about a minute. Remove from the fire, add a tablespoonful of butter, season, and serve.

Sauce Hollandaise No. 2.—Prepare as in last formula, and add the whites of the eggs, beaten stiff, after removing the sauce from the fire.

Sauce Tartare.—To one cup of mayonnaise dressing

seasoned with mixed seasoning, add a teaspoonful of French mustard and a tablespoonful each of pickled onions, capers, water cress, and parsley minced fine before measuring, also a teaspoonful of tarragon vinegar. Mix all well together and serve.

Glaze.—Put a quart of simple or compound stock into a granite-ware or porcelain-lined sauce-pan, and cook very slowly until as thick as syrup and light brown in color. Let cool and use.

Tomato Sauce No. 1.—Simmer gently for an hour four medium-sized tomatoes cut in slices, one tablespoonful of minced onion, and three cloves. Rub through a sieve, add a cup of water with which a teaspoonful of cornstarch is mixed, and a teaspoonful of sugar. Simmer five minutes, add a tablespoonful of butter, season, and serve.

This sauce is especially appropriate with boiled tongue, ham, or corned beef.

Tomato Sauce No. 2.—Cook together one tablespoonful of butter and two tablespoonfuls of flour, add one cup of cooked, strained tomato, and one cup of compound stock. Simmer five minutes, season, and serve.

Tomato Sauce No. 3.—Cook together one tablespoonful of butter and two tablespoonfuls of flour, add one cup of strained tomato, and one cup of celery or chicken broth. Simmer five minutes, season, and serve.

This is an appropriate sauce for chicken croquettes, veal cutlets, and fried or sautéd sweetbreads.

Tomato Sauce No. 4.—Cook together one tablespoonful of butter and two tablespoonfuls of flour, add one cup of strained tomato, simmer five minutes, add one cup of sweet cream, bring to boiling point, season to taste, and serve.

This sauce can be served appropriately with either croquettes or cutlets of chicken, sweetbreads, lobster, or fish.

Tomato Sauce No. 5.—Cook together one tablespoonful of butter and two tablespoonfuls of flour until brown, add one cup of strained tomato, one cup of mixed stock, and a tablespoonful each of sugar caramel and glaze, or extract of beef. Simmer five minutes, season to taste, and serve.

This is an appropriate sauce to serve with mutton chops, Hamburg steak, or croquettes of beef, veal, or mutton.

CHAPTER XII.

FRYING.

The average individual entertains the idea that when meat, vegetables, and other edibles are cooked in grease they are fried. And, with that idea in mind, writers and lecturers on cookery and hygiene have for a good many years been denouncing fried food and heaping anathemas upon the frying pan. There is no doubt that food of any kind that becomes saturated with grease while being cooked is unhealthful and productive of disease. But it does not, therefore, follow that articles of food properly fried are less healthful than the same articles cooked in any other manner. And until it is proven that they are, it is unjust to hold the frying pan responsible for the evils that arise from its misuse, or are incident to its abuse, by ignorant or unskilled cooks. Are not the under-baked rolls, the leathery pan-cakes, the soggy boiled vegetables, the wretchedly roasted meats, the half-broiled fish, the insipid stewed fruit, the smoky-tasting tea, the sloppy coffee, and the other badly-cooked articles that are served every day at a majority of tables equally as detrimental to health as the denounced products of the frying pan? And would it not be wiser to endeavor to improve the methods, rather than to attempt to abolish the process, of frying?

Frying is the cooking of food in oil or fat, and is one

of the most convenient and appetizing methods of preparing many articles of diet. But for the performance of the process three things should be carefully considered: 1st, the temperature of the oil or fat; 2d, the quantity of grease to be used; 3d, the form or shape of the article to be fried.

In order to fry properly the grease must be hot enough to instantly sear the surface of the article put into it. This instantaneous searing or cooking of the surface retains the juices and flavors inside the article being cooked, and prevents the absorption of grease. Butter cannot be used for frying, as it will burn before reaching a sufficiently high temperature to cook the food. And olive oil or cotton-seed oil can be heated to a much higher temperature without burning than lard or beef drippings. The temperature of grease should always be tested before there is danger of its burning, by dropping a slice of raw potato into it. As soon as the potato becomes brown the grease is hot enough for frying most things. The quantity of grease used should be sufficient to entirely submerge the article put into it. The most desirable shape or form for articles of food that are to be fried, if reference is had only to perfect frying, is the spherical or round, as articles of that shape can touch each other at but few points, while nearly their entire surface is at once exposed to the direct action of the hot grease. Thin slices of potato, if the potato is sliced lengthwise, given a twist and dropped into ice water, will fry more perfectly than without the twist. All articles of food that have been wet should be freed from water by shaking in a sieve or towel before they are put to fry. Only a few articles should be put into the fat at a time, lest the heat of the grease be reduced below the frying temperature. A frying basket is convenient if properly used. But it should not be filled with food and lowered into the frying kettle unless the food be of a delicate nature, like oysters and croquettes; and then the basket should be lowered into the hot grease very slowly. As a general rule the basket should be lowered into the grease empty, and the articles to be fried then put into it one by one.

Fried food may be divided into three classes: 1st, That class of food which requires no special protection to prevent the absorption of the grease. To this class belong potatoes, doughnuts, fritters, etc. 2d, That class which needs a special protection called a grease-proof coating. To this class belong chicken, fish, chops, etc. 3d, That class which is very soft or moist, or of perfectly smooth surface, and which, on account of one or more of these conditions, must be given all the protection possible. Articles of this class of food should be wrapped in a mixture of equal parts of wheat flour and corn-meal, in order that their surfaces may be rendered dry and rough before applying a coating of egg batter. To this class belong oysters, scollops, croquettes, etc.

Fried Potatoes.—Prepare the potatoes in any form desired. Let them soak in cold water until wanted for frying. Heat the grease in the frying kettle. Test its temperature with a slice of potato, and if hot enough lower the frying basket into it, and having drained the potatoes in a sieve and shaken them in a towel to free them of moisture, add a few slices at a time until the bottom of the basket is covered. The rapidity with which the potatoes may be dropped into the basket must be determined by the appearance of the fat. If the surface of the grease becomes covered with bubbles, it is an indication that its temperature is too low for perfect frying. Wait until the bubbles disappear before adding more potatoes. This test of temperature will apply to the frying of all articles. As soon as the potatoes are sufficiently cooked lift the basket from the grease, shake it over the kettle to free it and its contents from grease, dust the potatoes with salt and pepper, and pour into a warm dish lined with several folds of cheese-cloth. Serve on a napkin in a platter.

Fried Apples.—Wash and wipe the apples. Remove the blossom ends and all imperfections of the skin. Slice an eighth of an inch in thickness, cover the bottom of the frying basket with these slices, and fry in hot grease until a light brown color. Shake the basket to free the apples from grease, and serve with either broiled or sautéd ham, breakfast bacon, or pork chops.

Fried Onions.—Slice onions, after removing the dry skins, about a sixteenth of an inch in thickness. Cover the bottom of the frying basket with these slices and fry in hot grease until a rich brown color. Shake the basket to free them of grease, and dust lightly with salt and pepper. Serve with beefsteak, or with any kind of chops.

Fried Doughnuts.—Sift three pints of flour into a mixing bowl. Make a well in the center into which put half a pint of sugar, a quarter of a pint of sour milk, two eggs, two tablespoonfuls of butter, a teaspoonful of soda, and an eighth of a nutmeg, grated. Mix these ingredients well together, and work in the flour gradually until a dough is formed sufficiently stiff to be rolled upon a well-floured board into a sheet half an inch in thickness. Cut in any shape desired, fry in hot grease, and drain on cheese-cloth. When cold dust with pulverized sugar. Sweet milk and a heaping teaspoonful of baking powder can be used in place of sour milk and soda.

Fried Corn Muffins.—Take one cup of corn-meal, half a cup of flour, two cups of boiling sweet milk, one teaspoonful of sugar, half a teaspoonful of salt, two eggs.

Scald the meal with the boiling milk and let it stand until cold, then add the eggs unbeaten and sift in the flour lightly. Fry in spoonfuls in deep fat.

Fried Corn-bread.—Mix together a pint of corn-meal, a teaspoonful of sugar, and half a teaspoonful of salt. Pour over the mixture a pint of boiling water, and stir into it a teaspoonful of butter. Add gradually half a pint of cold milk, and then an unbeaten egg. Stir well and fry by dropping a spoonful at a time into hot grease. Drain on cheese-cloth and serve.

Plain Fritters.—Stir together a pint of flour, half a pint of cold water, the yolks of four eggs, two tablespoonfuls of sugar, two tablespoonfuls of olive oil or melted butter, and half a teaspoonful of salt. Beat with a Dover beater until very light, then mix in the whites of the eggs beaten stiff and fry in hot grease, dropping in a tablespoonful at a time. Drain on cheese-cloth, dust with pulverized sugar, and serve. Or omit the dusting of sugar, and serve with orange, lemon, raspberry, or any simple fruit sauce.

Apple Fritters.—Select smooth, medium-sized, sour apples. Pare whole, remove the cores, slice in rounds an eighth of an inch in thickness, dip in batter prepared as for plain fritters, fry in hot grease until a nice brown, drain on cheese-cloth, dust with pulverized sugar, and serve.

Peach Fritters.—Select hard, ripe peaches, separate into halves, and remove from the stone. Pare and divide each half into two slices, not quarters, lengthwise. To a batter made as for plain fritters, add a teaspoonful of peach extract, dip each slice of peach into the batter, fry in hot grease, drain, dust with pulverized sugar, and serve.

Pine-Apple Fritters.—Pare a pine-apple, cut it in slices an eighth of an inch thick, and divide the slices into quarters. Dip each quarter in batter prepared as for plain fritters, fry a light brown in hot grease, drain on cheese-cloth, dust with pulverized sugar, and serve.

Banana Fritters.—Peel the bananas, split in halves lengthwise, divide the halves in the middle crosswise, dip in batter prepared as for plain fritters, fry brown in hot grease, drain on cheese-cloth, dust with pulverized sugar, and serve.

Corn Fritters.—To a pint of sweet corn, either canned or cut uncooked from the cob, add an even teaspoonful of salt and a quarter of a teaspoonful of white pepper. Mix well and stir into a pint of batter prepared as for plain fritters. Fry in hot grease, dropping in a tablespoonful at a time, drain on cheese-cloth, and serve.

Sweetbread Fritters.—Soak the sweetbreads in salted cold water half an hour. Then put them into slightly salted boiling water, simmer gently until tender, remove from the fire, and let cool in the water in which they cooked. When cold remove the skin from them, then separate into their natural divisions, cut the larger pieces in two, so as to render them uniform in size, season lightly with salt and pepper, and mix with an equal quantity of batter prepared as for plain fritters. Drop a tablespoonful of the mixture at a time into hot grease, fry until brown, drain on cheese-cloth, and serve.

Oyster Fritters.—Prepare a batter as for plain fritters, omitting the sugar, and season to taste with salt and pepper. Drain the oysters in a colander. If they are large stick a small skewer through the thin edge of each oyster, dip into the batter, and fry in hot grease until brown. If they are small mix equal quantities of oysters and batter together, and fry, a tablespoonful at a time, in hot grease. Drain on cheese-cloth and serve.

Nun's Puffs.—Put a cupful of water in a sauce-pan over the fire, add half a cupful, light measure, of butter, and when it boils stir in three fourths of a cupful of flour, and cook five minutes, stirring constantly with a wooden spoon. Remove from the fire, and when cool, not cold, stir in, one by one, four eggs. Drop, a teaspoonful at a time, into hot grease, being careful not to get the frying kettle too full, as the puffs enlarge very much while cooking. Let them remain in the kettle about five minutes, drain carefully on cheese-cloth, and when cold dust with cinnamon and pulverized sugar. Or omit the cinnamon and sugar, make an incision in each puff, and fill with whipped cream flavored with vanilla and sweetened.

Rice Croquettes.—To a cupful of boiled, drained rice add half a cupful of sweet milk, a tablespoonful of sugar, and a teaspoonful of butter. Put in a sauce-pan over the fire and simmer gently, stirring frequently, until the rice has absorbed the milk. Remove and, when slightly cooled, flavor with half a teaspoonful of lemon extract, add the white of one egg, unbeaten, fry in hot grease, dropping in a spoonful at a time, drain on cheese-cloth, and serve with pulverized sugar or with any fruit sauce.

Hominy Croquettes.—To a cupful of granulated or fine hominy, well cooked, add a fourth of a cupful of sweet milk, a tablespoonful of sugar, a teaspoonful of butter, and the unbeaten white of one egg. Mix well, and fry and serve in the same manner as rice croquettes.

Fresh Fish Croquettes.—To a cup of any kind of cold fresh fish, from which the bones and skin have been removed, add half a cup of fine bread crumbs that have soaked for half an hour in half a cup of sweet milk, a teaspoonful of melted butter, salt and pepper to taste, and the unbeaten white of an egg, mix well together, fry by the spoonful in hot grease, drain on cheese-cloth, and serve with poached eggs or breakfast bacon.

Lobster Croquettes.—To a cup of picked up lobster add half a cup of bread crumbs softened in half a cup of sweet milk, salt and pepper to taste, a dust of mustard, and the unbeaten white of an egg. Mix well together, fry in spoonfuls in hot fat, drain on cheese-cloth, and serve.

Shrimp Croquettes.—Prepare like lobster, omitting the mustard, and fry and serve in the same manner.

Codfish Balls.—To a cup of salt codfish, cut in small pieces, freed from skin and bone, and well washed in cold water, add a cup of raw potato cut also in small pieces. Put in a sauce-pan, cover with boiling water, and simmer gently until the potato is cooked. Then drain, dry off carefully, mash the codfish and potato together, add a dust of white pepper, a tablespoonful of sweet milk, a teaspoonful of butter, and the unbeaten whites of two eggs, or one whole egg. Fry in spoonfuls in hot fat, drain on cheese-cloth, and serve with poached eggs on toast.

Chicken Croquettes No. 1.—To one cup of finely chopped chicken, either boiled, stewed, or roasted, add half a cup of bread crumbs, softened in half a cup of sweet cream, one teaspoonful of melted butter, salt and pepper to taste, and the unbeaten white of an egg. Mix well together, fry in spoonfuls in hot fat, drain on cheese-cloth, and serve in a napkin, garnished with lemon points and curled parsley.

Chicken Croquettes No. 2.—To half a cup of White Sauce No. 2 add a cup of cooked chicken, finely hashed, a teaspoonful of minced onion, half a teaspoonful of minced parsley, and salt and pepper to taste. Spread on a greased plate to cool, and when cold form into croquettes, cover with egg batter, roll in crumbs, fry in a basket in hot fat, and drain on cheese-cloth.

Chicken Croquettes No. 3.—To a cup of finely hashed cooked chicken add half a cup of finely chopped mushrooms, half a cup of White Sauce No. 1, and salt and pepper to taste. Let cool, form into croquettes, cover with egg batter, roll in crumbs, fry in a basket in hot fat, drain on cheese-cloth, and serve in a napkin, garnished with cresses or lemon points.

Chicken Croquettes No. 4.—To a cup of finely hashed cooked chicken add half a cup of boiled calf's brains, an eighth of a teaspoonful of grated lemon peel, half the quantity of nutmeg or mace, and a tablespoonful of White Sauce No. 1. Season to taste with salt and pepper, form into croquettes, cover with egg batter, roll in crumbs, fry in a basket in hot fat, and serve like Chicken Croquettes No. 1 or 2.

Sweetbread Croquettes.—Prepare the sweetbreads as directed for sweetbread fritters and make the croquettes like Chicken Croquettes No. 1 or No. 3.

Veal Croquettes.—Use boiled, stewed, or roasted veal, and follow the directions given for making chicken croquettes of either kind.

Fried Chicken.—Cut the chicken in pieces a suitable size for serving. Lay the pieces, skin side down, on a plate or board, dust freely with salt and lightly with pepper, cover with egg batter, roll in cracker crumbs, and fry in hot fat until they are a rich brown color and can be pierced easily with a fork. Then drain on cheese-cloth and serve in a napkin, garnished with cresses, celery tips, or curled parsley.

Fried Prairie Chicken.—Fry and serve prairie chicken in all respects like chicken.

Fried Quail.—Fold back the wings and use small wooden skewers to hold the legs in place; season with salt and pepper, dip in egg batter, fry in hot fat until a light brown color, drain on cheese-cloth, and serve in a napkin, garnished the same as chicken.

Fried Fish.—Cut fresh fish of any kind in pieces a suitable size for serving, and season with salt and pepper. Fry and serve the same as chicken.

Fried Oysters.—Select large oysters, drain on a sieve, lay singly on a plate, and season with salt and pepper. Lift each oyster by sticking a small skewer through its thin edge, dip it in white corn-meal and flour sifted together in equal proportions, cover with egg batter, then with crumbs, fry in a basket in very hot fat, drain on cheese-cloth, and serve on a warm platter, garnished with lemon points.

Fried Mush.—Cut cold mush into squares, cubes, or oblong pieces a suitable size for serving, cover with flour and meal sifted together, dip in egg batter, roll in crumbs, fry in a basket in hot fat, until a rich brown color, drain on cheese-cloth, and serve in a napkin; or use to garnish broiled or fried chicken or fish.

Fried Veal Chops.—Select rib or loin veal chops an inch in thickness, dust lightly with pulverized sugar and pepper and more freely with salt, dip in corn-meal and flour sifted together, cover with egg batter, roll in cracker crumbs, fry in hot fat, drain on cheese-cloth, and serve.

SAUTÉING.

Sautéing, which means cooking by tumbling or tossing about in a small quantity of hot fat, is a modified form of frying, and a very excellent method of cooking many articles of food. As in frying, the oils or fats which will bear the highest degree of heat are most perfectly adapted to sautéing. But butter, which will burn at a low temperature, may, if clarified, be used alone or mixed with lard or drippings quite satisfactorily for the purpose. Many things are more palatable when sautéd than when fried, notably oysters, egg-plant, onions, and apples.

If a pan or griddle is to be used more than once for sautéing it should be wiped each time it is used, so as to remove all grease and crumbs. The best utensil for sautéing is a flat-bottomed steel spider or griddle.

Clarified Butter.—To clarify butter heat it to boiling point, and let simmer gently until the salt settles and a frothy scum arises, leaving the oily portions transparent. Remove the scum, drain the oil carefully from the salt, and the clarified butter is ready for use. Butter in being clarified should never be allowed to scorch or become brown.

To Saute Egg-Plant.—Slice the egg-plant in slices about a fourth of an inch in thickness. Pare off the rind, dust lightly with white pepper and freely, on both sides, with flour. Put two tablespoonfuls of clarified butter in a spider over a brisk fire, and, as soon as the butter is hot, cover the bottom of the spider with the prepared slices of egg-plant, brown on the lower side, and turn them over. When brown on both sides, if the egg-plant is not soft in the center, shove to a cooler place on the range and let it finish cooking. Serve on a warm platter.

To Saute Squash.—Summer squash, when young and tender, may be sautéd in the same manner as egg-plant.

To Saute Onions.—Remove the dry skins from the

onion, and slice the onion in thin slices crosswise. To a pint of sliced onions allow three tablespoonfuls of clarified butter. Put the butter in a spider over the fire, and when sufficiently hot add the onions. As soon as the onions in the lower layer become brown lift them with a limber knife from the bottom of the spider, and let those not brown take their place. After they are brown, if the onions are not cooked enough the spider can be covered, shoved to a cooler part of the range, and the cooking be continued a few minutes longer. Serve on a warm platter, or as a garnish to beefsteak or pork chops.

To Saute Tomatoes.—Select smooth tomatoes of medium size, wash, wipe, and cut each of them in three slices. Dust the slices on both sides with salt, pepper, and flour, a little sugar also, if liked, and brown in clarified butter over a hot fire. Serve on a warm platter, or as a garnish for beefsteak, ham, breakfast bacon, pork, mutton, lamb, or veal chops.

To Saute Mush.—Cut cold mush in slices a quarter of an inch thick, brown on a griddle well greased with clarified butter, and serve on a warm platter.

To Saute Scrapple.—Slice, cook, and serve the same as mush. If the scrapple be rich the griddle need not be greased.

To Saute Breakfast Bacon.—Slice thin, remove the rind and brown edges, lay upon a hot spider over a moderate fire until brown on both sides and crisp. Serve as a relish with beefsteak, fresh fish, fish balls, or poached eggs.

To Saute Ham.—Have the slices of ham about a sixteenth of an inch thick, remove the rind and brown edges, lay upon a hot spider or pan over a quick fire until the under side is brown, then turn the slices and brown the other side. Put two or three tablespoonfuls of boiling water in the spider, cover it closely so as to shut in the steam, shove to the back of the range, and let simmer ten minutes. At the end of that time lift the slices of ham upon a warm platter, drain the grease from the pan, add a small piece of butter, or a spoonful of cream, mix with the browning in the pan, pour over the ham on the platter, and serve.

To Saute Potatoes.—Slice cold boiled potatoes in slices a sixteenth of an inch in thickness, season to taste with salt and pepper, and brown on both sides in clarified butter. Serve in a warm, covered dish, or as a garnish to beefsteak or chops of any kind.

To Saute Sweet Potatoes.—Boil until soft enough to be pierced easily with a fork, remove the skins, slice lengthwise, dust lightly with salt, pepper, and sugar, and brown in clarified butter in a spider. Or split in halves or quarters lengthwise, roll in melted butter, put in a dripping pan, and cook in the oven. Serve in a warm covered dish, or as a garnish for beefsteak or chops.

To Saute Apples.—Wash and wipe sour apples, remove the blossom end and all blemishes of skin, slice in rounds a sixteenth of an inch thick, dust with flour, and cook in clarified butter in a spider till brown on both sides. If the slices are not soft when brown, cover the spider and let them simmer a few minutes on a cooler part of the range. Serve with broiled ham, breakfast bacon, pork chops, or tenderloin.

To Saute Bananas.—Peel the bananas, split them in halves lengthwise, dust in sugar, roll in melted butter, and cook till brown in a spider over the fire, or in a roasting pan in a hot oven.

To Saute Salsify.—Boil the salsify in a small quantity of water, drain, dry off, and mash. To half a pint of mashed salsify add a teaspoonful of butter and season to taste with salt and pepper. Form into cakes, cover with egg batter and cracker crumbs, and brown in clarified butter.

To Saute Parsnips.—Boil in a large quantity of water until tender, split in halves or in slices, season with salt and pepper, and brown in clarified butter; or mash, form into cakes, and cook like salsify.

To Saute Lamb Chops.—Remove the outer skin from the chops, trim them neatly, lay on a smoking hot spider, brown the under side, then turn them over in the spider. When they are brown on both sides drain all the grease from the spider, season to taste with salt and pepper, add a small piece of butter and a tablespoonful of hot water, cover the spider closely, shove back on the range, and let stand for five minutes, then serve. Sauté mutton chops in the same manner.

To Saute Veal Chops.—Cut the chops an inch thick from the ribs or loin, remove the outer skin, dust lightly with pulverized sugar, season with salt and pepper, and dredge with flour. Have a spoonful of hot clarified butter in a spider over the fire, lay in the chops, brown the under side, and turn them over in the spider. When brown on both sides, cover the spider closely, shove it to the back of the range, let the chops simmer ten minutes, then lift them to a warm platter. Add a tablespoonful of sweet milk to the gravy in the skillet, stir well, and strain over the chops.

To Saute Pork Chops.—Season with sugar, salt, and pepper, the same as veal, and cook in a similar manner if the chops are lean; if they are fat, cook like lamb chops.

To Saute Tough Beefsteak.—Prepare, cook, and serve like veal chops, omitting the sugar. This method of cooking a tough beefsteak will make it tender and palatable.

To Saute Salisbury Steak.—Chop or grind lean round steak very fine, form into cakes, like sausage, dust with flour, and brown on both sides in clarified butter on a griddle or in a spider, lift to a warm platter, and season with salt, pepper, and butter.

To Saute Hamburg Steak.—To a pint of meat chopped or ground as for Salisbury steak add a tablespoonful of finely minced onion, or a teaspoonful of sage, thyme, or summer savory, form into cakes, and cook the same as Salisbury steak.

Either Salisbury or Hamburg steak may be cooked by covering the bottom of a greased spider about half an inch thick with the chopped meat, and, when nicely browned, folding like an omelet, and turning upon a warm platter.

To Saute Chicken.—Separate the joints of the chicken, and cut into pieces a suitable size for serving, season with salt and pepper, and brown in the spider in clarified butter or the drippings obtained from salt pork or breakfast bacon. When nicely browned cover the spider closely, shove to the back of the range, and let the chicken simmer ten or fifteen minutes, then lift to a warm platter. If gravy be desired, add a spoonful of flour to the fat in the spider, mix well, pour in half a pint of sweet cream, milk, or water, season to taste with salt and pepper, and serve in a tureen. Breakfast bacon, or thin, crisp slices of pork, may be served with chicken.

To Saute Prairie Chicken.—Prepare and cook like chicken. Currant or grape jelly is suitable to serve with prairie chicken, quail, wild duck, and venison.

Grouse and quail are sautéd in the same manner as prairie chicken.

To Saute Scollops.—Pour boiling water over the scollops and let them remain in it five minutes. Drain and dry on a towel. Sprinkle with pepper and salt, roll in flour, and sauté in clarified butter in a spider.

To Saute Soft-shell Crabs.—Remove the loose shell of the crabs and the spongy substance on both sides of the upper shell. Sprinkle the crabs with salt and pepper, roll them in flour, and sauté till nicely brown in a little clarified butter in a spider. Soft-shell crabs should be browned on both sides.

To Saute Calf's Brains.—Separate the prepared brains into pieces about the size of an oyster, sprinkle with salt and pepper, roll in flour, and cook until nicely brown on both sides, in a little clarified butter, in a spider.

To Saute Rabbit or Squirrel.—Prepare and cook like chicken, but add a little minced parsley to the seasoning.

To Saute Fish.—Remove the head, tail, and fins, also

the bones if desired, cut the fish crosswise in slices a suitable size for serving, season with salt and pepper, roll in white corn-meal, or meal and flour mixed, and cook in the drippings from breakfast bacon or salt pork. Serve the bacon or pork with the fish. As great heat as the fish will bear without burning is essential to develop its finest flavor. Clarified butter can be used in place of bacon or pork drippings, if preferred.

To Saute Oysters.—Drain the oysters in a colander or on a sieve, season with salt and pepper, roll in white corn-meal or crumbs, and brown quickly in a little clarified butter in a spider. Serve on a warm platter, garnished with lemon points.

To Saute Corn Oysters.—To half a pint of sweet corn, cut from the cob or canned, add salt and pepper to taste, three tablespoonfuls of sweet cream, one rounding tablespoonful of flour sifted in, and the beaten white of an egg. Stir lightly with a fork. Have two tablespoonfuls of clarified butter smoking hot in a spider over the fire. Put a tablespoonful at a time of the mixture in the spider until it is filled, without the spoonfuls touching each other, then with a broad-bladed knife or a spoon gently press each spoonful into the shape of an oyster. Let brown on the lower side, turn over in the spider, and let brown on the other side, then lift to a warm platter. Do not pile on top of each other.

To Saute Hominy.—Slightly soften a pint of cold boiled hominy, either coarse or fine, by warming in a sauce-pan with two or three tablespoonfuls of milk. Put two tablespoonfuls of clarified butter in a spider, and when hot put in the hominy, press it against the bottom of the spider with a spoon, let it cook slowly until nicely browned on the under side, then fold like an omelet, and serve on a warm platter.

To Saute Hash.—Mix together a half pint of cold cooked fresh meat, or corned beef hashed, and half a pint of cold hashed potato. The fresh meat may be either broiled, roasted, boiled, or stewed, and the potatoes either boiled or baked. Season the mixture to taste with salt and pepper, moisten with four tablespoonfuls of broth, gravy, milk, or cream, brown in a spider, with two tablespoonfuls of butter, fold like an omelet, and serve on a warm platter garnished with breakfast bacon. Serve with it sour baked or stewed apples.

To Saute Fish Cakes.—Mix together half a pint of boiled codfish freed from bones and skin, half a pint of mashed, boiled potato, two tablespoonfuls of sweet milk, and one tablespoonful of butter. Season to taste with salt and pepper, form into cakes half an inch thick, and brown in a spider in hot butter, or the drippings of salt pork or breakfast bacon.

To Saute Sausage.—Form the prepared sausage meat into small cakes half an inch in thickness. Lay in a spider or on a griddle, without grease, and as soon as the under side is browned turn over and brown the upper side, then cover the spider, shove it to the back of the range, and let the sausage simmer five minutes. To cook sausage in skins, pierce the skins in several places with a skewer or fork, put in a spider, add a few spoonfuls of boiling water, cover closely, simmer gently for twenty minutes, then remove the cover and let the sausage become brown before serving it.

To Saute Calf's Liver.—Remove the skin from the liver, cut in slices half an inch in thickness, soak in salted cold water half an hour, dry on a towel, dust lightly with pepper and freely with flour, and cook gently in a spider in a little clarified butter, or drippings from salt pork or breakfast bacon, until thoroughly done. Serve crisp slices of breakfast bacon or salt pork with the liver.

CHAPTER XIII.

SICK-ROOM COOKERY.

COOKERY for invalids and sick-room cookery, as indicating a particular kind of cookery, are misleading terms, if not gross misnomers. Nearly all articles of food that are suitable for people in ordinary health are suitable, under certain conditions, for invalids at some periods of their sickness or convalescence. For the principles that govern the scientific preparation of food apply in all cases—whether the food be prepared for invalids or for persons in robust health. The province of a physician is to prescribe the articles of diet best adapted to the special needs of each patient. To prepare those articles according to the most approved culinary methods is the duty of the nurse. Therefore, to be a good nurse one must understand the principles of cookery and be able to apply them practically in the preparation of such articles as are prescribed by the physician.

There are, however, a number of simple gruels, beverages, and toasts, seldom relished by people in health, that are craved by invalids, and may be beneficial to them. Most of these are permissible in all sick rooms, and can be used, at suitable times, by a judicious nurse without consulting a physician or without fear of their proving detrimental to the patient. To indicate the general principles underlying the preparation of such articles of invalid diet a few formulas are given :

Corn-meal Gruel.—To one quart of boiling water, slightly salted, add one fourth of a cup of corn-meal, wet with a fourth of a cup of cold water. Boil the mixture rapidly for a few minutes in a granite-ware sauce-pan, then let it simmer for an hour and a half, or until thoroughly cooked.

Oatmeal Gruel.—Into one quart of boiling water, slightly salted, sprinkle slowly, stirring meanwhile, one fourth of a cup of oatmeal, and cook slowly two hours in a granite-ware sauce-pan or a double boiler.

Gruels may be made from rolled wheat, barley, and some other cereals in a similar manner.

Farina Gruel.—To one quart of boiling water, slightly salted, add one tablespoonful of farina and cook slowly in a granite-ware sauce-pan or a double boiler three quarters of an hour. Gruel can be made of farinose in the same manner. All gruels may be strained through a fine hair sieve, or a piece of muslin, if it is desirable to remove the particles of grain that may be in them.

Gruels may be served with or without cream or milk ; and, if desired, the milk or cream may be added to them just before they are removed from the fire.

Rice Gruel.—To one quart of boiling water, salted to taste, add a quarter of a cup of prepared rice, and cook slowly in a sauce-pan an hour and a half.

White Flour Gruel.—To a quart of boiling water, slightly salted, add half a cup of white flour wet with a quarter of a cup of cold water, and cook slowly in a sauce-pan for an hour.

Browned Flour Gruel.—Brown flour by placing it in a shallow pan in the oven and stirring occasionally until it is scorched to a uniform brown color. Then prepare the same as white flour gruel.

Gruels may be made from graham, whole wheat, peeled wheat, gluten, or any other brand of flour, in a similar manner. Gruels made of farina, farinose, rice, or flour of any kind are richer in flavor when made with equal portions of sweet milk and water; and when so made it is better to add the milk just before removing the gruel from the fire. When equal quantities of milk and water are to be used in preparing gruels only half the quantity of water mentioned in the formulas should be used.

Irish Moss Gruel.—Soak a small handful of Irish moss for five minutes in a quantity of cold water. Rinse thoroughly, put into a pint of milk or water, or equal quantities of milk and water, and let stand where it will be very hot, but will not boil, for fifteen or twenty minutes, then strain, season to taste with salt or sugar, as desired, and serve.

All sea moss gruels are made in a similar manner.

Crust Coffee.—Brown gradually, until a rich dark color, two or three crusts or slices of bread, put them in a warm pitcher, add a pinch of salt, pour a quart of boiling water over them, and cover the pitcher closely. This makes a very refreshing drink for invalids. It is sometimes called "toast tea."

Toasted corn-bread or parched corn or wheat may also be used for making drinks for invalids.

Apple Water.—Bake before the fire two or three

medium-sized sour apples until soft and richly browned. Put them in a warm pitcher or bowl, add a pinch of salt and a little sugar, if desired, mash and break them until the seeds are released from the cores, then pour a quart of boiling water over them. Cover the pitcher, let stand five minutes, then strain off the water. Apple water can be used either warm or cold.

A great variety of refreshing drinks may be made for invalids by pouring boiling water over crushed fruit, adding a dust of salt and sugar to taste, and stirring well together. Such heavily flavored and comparatively sweet fruits as bananas, raspberries, etc., make a much more refreshing drink when a small quantity of lemon juice is added to the fruit. Very acceptable drinks may also be prepared from such dried or evaporated fruits as apples, peaches, plums, apricots, prunes, prunellas, and raisins by soaking the prepared fruit a few hours, and then cooking it gently until the water is of the desired flavor. All fruit-juice preparations for invalids may be served either hot, warm, or cold to suit the taste, or fancy of the invalid.

Egg Whips.—A great variety of palatable and nutritious drinks for invalids may be prepared by combining whipped eggs with cream, coffee, cocoa, chocolate, fruit juices, fruit syrups, flavoring extracts, etc.

Egg Nog without **Wine or Brandy.**—Put the yolk of a fresh egg in a small bowl or cup, add a teaspoonful of lemon juice, a tablespoonful of sugar, a grating of nutmeg, and five drops each of ginger and lemon extract. Whip until light and thick. Beat the white of the egg to a stiff froth, and mix with the beaten yolk, then add three tablespoonfuls of cream, whipped or unwhipped, and serve.

Egg Whips with Syrup.—Put the yolk of a fresh egg in a small bowl or cup, add a teaspoonful of cold water, and whip very light and thick. Mix with it the white of the egg beaten stiff and a tablespoonful of any fruit syrup preferred, then add three tablespoonfuls of cream, milk, or ice water, and serve. A tablespoonful of cold coffee, cocoa, or chocolate may be used in place of a fruit syrup; or the egg may be whipped as directed, and sugar, orange, lemon, vanilla, nutmeg, or any flavoring extract desired be added, with cream, milk, or water in the proportion liked.

Lemonade No. 1.—To half a cup of lemon juice add two cups of sugar, or sugar to taste, four cups of water, a quarter of the peel of one lemon in thin strips, and a pinch of salt. Stir well and serve.

Lemonade No. 2.—To four cups of freshly boiled water add one and a half cups of sugar, and a dust of salt, boil two minutes, strain upon half a cup of lemon juice and two or three strips of lemon peel. Serve hot or cold.

Lemonade No. 3.—Omit the lemon peel and prepare like Lemonade No. 2. When cold add a cup each of crushed strawberries and flaked or grated pine-apple.

Orangeade.—To one cup of orange juice add a cup of sugar, the juice of one lemon, a pinch of salt, a quarter of the peel of one orange cut in very thin strips, or half a teaspoonful of orange extract, and four cups of water.

Strawberryade.—To one cup of strawberry juice add the juice of one lemon, one cup of sugar, or sugar to taste, a pinch of salt, and four cups of water. Stir until the sugar dissolves, then serve.

Pine-Appleade.—To one cup of pine-apple syrup or juice add the juice of one lemon, a pinch of salt, sugar to taste, and three cups of water. Stir until the sugar dissolves, then serve. Half a cup of pine-apple juice or syrup may be added to the strawberryade, or half a cup of strawberry juice to the pine-appleade. Other berries and fruits may be used in a similar manner for making palatable drinks for invalids.

Cocoa No. 1.—Put a teaspoonful of cocoa and a teaspoonful of granulated sugar into a heated cup, mix well together, add sweet cream to taste, fill the cup with boiling water, and serve.

Cocoa No. 2.—Put four teaspoonfuls of cocoa into a heated cup, and pour upon it, gradually, stirring meanwhile, one cup of boiling water. When perfectly mixed, pour into a chocolate pot, add one cup of boiling water and two cups of hot milk. Beat with a chocolate whip until light and foamy. Serve with whipped cream.

Cocoa No. 3.—Prepare like Cocoa No. 2, but just before whipping the mixture add to it a fresh egg, beaten very light, then whip and serve.

Chocolate.—If the chocolate is finely grated, prepare the same as cocoa. If it is coarsely grated, mix with the quantity of water to be used, and simmer in a sauce-pan until perfectly smooth before adding hot milk.

Shells.—Put a quarter of a cup of cocoa shells into a sauce-pan, add two cups of boiling water, and let stand where it will keep hot, but not boil, for fifteen minutes. Serve with either hot milk or whipped cream.

Beefsteak Toast.—Toast thin slices of bread until a nice brown color, then moisten them with the juice pressed from rare broiled beefsteak. Serve hot.

Broth Toast.—Dip slices of toast into very hot, well-salted chicken, beef, or mutton broth, and serve.

Frizzled beef or creamed codfish may be served on toast; or the beef and fish may be strained out and the slices of toast moistened with the cream gravy.

Oyster Toast.—Cover thin slices of hot, dry toast with stewed, broiled, or panned oysters until they are well saturated with the juices, then remove the oysters and serve the toast.

Fruit Toast.—Spread over thin slices of buttered toast a small quantity of freshly cooked fruit, sweetened to taste. In using berries, if the seeds are objectionable, the juice alone may be used to moisten and flavor the toast.

Blackberry Mush.—To a quart of ripe blackberries add a pint of water and cook in a sauce-pan until the berries are soft. Stir to a smooth paste three fourths of a cup of flour and half a cup of cold water, and add to the cooked berries in the sauce-pan. Let the mixture simmer five minutes, or until the flour is well cooked, stirring constantly meanwhile, then sweeten with three fourths of a cup of sugar. Serve cold with sweet cream.

Mush can be made of dewberries, strawberries, or raspberries in a similar manner.

CHAPTER XIV.

CANNING, PRESERVING, AND PICKLING.

Our groceries are so crowded with the products of canning establishments that the canning, preserving, and pickling of fruits and vegetables is almost a neglected art in the average family. But as nearly all fruits and vegetables are finer flavored and give better satisfaction when properly canned, preserved, pickled, or made into jams and jellies at home than when done at canning establishments, a few general directions are given in regard to doing such work, and the principles that underlie the canning, preserving, and pickling of various fruits and vegetables are illustrated by a number of select and well-tested formulas.

General Directions.—To retain the color and flavor of fruit or vegetables most effectually in canning or preserving—and to do this should be a prominent aim—the fruit or vegetables should be cooked slowly, in small quantities, in granite-ware or porcelain-lined vessels, and be stirred with a wooden or a silver spoon. Hard, tough fruit that is to be canned or preserved should be cooked in water until tender before any sugar is added; but soft fruit should be cooked in a syrup made from sugar and water, or sugar and the juice of the kind of fruit to be canned or preserved. It is not necessary to use sugar in canning fruit, as nearly all fruits, when properly canned, will keep perfectly without it. Some fruits retain their color and flavor best when canned with sugar, others when canned without it. If fruit is canned without sugar, it can be sweetened to taste at the time of serving. The use or non-use of sugar is therefore an open question and largely a matter of individual opinion.

All canned fruits and vegetables should be put up boiling hot, in air-tight cans; and all fruits and vegetables put up in glass—whether canned or preserved—should be wrapped in paper to exclude the light, and be stored in a cool, dry closet.

Many seedy fruits, such as strawberries, blackberries, etc., retain their color and flavor better when crushed and made into jams than when kept whole and canned or preserved. In making jams only the quantity of sugar that will render them most palatable need be used; but in making preserves it is often necessary to use an equal weight of sugar and fruit.

To Can Strawberries.—Crush one fourth of the berries selected for canning, strain out the juice, and put it in a preserving kettle. To each pint of juice add one pint of granulated sugar and one half pint of water, let simmer twenty minutes, and remove the scum. Fill glass cans with the remaining berries and set on racks or rests in a boiler containing sufficient warm water to cover the racks. Fill the cans of fruit with the prepared syrup and screw on the caps loosely. After all the cans have been filled, add hot water to that in the boiler until it comes half way to the top of the cans, put the lid on the boiler, let the water boil half an hour, then screw the caps tightly on the cans, cover them with a towel **to**

protect them from exposure to cold air, remove from the boiler, and set away to cool. When perfectly cold tighten the caps, if necessary, wrap the cans in paper, and keep in a cool, dry closet. Other berries may be canned in a similar manner, either with or without sugar.

To Can Peaches.—Halve and pare the peaches intended for canning, put them in glass cans, and set the cans on racks in a boiler as directed for canning strawberries. Fill the cans of fruit with a syrup made by adding one pound of granulated sugar to each pint of water used and letting it simmer five minutes, put on the caps loosely, cover the boiler, let the fruit cook half an hour, if the peaches are soft, an hour if they are hard, then screw the caps tightly on the jars, and proceed as directed for canning strawberries.

To Can Pine-Apples.—Pare the pine-apples, flake from the cores with a fork, fill heated glass cans with the prepared fruit, and set them on a rack in a boiler. Make a syrup by cooking together, five minutes, one pound of sugar to each pint of water. Remove the scum from the syrup, fill the cans containing the fruit with the hot syrup, screw on the caps loosely, cook half an hour, tighten the caps, and remove the cans from the boiler. When the cans are cold again tighten the caps, wrap in paper, and set in a cool, dry closet.

To Can Quinces.—Quarter, pare, and core the quinces. Put the prepared fruit into a preserving kettle, cover with water, simmer until tender enough to pierce with a straw, then put into glass cans and set in a warm place. To each pint of the water in which the quinces were cooked add half a pound of granulated sugar, simmer five minutes, remove the scum, fill the cans containing the fruit with the syrup, screw on the caps, and when cold wrap in paper and put in a dry closet.

To Can Pears.—If the pears are ripe and soft can like peaches; if they are hard can like quinces.

To Can Plums.—Pierce the plums with a fork, or girdle them with a knife. If they are very acid use three fourths of a pound of sugar to each pound of plums, if very mild use but a quarter of a pound of sugar to each pound of plums. Put the sugar, with half a pint of water to each pound of sugar, into a preserving kettle, simmer five minutes, remove the scum, then put the plums into the syrup and cook fifteen minutes, or until the fruit is soft and looks cooked. Stir the plums frequently while cooking, and when soft put them in heated glass cans, filling the cans quite full, screw the caps on tightly, and after the cans are cold wrap in paper and set away.

To Can Cherries No. 1.—Fill glass cans with large, ripe cherries and set them on racks in a boiler partly filled with warm water. Make a syrup, using one pound of sugar to each pint of water, and after it has simmered five minutes fill the cans containing the fruit with it, screw on the caps lightly, cook half an hour, then tighten the caps and remove the cans. When cold tighten the caps again, wrap the cans in paper, and set in a dry, cool closet.

To Can Cherries No. 2.—Pit the cherries, put them in a preserving kettle, add half a cup of water to each quart of cherries, cover closely, heat to boiling point, simmer ten minutes, then add sugar to taste. If the cherries are sweet a quarter of a pound of sugar to each pound of cherries will be sufficient, if they are very sour three quarters of a pound of sugar will be required to each pound of cherries. After adding the sugar cook until it dissolves and the fruit boils, then fill heated cans with it, screw the caps on the cans, let them cool, wrap in paper, and set in a cool, dry closet.

To Can Corn.—Cut the corn from the cob and pack it, as compactly as possible, in glass cans. Screw the caps loosely on the cans, set them on a rack in a boiler, add warm water until the cans are half covered, put the lid on the boiler, and cook the corn three hours, then screw down the caps on the cans and remove them from the boiler. When cold tighten the caps, wrap the cans in paper, and set in a cool, dry closet.

To Can Peas.—Fill glass cans, as compactly as possible, with peas. Set the cans on a rack in a boiler, fill with warm water, add a teaspoonful of salt to each quart of peas, screw the caps on the cans loosely, cook an hour, and then proceed as for canning corn.

To Can Lima Beans.—Cook the beans five minutes in slightly salted water, then drain off the water, pack the beans compactly in glass cans, set the cans on a rack in a boiler, fill them with warm water, add a teaspoonful each of salt and granulated sugar to each quart of beans, screw the caps on the cans loosely, cook an hour, and proceed as for canning corn.

To Can String Beans.—Follow the directions given for canning lima beans.

To Can Asparagus.—Wash the stalks of asparagus, cut them of the same length, place them, with the tips upward, compactly, in glass cans, set the cans on a rack in a boiler, fill them with warm water, add a teaspoonful of salt to each quart can of asparagus, screw on the caps loosely, cook half an hour, and proceed as for canning corn.

To Can Tomatoes No. 1.—Skin the tomatoes, put them in a preserving kettle, cook for half an hour, if in small quantities, longer if in large quantities, dip off the water occasionally while the tomatoes are cooking, as a pint of water can be removed from two quarts of tomatoes and their quality and flavor be greatly improved thereby. When sufficiently cooked fill heated glass cans with the hot tomato, screw the caps on the cans, set aside till cold, then tighten the caps, wrap the cans in paper, and keep in a cool, dry closet.

To Can Tomatoes No. 2.—Fill heated glass cans compactly with smooth, medium-sized tomatoes that are not over-ripe. Fill the cans with boiling water, add a tablespoonful of salt to each quart of tomatoes, screw on the caps tightly, let stand till cold, then tighten the caps on the cans, wrap in paper, and put in a cool, dry closet.

To Can Tomatoes No. 3.—Remove the skins from smooth, medium-sized tomatoes as directed on page 26, and fill heated glass cans compactly with them. Fill the cans with boiling water, add two whole cloves and a tablespoonful each of sugar and salt to each quart of tomatoes, screw the caps tightly on the cans, let them stand until cold, then tighten the caps, wrap the cans in paper, and put in a cool, dry closet.

To Preserve Peaches.—Cut a pound of select peaches in halves, remove from the stones, and pare. Put a pound of cut-loaf or granulated sugar, a pint of water, and the pits from half the peach stones, into a preserving kettle and cook until the sugar is dissolved and the syrup boils, then put enough of the prepared peaches into the kettle to cover the surface of the syrup. Simmer gently, turning the fruit over occasionally until cooked and transparent, then put in glasses, filling them three quarters full. After all the peaches have been cooked and put in glasses in this manner simmer the syrup two or three minutes, skim and pour over the fruit in the glasses, cover securely, wrap in paper when cold, and keep in a cool, dry closet.

To Preserve Pine-Apples.—Pare the pine-apples, cut them in slices half an inch thick, and divide the slices into halves or quarters. Make a syrup by using one pound of sugar to each half pint of water, boil, skim, and then proceed as directed for preserving peaches.

To Preserve Quinces.—Cut the quinces in halves or quarters according to size, remove the seeds, and pare and core the quinces. Put the prepared fruit and the seeds into a preserving kettle, barely cover with hot water, and simmer very gently until the fruit can be pierced with a straw, then carefully remove from the water and lay upon plates. Measure the water in which the quinces cooked and to each pint of water add a pound of sugar. Cook in a preserving kettle until the sugar dissolves and the syrup boils, then cook the quinces in the syrup, as directed for preserving peaches.

To Preserve Pears.—Prepare, cook, and preserve as directed for preserving quinces if the pears are of a hard variety, as for preserving peaches if of a soft variety.

To Preserve Plums.—With a sharp knife cut through the skin of each plum and girdle it. Put three pounds of the girdled plums and one pint of water into a preserving kettle, cover, and simmer gently ten minutes, or until the plums are soft, add three pounds of granulated sugar and stir and cook gently ten minutes more, or until the fruit looks clear and cooked, then put in cans, cover closely, wrap in paper, and store in a cool, dry place.

To Preserve Cherries.—To three pounds of pitted cherries add the juice squeezed from the cherries in pitting and one pint of water. Cook and preserve as directed for preserving plums.

To Preserve Strawberries No. 1.—From two pounds of firm, dark-red strawberries pick out a pound of the smallest berries, put them in an earthen bowl with one pound of granulated sugar and mash with a wooden spoon or a pestle until perfectly crushed and well mixed. Let them stand in a cold place for half an hour, then strain through a strong, thin cloth and press out all the juice. Put the juice in a granite-ware or porcelain-lined kettle or sauce-pan and simmer gently twenty minutes, removing the scum. After the large berries have been washed and drained, roll them carefully on several thicknesses of cheese-cloth so as to dry and not bruise them, and put them carefully into hot glass cans. Fill the cans perfectly full with the berries and stand them on a folded wet towel in a warm place. Add to the juice, after it has simmered twenty minutes, one pound of rock candy, broken in small pieces, stir gently, with a wooden spoon, until dissolved, then pour the syrup over the berries in the cans. When the cans are completely filled with the syrup, screw on the caps, which should be first heated, cover with a towel, and place where they will cool gradually. When perfectly cold tighten the caps, wrap the cans in paper to exclude the light, store in a cool, dry place, and turn upside down once a week for six or eight weeks.

To Preserve Strawberries No. 2.—Prepare and cook the syrup as directed for preserving strawberries in formula No. 1, adding cut-loaf sugar in place of rock candy. Spread the large berries, after they have been washed, drained, and dried, on deep platters that have been first heated, dip or pour the boiling syrup over them, set in the sunshine, and cover with fine wire netting or screens. Press the berries gently under the syrup, or pour the syrup over them, two or three times a day, until jelly begins to form, which will be after an exposure of the mixture to a hot sun for about three days, put into small cans or tumblers, filling them quite full, expose to a bright sunshine until the surface is slightly dried over and a skin formed, then cover closely, wrap in paper, and keep in a cool, dry closet.

To Preserve Strawberries No. 3.—To two pounds of granulated or cut-loaf sugar add one pint of water and simmer in a sauce-pan five minutes. Have two pounds of large, firm strawberries prepared for cooking. Put enough of them into the syrup to cover the surface, simmer very gently, shaking the sauce-pan occasionally to keep the berries submerged in the syrup, until they look cooked and transparent, then skim them from the syrup and put into glasses. Cook and dispose of all the berries in a similar manner, filling each of the glasses three fourths full of the cooked fruit, then simmer the syrup until about the consistency of ordinary syrup, fill the glasses containing the berries quite full with it, cover closely, wrap in paper, and store in a cool, dry place.

To Preserve Raspberries.—Large red raspberries can be preserved according to either of the formulas given for preserving strawberries; but, whichever formula is followed, the juice of a lemon should be added to increase the acidity of the syrup.

Raspberry Jam.—From two quarts of red raspberries pick out one third of the smallest berries. Crush, press out the juice, and strain it. Crush the remainder of the berries, put them, with the strained juice, into a porcelain-lined kettle, and, after they begin to boil, simmer gently for twenty minutes, stirring frequently, then add a pound and a half of granulated sugar, simmer five minutes more, remove the scum that rises, take the kettle from the fire, put the jam in glasses, cover closely, wrap in paper, and set in a cool, dry closet.

Strawberry Jam.—From two quarts of strawberries pick out one third of the smaller ones. Crush, press out the juice, and strain it from the crushed fruit. Crush the remainder of the two quarts of berries, put them, with the juice and one pound of granulated sugar, into a preserving kettle, simmer twenty minutes, add another pound of sugar, and as soon as the sugar is dissolved and the fruit begins to boil, remove the kettle from the fire, put the jam into glasses, cover closely, wrap in paper, and put in a cool, dry place.

If the strawberries are not very acid omit half a pound of the sugar.

Blackberry Jam.—Prepare and cook the berries as directed for raspberry jam, using only one pound of sugar to two quarts of blackberries.

Currant Jam.—Prepare and cook the currants as directed for raspberry jam. Or use two thirds currants and one third red raspberries for making the jam.

Pine-Apple Marmalade.—Pare and grate the pine-apples. Put the grated pine-apple into a preserving kettle, add a pound of granulated sugar for each pound of pine-apple, stir with a wooden spoon, and cook fifteen minutes, or until transparent. Put in cans, cover closely, wrap in paper, and put in a cool, dry place.

Orange Marmalade.—Take twelve oranges, six lemons, ten pounds of granulated sugar, and a gallon of cold water. Scrub the oranges and lemons with a stiff brush and warm water, and wipe them dry. Then cut them crosswise with a sharp knife, in as thin slices as possible, and reject the end pieces. Pick out the seeds, put them in a bowl, and pour over them a pint of water. Pour the balance of the water over the sliced fruit, and set both seed and fruit aside and let soak for thirty-six hours. At the end of that time put the sliced fruit, with the water in which it soaked, into a preserving kettle, drain the water from the seeds into it, and cook slowly for two hours, then add the sugar and cook for another hour, or until the mixture jellies. Stir occasionally during the last hour's cooking. Put the marmalade while warm into tumblers or fruit jars, cover closely, and keep in a cool place.

Grape Marmalade.—To four quarts of grapes, picked before they are fully ripe, add one quart of water, cook till soft, then rub through a sieve. To each pint of pulp add a pound of granulated sugar, stir while cooking, and cook twenty minutes. Put in cans and cover closely.

Marmalade may be prepared in a similar manner from peaches, plums, gooseberries, and all pulpy fruits.

Strawberry Jelly.—Put three pints of strawberry juice into a preserving kettle, add one pound of cut-loaf sugar, simmer twenty minutes, add two more pounds of sugar, simmer five minutes, and remove from the fire. Put the jelly in glasses, cover securely, and keep in a cool, dry place.

Raspberry Jelly.—Simmer three pints of raspberry juice twenty minutes, add two and a quarter pounds of sugar, simmer five minutes, or until it will jelly when cooled on a plate, then remove from the fire, fill into glasses, cover closely, and set away.

Blackberry Jelly.—Prepare and cook as directed for raspberry jelly, using half a pound of sugar to each pint of juice; or, if preferred, add the juice of a lemon to every three pints of blackberry juice and use a pound of sugar to each pint of liquid.

Apple Jelly.—Select very tart, red-skinned apples, wash, remove all imperfect spots, and cut in quarters. Put the quarters into a preserving kettle and cook gently for half an hour, or until tender, then put into a jelly bag and let the juice drip into an earthen bowl. Do not squeeze the fruit. Put three pints of the apple juice into a preserving kettle, simmer twenty minutes, add three pounds of granulated sugar, simmer five minutes, then remove from the fire and put in glasses. When cold cover closely, and keep in a cool, dry place.

Crab-Apple Jelly.—Follow the directions given for making apple jelly.

Quince Jelly.—Follow the directions for making apple jelly, but cook the prepared fruit a greater length of time.

Currant Jelly.—Select currants that are not over-ripe. Pick from the stems, crush in small quantities, and strain out the juice. Allow one pound of cut-loaf or granulated sugar to each pint of juice. Put three pints of juice at a time into a preserving kettle, let it simmer gently for twenty minutes, removing the scum occasionally, then add the sugar, stir occasionally, and as soon as it dissolves and the jelly boils remove from the fire and put in glasses, cover closely, and set in a cool, dry closet.

Grape Jelly.—Select grapes that are not over-ripe. Pick from the stems, put into a preserving kettle, add half a pint of water for each pound of grapes, simmer till soft, then put the cooked fruit into a jelly bag and let the juice drip into a bowl. Do not squeeze the bag. Put the strained juice into the preserving kettle and simmer twenty minutes. Add a pound of granulated sugar to each pint of juice, simmer five minutes, skim, put into jelly glasses, cover closely, and set in a cool, dry place.

Pickled Cabbage.—Select crisp, white cabbage and chop it fine. To each quart of chopped cabbage add a tablespoonful each of salt, white mustard seed, and sugar, with pepper to taste. Put the mixture in a jar and cover with cold cider vinegar. Scatter half a dozen cloves over the top of the cabbage, cover the jar, and in a few days the pickle will be ready for use. If the vinegar is pure and strong the cabbage will keep almost indefinitely.

Cold Catsup.—Select firm, ripe tomatoes and scald, cool, and skin them as directed on page 26. Slice the prepared tomatoes in slices a quarter of an inch thick and dice the slices. Put on a large platter and to each quart of diced tomato add a teaspoon of salt, sifting the salt uniformly over the tomato. Place a folded towel under one end of the platter so the water that drains from the tomato may be dipped off. When the tomato is well drained add a cup of finely chopped celery, two tablespoonfuls of granulated sugar, one tablespoonful of white mustard seed, one of minced onion, half a dozen whole cloves, and pepper to taste. Mix lightly together, put in glass cans, filling them nearly full, cover with cold cider vinegar, screw on the caps tightly, wrap the cans in paper, and set them in a cool, dry place.

Cucumber Catsup.—Grate six fresh cucumbers and three onions of medium size. Add a teaspoonful of salt, half a teaspoonful of pepper, and half a cup of vinegar. Mix all well together, bottle, wrap in paper, and put in a cool place.

Green Tomato Pickle.—Slice together a peck of green tomatoes and a quart of onions, and sprinkle the mixture with half a cup of salt. Let stand six or eight hours, drain off the water, put the prepared tomatoes into a preserving kettle, add six quarts of vinegar, three sweet peppers chopped fine, a quarter of a pound of white mustard seed, and an ounce of whole cloves. Boil slowly three or four hours, stirring frequently, and half an hour before removing from the fire add a pound of sugar. Put in cans or jars, cover securely, and set away.

Cucumber Pickles.—Fill a jar with small, freshly gathered cucumbers, sprinkle lightly with salt, fill the jar with boiling water, and let stand till cold. Drain the water from the cucumbers, put them in a preserving kettle, cover with equal portions of cider vinegar and water, heat to boiling point, then pour off the liquid. Put the cucumbers in the jar, add three small sweet peppers, half a dozen whole cloves, and a cup of sugar. Cover with cold vinegar and put away.

Spiced Peaches.—Take seven pounds of peaches, three pounds of sugar, a quart of vinegar, an ounce of cinnamon, and half an ounce of cloves. Make a syrup of the sugar by adding a quart of water, and, when boiling, cook as many of the peaches as the kettle will hold without piling one upon another. Simmer gently, shaking and turning them about until tender and somewhat transparent, then remove with a skimmer and place in a jar. Cook all the fruit in this manner, then simmer the syrup until it is thick, add to it the vinegar and spices, simmer five minutes more, pour it over the pickles in a jar, cover, and set them away.

Spiced Damsons.—Puncture seven pounds of damsons with a fork and lay them in a jar. Heat to boiling one quart of vinegar and four pounds of sugar with spice the same as for peaches. Pour the hot liquid upon the plums, cover closely, and let stand for twenty-four hours. Repeat this process every morning for a week. Then heat the fruit with the syrup, simmer for ten minutes, put in jars, cover closely, and set away.

PART IV.—MIXING.

INTRODUCTION.

THE most important departments of cookery are those of mixing and seasoning. And all articles of food that have to be mixed and seasoned, in their preparation for the table, belong legitimately to those departments. For the purpose, however, of showing clearly that the four primary methods of broiling, roasting, boiling, and frying cover all the different ways in which food can be cooked, it has been deemed advisable, in the arrangement of this book, to place under those respective heads quite a number of articles that belong, and would otherwise have appeared, under the heads of mixing and seasoning.

The general name of wetting is given to all liquids used for mixing doughs or batters, whether the liquid used be water, sweet milk, sour milk, buttermilk, cream, or a combination of these liquids, and the proportion of flour required to a given quantity of wetting, for making a certain kind of batter cake or muffin, can only be given approximately, as the quality and condition of the flour affects the character and consistency of the batter in making batter cakes and muffins more materially even than it does that of dough in bread-making. Still, by keeping in mind a few well-established principles, the careful cook will have no difficulty in handling any brand of flour so as to produce satisfactory results, in all kinds of muffins, waffles, griddle cakes, etc.

These soft mixtures of dough, or batters vary in consistency or stiffness from one cup of flour for each cup of wetting to two cups of flour for each cup of wetting, but the largest proportion of them are graded between the two extremes, and the most desirable occupy a middle ground, varying little from a cup and a half of flour to each cup of wetting—provided winter or soft wheat flour, which is preferable for all soft doughs and batters, be used.

But before mixing any of them the effect that will be produced by the introduction of eggs into such mixtures should be carefully considered. Four medium-sized eggs beaten lightly and mixed with a pint of milk will, when baked, thicken the milk into a custard stiff enough to retain its form when cold. And by this standard the thickening quality of egg when beaten lightly and mixed with milk may be approximated. If the egg be beaten until very light its thickening power diminishes; but it then contributes materially to the lightness of the mixture. The white of the egg is much more valuable for imparting lightness to a batter of soft dough than the yolk, while the latter on account of its richness is most valuable for use in creams, custards, sauces, and puddings.

The effect of butter on these mixtures is to make them short or tender and to enrich them. If many eggs are used in batter mixtures, butter, or "shortening" of some kind, is necessary to counteract the toughening tendency of the eggs.

To make a perfect batter cake or muffin the manner of mixing or putting the ingredients together is equally as important as a careful adjustment of the proportions of those ingredients, and the methods of mixing may with propriety be varied when different proportions of the same ingredients are used.

It is always best to sift baking powder and salt with the flour, that they may be freed from lumps and equally distributed through it. It is also best to sift the flour just before using it.

In making a very thin batter the flour should be put in the mixing bowl, and the milk or other wetting added, a portion at a time, so the batter may be well whipped or beaten before being made too thin.

CHAPTER XV.

BREAD-MAKING.

BREAD-MAKING is a neglected art. In hotels, restaurants, boarding houses, and private families, bad bread is abundant, and good bread seldom found. Everywhere bad bread is the rule, good bread the exception. Yet good bread is one of the most nutritious, satisfying, and inexpensive articles of human food, while bad bread is one of the most innutritious, unsatisfying, and expensive.

The general belief that numerous ingredients and much hard labor are necessary for successful bread-making has no foundation in fact. Bread-making, when the principles are understood, is one of the easiest of culinary processes; and the only ingredients needed for bread of the choicest quality are flour, yeast, milk, water, and salt. Women will use salt rising, dry yeast cakes, potato balls, yeast foam, and innumerable other ferments to lighten their dough, and supplement them with grease, sugar, alum, vinegar, charcoal, and almost every other conceivable thing, and invariably have bad bread. Yet it seems never to occur to them to use only the proper ingredients. Why do people take such infinite pains to make bad bread? Why, in this enlightened age of the world, should any person of ordinary sense want salt rising, dried yeast cakes, potato balls, or any false or putrefactive ferments in bread-making, when compressed yeast or pure home-made yeast is so readily obtainable, and is so superior in all respects for the purpose? Or why should any intelligent person put aught else into dough than flour, yeast, milk, water, and salt, when these ingredients alone produce the very best of bread?

In the good old times of which we are so frequently reminded by pessimistic croakers, wheat with a year's accumulation of dirt clinging to it was emptied from a dirty sack into a dirty hopper, crushed by dirty stones into dirty flour, and then mixed with a dirty ferment into grandmother's bread. Was there not, under such conditions, a basis of truth for the then prevalent belief that it was the allotted task of each member of the family to eat his or her peck of dirt? But those conditions have passed away. Through the agency of an improved method of milling, each grain of wheat is carefully brushed free of dirt and furze before it passes under the polished steel or porcelain rollers to be converted into flour, and by the aid of science pure yeast is made expressly for family use. Should not such an advance in preparing flour and yeast be followed by a similar advance in making bread? The flour and yeast of to-day are far superior to the flour and yeast used by our grandmothers. Why should not the bread made to-day be far superior to the bread made by our grandmothers? The flour and yeast furnished by American men to-day are unequaled anywhere in excellence. Why shouldn't the bread made by American women to-day be the best bread in the world?

Flour.—Under the system of milling that was almost universal until thirty years ago the only fine flour that could be produced was mostly starch, and the finest white flour was then deficient in nitrogen and the phosphates. Millers had no facilities for separating and purifying the middlings which contained the hard, nitrogenous parts of the grain, and they were largely used for pig and cattle feed. The new system of milling, known as the roller process, has, however, entirely revolutionized things, and the middlings which contained those parts of the wheat are now purified and milled with care into patent or new process flour. The idea is still entertained by many that the choice, high-priced, patent flours are deficient in nitrogenous matter, and that coarse flour is more nutritious and healthful than fine. The reverse is the fact. The finest flours contain all the best elements of the wheat berry, without any admixture of pulverized wood fiber, bran coating, or germ grease; and, all things considered, the very finest patent flour holds the leading place both hygienically and economically among cereal foods or grain products.

The highest grade of patent flour is made from middlings cleansed from impurities by "middlings purifiers." The inferior middlings go into other grades in due proportion. And the highest grade contains more gluten in proportion to the quantity of starch than the other grades. But any of the different grades of flour made at a certain mill can be raised or lowered in quality at the option of the miller, by increasing or decreasing the amount of gluten and starch in a given quantity of flour. Where the first patent made from a given quantity of wheat is of the choicest quality, it contains a large percentage of the best constituents of the wheat, and the other grades made from the same wheat must be correspondingly low in those constituents. Of course where only one grade of flour is made at a mill all the constituents of the wheat berry go into the flour; but in a hundred pounds of such flour the quantity of starch is greater in proportion to the quantity of gluten than it is in a hundred pounds of the highest grade patent flour. There is usually considerable difference in the price of first and second grade flour, and frequently a difference of fifty per cent in price between a sack of the highest and a sack of the lowest grade flour. In other words, when the best patent flour made by a certain mill sells for $1.50 a sack, the lowest grade flour made by the same mill sells for 80 cents a sack. As a general rule, however, the highest priced flour is the cheapest, as it contains twice the amount of nutritious material and will, with half the labor, produce more than twice the quantity of good, wholesome bread.

Strength, when applied to flour, means the measure of its power to absorb and retain water; or indicates rather the measure of water that the flour will absorb to produce dough of a certain consistency, without any regard to the delicacy or nutritive qualities of the bread obtained from such dough. And when millers and bakers talk of "a strong flour," they mean that a certain grade of flour will absorb more water, and make more loaves of bread, than another grade will, and that a sack of flour of a special grade will take more wetting into its mixture and yield a greater quantity of bread than a sack of another grade will, the quality of the bread not being taken into account.

Spring wheat has a harder grain than winter wheat and yields a harder and grittier flour, which absorbs more water and is easier to handle successfully than winter wheat flour, in bread-making. But equally good bread can be made from either variety, although more delicate cake and pastry can be made from winter wheat than from spring wheat flour, and what is known in the market as "pastry flour" is simply flour made of winter wheat.

Compressed Yeast.—Yeast is a vegetable germ found upon the skin of grapes, plums, and some other fruits—in fact, the beautiful shade upon the skin of those fruits known as "bloom" is produced by the yeast plants that float in the atmosphere settling upon them. If yeast germs get, or are put, into a substance in which they find material adapted to their development they increase very rapidly, and by their vegetative action during the period of growth cause the substance in which they are growing to bubble or ferment. The manufacturers of yeast multiply these germs indefinitely by inducing fermentation in a sweet infusion of malt, rye, and corn, and millions of the germs rise to the surface of the fermenting liquid, forming a scum resembling the froth of new milk. This scum is removed, run into vats of cold water, and allowed to settle to the bottom. The water is then pumped off, and the yeast pumped into hydraulic presses and reduced by pressure to the consistency desired, when it is made into cakes and put upon the market as "compressed yeast." And from the fact that compressed yeast is the purest yeast that scientific research has yet discovered, and that it is impossible by mechanical skill to crowd a greater number of yeast germs into a given space than are crowded into a cake of compressed yeast, it goes almost without saying that compressed yeast is the best ferment known to the world to-day for bread-making.

It has been demonstrated over and over again that a certain quantity of pure, strong yeast is necessary to produce the best results in bread-making—that it is, in fact, impossible to make the best quality of bread unless the proper quantity of yeast be used; and housekeepers who, to save two or three cents on each baking, buy liquid yeast at the bake shop, or dry yeast cakes at the corner grocery, always have inferior bread and are losers in nearly every way, in the long run. In yeast fermentation the decomposition of the starch in flour yields the gas that lightens the dough, while in these other fermentations it is the gluten that suffers; and as starch is the most plentiful and least valuable portion of the flour, economical considerations alone should induce the use of compressed yeast in preference to any other ferments. Pure yeast produces sweet, nutty-flavored, wholesome bread, while diseased and putrefactive ferments produce the coarse, rough crumb, the pale, flinty crust, and the flat, sour loaf that are so disappointing and discouraging to the bread-maker. The alleged costliness of compressed yeast would be a serious objection to its use in many families, if the allegation were correct. But no one whose time is of any value can afford to dabble with dry yeast cakes or any of the other ferments. They generally cost a hundred fold more than compressed yeast by annoying the user, by robbing the flour of nutrition, and by yielding inferior bread. How much is gained in a baking by using one cent's worth of common yeast and losing four cents' worth of nutritive matter from the flour, over using four cents' worth of compressed yeast and retaining all the nutrition in the bread?

The liability of compressed yeast to spoil in a short time by exposure is an objection that is frequently made to its use. But a similar objection can, with equal propriety, be made to the use of fresh fish, fowl, and flesh generally. And as a large proportion of so-called perishable articles of food require greater care for their perfect preservation than compressed yeast, this objection is more imaginary than real. As long as compressed yeast remains firm and has an alcoholic smell it can be depended upon to give better results than dry yeast cakes or liquid yeast; but the fresher it can be had the better it is for bread-making, and in localities where it is readily attainable housekeepers should always get it as fresh as possible.

Given good flour and good yeast any one should be able to make good bread. For the only other ingredients needed are a little salt and sufficient wetting to mix the flour into a dough of the proper consistency. And the wetting may be either water, or milk, or milk and water—provided always the milk is sweet. Bread mixed with water alone is tougher and sweeter, and will keep moist longer than bread mixed with milk and water, or with milk alone. French bread is mixed with water alone, Vienna bread is mixed with milk and water in equal proportions, and several varieties of bread are mixed with milk alone.

Comparatively good bread can be made with liquid yeast, or even with dry yeast cakes if fresh and sweet; but the best quality of bread can be made only with compressed yeast. And bread can be made so much easier with compressed yeast than with either liquid yeast or dry yeast cakes, that no housekeeper who can get compressed yeast can afford to use any other kind.

Compressed Yeast Bread.—To each pint of lukewarm wetting, composed of equal portions of sweet milk and water, add a teaspoonful of salt and one half-ounce cake of compressed yeast dissolved in about three tablespoonfuls of cold water, then stir in flour with a spoon until a dough is formed sufficiently stiff to be turned from the mixing bowl in a mass. Put this dough on a molding board, and knead well, adding flour until it ceases to stick to the fingers or the molding board, then put it in a well-greased earthen bowl, brush the surface lightly with melted butter or drippings to keep it from crusting over, cover it with a bread towel, set to rise, and let stand for three hours, at a temperature of seventy-five degrees. At the end of that time form into loaves or rolls, put into greased pans, brush the surface with melted butter or drippings, cover as before, and again set to rise for an hour, at the same temperature, then bake.

Dough when light enough to bake should be double

the size in bulk it was when set to rise, and should be so aërated all through that when lifted, in the pan, the sense of weight will be scarcely perceptible.

Bread should be put to bake as soon as it is sufficiently light; and the oven, at the time the dough is put into it, should be at a temperature of 375 degrees—or hot enough to nicely brown a spoonful of flour, if put in it, in two minutes, and it should be kept at almost the same temperature throughout the baking. At that temperature rolls will bake in twenty or twenty-five minutes, and ordinary sized loaves in from forty-five to fifty minutes. A loaf of bread when perfectly baked is a beautiful chestnut brown all over. If either the ends, sides, or bottom have a sickly hue, or are perceptibly lighter in color than the top, the loaf has been imperfectly baked, and should be returned to the oven. A loaf of bread when sufficiently baked will not burn the hand, if lifted from the baking pan and laid on the open palm; and if tapped on the bottom with the finger it will emit a hollow sound. Bread not sufficiently baked deteriorates rapidly and will begin to grow moldy, and frequently ropy, in three or four days, while perfectly baked bread may be kept from mold, and in very good condition, for a week or ten days.

Bread as soon as taken from the oven should be turned from the pans, and placed, uncovered, in such position as will expose the greatest amount of surface to the fresh air, without allowing it to come in contact with anything likely to give it an unpleasant taste or odor. And when cold it should be put in a box or jar to which the air can have access, and be kept in a dry, cool room or closet. To wrap bread in cloths while warm prevents the escape of gas or steam, destroys the crispness of the crust, and robs the bread of much of its fine, nutty flavor.

The quantity of flour necessary to be mixed with a certain quantity of wetting to make dough of the proper consistency for bread cannot be given accurately by weight or measure, without knowing the special brand of flour to be used, as the quantity varies according to the quality. But each quart of wetting will require from three pounds and ten ounces to three pounds and twelve ounces, or from seven to seven and one half pints of the best flour, and the amount of dough mixed from these proportions of wetting and flour will make four medium-sized loaves, or about five pounds, of good bread.

The quantity of yeast used in bread-making is quite important, and if an insufficient quantity is used the bread will be devoid of the rich, nutty flavor, which is a prominent characteristic of all good bread, and will frequently have a yeasty smell or taste.

Bread is never improved by the addition of grease or sugar. Grease interferes with the perfect action of the yeast, and sugar destroys much of the fine flavor of the flour. The simplest, easiest, and best method of making bread that has yet been discovered is the method given above. The formula is that used by the Vienna bakers, who have for many years had the reputation of being the best bread-makers in the world. And all bread made in that manner is known as Vienna bread.

Liquid Yeast.—Compressed yeast is on sale in most towns and villages, but as it cannot be obtained at all times and in all places every housekeeper should be acquainted with some approved method of making liquid yeast. Here is one that has been thoroughly tested: Steep an eighth of an ounce of pressed, or a small handful of loose, hops in a quart of boiling water for about five minutes. Strain the boiling infusion upon half a pint of flour, stirred to a smooth paste with a little cold water, mix well, let boil a minute, add a tablespoonful of salt, two tablespoonfuls of white sugar, set aside till lukewarm, then stir in two half-ounce cakes of compressed yeast dissolved in two tablespoonfuls of cold water, or a gill of good liquid yeast. Let stand twenty-four hours, stirring occasionally, cover closely, and set in a cool place. Yeast made according to this method will keep sweet two or three weeks, and can be used any time during that period for mixing bread, or for starting a fresh supply of yeast.

Liquid Yeast Bread.—Mash one medium-sized, well-boiled potato in an earthen bowl with half a teacupful of flour, and pour over it, stirring meanwhile, a quart of boiling water. Set the mixture aside until it gets lukewarm, then pour into it half a teacupful of liquid yeast, stir well, cover closely, and let stand till light. When it is perfectly light and foamy, which will be in about six hours if kept at the proper temperature, mix together equal portions of this ferment and warm sweet milk. Stir in sifted flour until a dough is formed sufficiently stiff to be turned from the mixing bowl to the molding board in a mass, then proceed in every respect as when making bread with compressed yeast. Bread made according to this method goes under the general name of home-made bread, and if all the conditions are carefully complied with, it will be of good quality, but not nearly so good as Vienna bread.

Imperial Rolls.—Divide a piece of Vienna bread dough, large enough for an ordinary sized loaf, into a dozen irregular pieces about half an inch in thickness. Take, separately, each of these pieces in the left hand, and slightly stretch with the thumb and forefinger of the right hand one of the irregular points over the left thumb, toward the center of the roll. Repeat this operation, turning the piece of dough as it proceeds, at each turn lifting the thumb and gently pressing it upon the last fold, until all the points have been drawn in, when the roll must be turned face, or smooth side, upward to rise, and when sufficiently risen must be reversed in position, or turned smooth side downward in the pan, and placed in the oven. If the folding is done properly, an imperial roll when baked will be composed of a succession of sheets or layers of delicate, tenacious crumb, surrounded with a thin, crisp, tender crust.

French Rolls No. 1.—Take enough dough for a small loaf of bread, and divide it into four pieces. Roll each piece under the palms of the hands, upon the molding board, into a long roll not much thicker than one's thumb, lay in a suitable roll pan, let rise till sufficiently light, then bake.

French Rolls No. 2.—Divide a piece of bread dough large enough for a small loaf of bread into twelve pieces. With the finger-tips knead each piece into a ball, then roll under the palms of the hands, upon the molding board, until each is five or six inches in length—rolling at last upon the ends only, so as to make them pointed and smaller. Place two of these rolls together, and lifting one end of each roll upon the other, pinch together, lay in a flat, broad pan to rise, and brush over with melted butter. Leave half an inch space between the rolls so the crust of each roll may be perfect, and, when sufficiently light, bake in the pan in which they were put to rise.

French Rolls No. 3.—Divide sufficient dough for a small loaf into twelve pieces. With the finger-tips knead each piece into a ball, and place these balls an inch apart, on a greased baking pan or floured board, to rise. Brush over with melted butter, and let stand half an hour at a temperature of seventy-five degrees, then take each ball separately, and with a rolling pin not larger than one's finger, press in the center of each roll, pushing the dough each way from the center, until the dough under the rolling pin is very thin and about an inch and a half in width. Lift up this double roll, stretch it until about an inch and a half longer, and lay it face downward upon a towel or cloth spread in a shallow pan, and close up against one side of the pan. Manipulate another of the rolls in the same manner and place beside the first, drawing up a portion of the towel between the rolls. Repeat the operation until all the rolls are in the pan. Let rise in this position half an hour, or until the rolls are very light, then lift carefully and place on a baking sheet or pan, face up, not allowing them to touch each other, and bake.

Crescents.—Roll the dough as directed for French Rolls No. 2, but twice as long, which will leave it only half as large. Roll down at the ends to make them pointed. Place two of these long, slender rolls beside each other, and throwing them alternately over each other, twist them together, and pinch the ends close. Put them on a baking sheet or pan in the form of a crescent or horse shoe, and let them rise for an hour, or until light, then bake.

Queen Ann Rolls.—Shape the dough as for French rolls, twist two of the rolls together as for crescents, lay in Queen Ann pans or large roll pans, let stand an hour, or until light, then bake.

Rolls of all kinds are more crisp and tender when baked quickly, and the oven should be hotter for rolls than for bread. They should also be considerably lighter than bread when put to bake, as they have but little opportunity to rise after they go in the oven, if it is hot enough to bake them properly.

Federal Bread.—To a quart of either milk or water add a level teaspoon of salt and a cup of liquid yeast or two cakes of compressed yeast dissolved, then stir in flour enough to form a dough somewhat softer than for bread. Add a tablespoonful of melted butter, and three well-beaten eggs, pour into a baking dish or pan, let rise six or eight hours, or until thoroughly light, then bake. When baked, split crosswise in three or four sections, butter generously, and replace so the loaf will have its original shape. Serve warm. This is a favorite bread for breakfast and tea in some sections.

Buns.—Two eggs, two cups boiling milk, half cup

sugar, half cup butter, one cake compressed yeast, flour enough to make a dough. Beat the eggs very light, pour over them, beating meanwhile, the boiling milk, then add the sugar and salt. Let the mixture cool until lukewarm, then add the yeast, dissolved in a little cold water, and stir in flour until a soft dough has been formed. Turn upon the molding board and knead in flour gradually until the dough becomes smooth and elastic, but not stiff enough for bread, then put in a greased bowl, and set to rise for five hours, or until light. When light work in the butter, but do not add any more flour, and let rise for an hour, or until light, then form into buns or balls the size desired, place in a greased pan about an inch apart, and again let rise for two hours, or until light, then bake in a moderate oven.

Cinnamon Rolls.—Roll small pieces of bun dough, after it has risen the second time, into small rolls or sticks. Flatten with a limber knife and cover with melted butter, sugar, and cinnamon. Fold over and roll into circular cakes with one end in the center, and the other pinched to the outer surface, and place in a baking pan, an inch apart. Let rise two hours, and bake in a moderate oven.

German Coffee Cake.—Roll a piece of bun dough after it has risen the second time into a sheet half an inch thick, lay on a shallow baking pan, cover with granulated sugar, then with cinnamon, and lastly with melted butter. Let rise for two hours, or until very light, then bake in a moderate oven. Sliced sour apple can be laid over the cake when light, or the sugar, cinnamon, and butter can be omitted, and the cake when light can be spread with preserves, jam, or jelly, and baked in a moderate oven.

Beaten Biscuit.—To two cups of flour add half a tablespoonful of lard and half a teaspoonful of salt. Rub the lard well through the flour, moisten gradually with half a cup of cold water, and work the dough until it will hold together, then beat with a mallet or heavy implement until it is pliable and blisters. When it reaches this condition roll out, cut into cakes the size desired, prick several times with a fork, and bake in a hot oven twenty-five minutes, or until nicely browned.

Baking Powder Biscuit No. 1.—Two cups of flour, one cup of sweet milk, two teaspoons baking powder, one half teaspoonful of salt. Sift the salt, baking powder, and flour together, add the milk, and beat to a smooth dough. Turn upon a well-floured molding board, dust with flour, and roll into a sheet about an inch in thickness. Dip the biscuit cutter in flour, cut the sheet of dough into cakes, lay in a baking pan, and bake in a quick oven until thoroughly done.

Baking Powder Biscuit No. 2.—Two cups of flour, one cup sweet milk, two tablespoonfuls melted butter, two teaspoons baking powder, and half a teaspoonful of salt. Mix as in No. 1, add the melted butter, after all the milk is in, beat well through the dough, then proceed as before.

Baking Powder Biscuit No. 3.—Two cups flour, one cup cold water, one tablespoon butter, two teaspoons baking powder, one half teaspoon salt. Sift the baking powder and salt with the flour. Rub the butter through it with a limber-bladed knife, add the cold water, mix well with a spoon, then proceed as in No. 1.

Wheat Muffins No. 1.—One and a half cups of flour, one cup of sweet milk, one egg, one tablespoonful of melted butter, a pinch of salt. Put the flour, yolk of egg, butter, salt, and half the milk together in the mixing bowl, and beat until very light, then gradually add the balance of the milk, continuing the beating, and lastly beat the white of the egg stiff, and fold carefully into the mixture. Bake half an hour in a hot oven.

Wheat Muffins No. 2.—Two cups of flour, one cup of sweet milk, two tablespoons of melted butter, two teaspoons of baking powder, a pinch of salt. Sift the baking powder and salt with the flour into the mixing bowl, add the milk, and beat well, then add the melted butter. Bake half an hour.

Wheat Muffins No. 3.—One and a half cups of flour, one cup of sweet milk, two tablespoons of melted butter, two teaspoons of baking powder, two eggs, a pinch of salt. Sift the baking powder, salt, and flour into the mixing bowl, add the milk and yolks of eggs, beat until very light, then add the melted butter, and lastly the whites of the eggs beaten stiff. Bake half an hour.

Rice Muffins.—One and a half cups of flour, one cup of sweet milk, one cup of boiled rice, two tablespoons of melted butter, two teaspoons of baking powder, two eggs. Sift the baking powder, salt, and flour into the mixing bowl, add the milk and yolks of eggs, beat until very light, add the melted butter, then the boiled rice, which stir evenly through the mixture with a fork, and lastly fold in the whites of the eggs, beaten stiff. Bake half an hour.

The formula for rice muffins is exactly the same as that

for Wheat Muffins No. 3, with the addition of a cup of boiled rice ; and although the rice enlarges the quantity of batter considerably it does not materially affect its consistency. The rice, in boiling, absorbs all the moisture it is capable of holding, hence in mixing it in the wheat muffin batter it is not necessary to use any additional wetting.

Wheat Griddle Cakes No. 1.—One and a half cups of flour, one cup of sweet milk, two level teaspoons of baking powder, one tablespoonful of melted butter, one egg, a pinch of salt. Sift the baking powder, salt, and flour together in the mixing bowl, add the milk, butter, and yolk of egg, beat until very light, then fold in the white of the egg beaten stiff, and bake in cakes on a hot griddle.

Wheat Griddle Cakes No. 2.—One and one half cups of flour, one cup of thick, sour milk, one teaspoon of soda, a pinch of salt. Sift the soda, salt, and flour together into the mixing bowl, add the sour milk, and stir with a spoon, but only until thoroughly mixed. Bake on a griddle.

Wheat Griddle Cakes No. 3.—One and one half cups of flour, one cup of buttermilk, one teaspoon of soda, one egg, a pinch of salt. Sift the soda and salt with the flour, add the buttermilk and the egg slightly beaten, stir all carefully together, and bake on a griddle.

French Pancakes.—One cup of milk, half a cup of flour, three eggs, one tablespoonful of olive oil or melted butter, one teaspoonful of granulated sugar, half a teaspoonful of salt. Sift the flour, sugar, and salt together, add the oil, the yolks of the eggs, and one third of the milk, and beat until very light, then gradually add the remainder of the milk, stirring meanwhile, and lastly fold in the whites of the eggs, beaten stiff. Put a teaspoonful of butter or olive oil on the griddle, and when hot pour upon it one third of the batter. Turn when brown, and when baked lift from the griddle, and spread with powdered sugar and cinnamon ; or spread lightly with any rich preserve or marmalade, roll up, dust the outside with pulverized sugar, sear with a hot iron, and serve at breakfast or luncheon, or as an entrée at dinner.

Flannel Cakes.—Two cups lukewarm water, one and one half cups flour, one and one half cups corn-meal, half a teaspoonful salt, half a cup of home-made, or half a cake of compressed, yeast. Add the yeast and salt to the water, mix the flour and meal together, and stir them into it. Let stand over night, or until light, then bake on a griddle. If the batter should become sour by standing over night stir into it half a teaspoonful of soda dissolved in warm water. Milk can be used instead of water for mixing the batter.

Bread Cakes.—Two cups bread crumbs, two cups boiling milk, one cup cold milk, one cup flour, one tablespoonful butter, one teaspoonful baking powder, two eggs. Pour the boiling milk over the bread crumbs, add the butter, cover, and let stand over night, or till cold. Mash to a smooth paste, beat into it the yolks of the eggs, add gradually the cold milk, then add the flour and baking powder sifted together, and lastly the whites of the eggs beaten stiff. Bake, in small cakes, on a griddle, until nicely browned.

Waffles No. 1.—Two cups sweet milk, three cups flour, one tablespoonful of butter, half a cake of compressed yeast, or half a cup of liquid yeast, a level teaspoon of salt. Boil the milk, add the butter and salt, and set aside till lukewarm, then stir gradually into the flour, and lastly add the yeast. Beat well and let stand over night. Give the batter a thorough beating in the morning and bake in greased waffle irons.

Waffles No. 2.—Two cups sweet milk, three cups flour, two tablespoonfuls melted butter, a level teaspoonful salt, three eggs, half a cake of compressed, or a gill of liquid, yeast. Boil the milk, and when lukewarm add the salt and yeast and stir gradually into the flour. Beat well and let stand over night. In the morning add the melted butter, then the yolks of the eggs, one at a time, beating each one thoroughly in the batter before adding another, and lastly add the whites beaten stiff.

Waffles No. 3.—Two cups cold sweet milk, three cups flour, two tablespoonfuls melted butter, two teaspoons baking powder, one level teaspoon salt, two eggs. Mix the baking powder, salt, and flour together, stir the cold milk in gradually, add the melted butter, then the yolks, and lastly the whites of the eggs beaten separately. Bake at once.

Buckwheat Cakes No. 1.—To a quart of cold water add a half ounce of compressed yeast dissolved, or a cup of liquid yeast, and a level teaspoon of salt, then stir in buckwheat flour enough to make a thick batter. Set in a warm place till light, then beat thoroughly, and put in a cool place till next morning. In the morning beat the batter, take out a cupful, and set aside to start the next mixing with; add a quarter of a teaspoonful of soda dissolved in warm water, and sufficient warm milk to thin the batter to the consistency desired. Set in a warm place for half an hour, or until ready to bake.

Buckwheat Cakes No. 2.—Stir into a quart of boiling water in which a teaspoonful of salt has been dissolved half a cup of corn-meal wet with a little cold water, and cook well. Let cool till lukewarm, then stir in half a cup of wheat flour, three cups of buckwheat flour, and a gill of soft yeast, or a small cake of compressed yeast, dissolved in two spoonfuls of cold water, and set in a moderately warm place until light. Just before baking, add half a teaspoonful of soda to the batter, and thin, if necessary, with a little warm water.

These cakes when intended for breakfast should be set to rise at noon the previous day. By eight or nine o'clock in the evening they will be light, and should then be well beaten and set in a cool place during the night.

Pop-Overs.—One cup of flour, one cup of sweet milk, one egg, and a pinch of salt. Put the egg, flour, salt, and half the milk together in a small bowl, and with a Dover beater whip very light, then gradually add the balance of the milk. Half fill deep gem pans, and bake forty-five minutes in an oven at the same temperature as for bread.

As a general rule it is advisable to beat the yolks of the eggs with the batter, and to beat the whites separately and fold them carefully into the batter at the very last. But in all very thin batters it is best to beat the eggs, without separating the whites and yolks, with the flour and a portion of the milk, as in pop-overs and similar mixtures.

Strawberry Shortcake.—Two cups of flour, one cup sweet milk, two tablespoons melted butter, two teaspoons baking powder, one half teaspoon salt. Sift the salt, baking powder, and flour together, add the milk, then the melted butter, and beat to a smooth dough. Turn on to a well-floured molding board, dust over with flour, and roll into a sheet half an inch in thickness. Cut into large cakes and bake in a moderate oven. When thoroughly baked, pull the crust apart with a fork, put bits of butter here and there over the inside, let stand a minute to soften, then spread gently so as not to pack the soft crumb of the surface. When all the cakes are buttered in this manner lay two or three of them, crust down, on a platter or shallow dish, cover with strawberries that have been sweetened and stood in a warm place while the cakes were baking, then place other halves, crust down, upon these, cover with the prepared strawberries in the same manner, and so place a third layer of the shortcake and again cover with berries, being careful to have the berries most plentiful upon the upper layer. Cut the shortcake into quarters and serve.

Orange Shortcake.—Stew sour apples and mix while warm with an equal portion of orange marmalade. Spread upon shortcake prepared as for strawberries.

Raspberry Shortcake.—Prepare, bake, and butter the shortcake exactly as directed for strawberry shortcake, then spread with raspberries, sweetened to taste and slightly warmed.

Banana Shortcake.—Prepare the shortcake as directed for strawberry shortcake and spread with bananas prepared in this manner: To the juice of one lemon add a cup of granulated sugar, warm enough to melt the sugar, slice into it four bananas, with a wooden spoon mash and beat into a pulp. Use the same as strawberries or raspberries.

Pine-Apple Shortcake.—Prepare and bake the shortcake the same as for strawberry shortcake. Cook together one cup of water and two cups of granulated sugar until the sugar is dissolved, then thicken with a tablespoonful of arrow-root mixed with two tablespoonfuls of cold water. Simmer five minutes, remove from the fire, add the syrup from a can of flaked pine-apple, and two tablespoonfuls of lemon juice. While slightly warm add the flaked pine-apple, mix well, and spread upon the buttered shortcake.

Cornstarch can be used in place of arrow-root, but it is not so delicate in flavor.

Graham Bread.—To each pint of lukewarm wetting composed of equal portions of sweet milk and water, add a tablespoonful of sugar, half a teaspoonful of salt, and a half-ounce cake of compressed yeast, dissolved in two tablespoonfuls of cold water. Then stir in with a wooden spoon a heaping quart of graham flour, or as much more as may be necessary to form a dough sufficiently stiff to be removed in a mass from the mixing bowl. Turn the dough on to the molding board well sprinkled with white flour, and knead, adding white flour until the dough ceases to stick to the fingers, or molding board. Then proceed exactly as for white flour bread, being careful not to make the dough so stiff as for white bread.

Molasses can be used instead of sugar, in making

graham bread, but it makes the bread dark-colored and sticky, and renders it liable to become sour or moldy in hot weather, if kept two or three days. Bread is made in the same manner from entire wheat, whole wheat, and peeled wheat flour. The sugar may be omitted from any of them, when desired. Graham bread requires to be baked a considerably longer time than white flour bread, as does also bread made of either whole wheat, entire wheat, or peeled wheat flour. Consequently the loaves should be smaller and should be baked at a somewhat lower temperature.

There is so much inferior graham flour in market—made by mixing an undue proportion of bran with low grade white flour—that the only way to make satisfactory or even half-way decent bread of it is to sift out a large portion of the bran, and mix with the residue at least twenty per cent of the highest grade white flour. And where good graham flour cannot be obtained it is always best to do this before using. When it is of good quality it does not need to have any bran sifted out, and no white flour should be added.

Graham Diamonds.—Add a teaspoonful each of granulated sugar and salt to a quart of graham flour. Pour boiling water upon it until thoroughly scalded. Work into a soft dough and roll out to about half an inch in thickness, then with a sharp knife cut into diamonds or squares, place in a baking pan, and bake in a hot oven half an hour, or until well baked and crisp.

Plain Graham Gems.—Dissolve a teaspoonful of sugar and half a teaspoonful of salt into two cups of cold milk and water mixed in equal proportions, and stir briskly into it three cups of graham flour. Pour the mixture into well-greased gem pans, filling each cup of the pan about half full, and bake in a quick oven until brown.

Graham Gems with Eggs.—To two cups of cold milk and water mixed in equal proportions add the beaten yolks of two eggs, stir in two cups of graham flour with which a teaspoonful of sugar and half a teaspoonful of salt have been mixed, then add the whites of the eggs beaten stiff, pour into greased gem pans, and bake half an hour, or until brown.

Graham Gems with Sour Milk.—Beat together one cup of sour milk or cream, one teaspoonful of salt, half a teaspoonful of soda, and a cup and a half of graham flour, and bake in greased gem pans.

Graham Gems with Sweet Milk.—Beat together one cup of sweet milk, one tablespoonful of melted butter, one teaspoonful of sugar, half a teaspoonful of salt, one egg, and two teaspoonfuls of baking powder. Stir in one and a half cups of graham flour, and bake in greased gem pans.

Muffin rings can be used for baking these gems in, but muffin pans are much better. If iron pans are used they should be hot when the batter is put into them, and should be placed in the oven where the greatest heat will be at the bottom, so the gems may rise to their fullest capacity before browning on top. It is frequently advisable to set the pan on top of the stove about a minute before putting it in the oven, that it may heat thoroughly and thus facilitate the rising of the gems.

Boston Brown Bread. — Two cups corn-meal, two

cups graham flour, one cup New Orleans molasses, three cups sour milk or buttermilk, three even teaspoons soda, two even teaspoons salt. Mix together the meal, flour, soda, and salt, add the molasses and milk, stir thoroughly, pour into a well-greased mold, cover closely, and steam four or five hours.

Oatmeal Rolls.—To a quart of cooked oatmeal, cold, add a cup of white, graham, or whole wheat flour, mix thoroughly, and pack smoothly into a broad pan an inch deep. When wanted for use cut into circular cakes with a floured biscuit cutter, or into strips any desired length, with a knife, lay in a greased or floured pan, and bake until nicely browned.

Cracked Wheat Rolls.—Use cracked wheat mush in place of oatmeal and make and bake in the same manner.

Oatmeal Muffins.—To four cups of oatmeal mush add one cup of flour, one tablespoonful of butter, one cup of cold sweet milk, and the yolks of two eggs. Beat well together, and then add the whites of the eggs beaten stiff. Bake in hot gem pans or in muffin rings.

Cracked Wheat Muffins.—Use cracked or rolled wheat mush instead of oatmeal, and make and bake in the same manner.

CORN-MEAL.

The roller mill has worked as great an improvement in corn-meal as it has in flour, and the corn-meal of to-day is vastly superior in quality to the corn-meal of twenty-five years ago, and requires very different handling. And yet the recipes given in most cook-books prescribe "one cup of wheat flour and two cups of corn-meal," or else "two cups of wheat flour and one cup of corn-meal," for making all kinds of corn-bread. These are the formulas that were in vogue when bolted corn-meal was the only meal manufactured and used, and if they produced satisfactory results with bolted meal, they certainly do not when granulated meal is used. Such a mixture—whether the meal be bolted or granulated—does not make bread of any kind of a very high character; but, be its character high or low, it has no legitimate claim to the title of corn-bread. For bread-making purposes wheat flour and corn-meal have no affinity whatever, as one requires scalding and the other does not.

Corn-meal requires a good deal of cooking to develop its finest flavor, and make it palatable and healthful; and the main point in making good corn-bread is to scald the meal thoroughly. The water used for scalding meal should be boiling, and that none of its efficacy be lost it is desirable that the vessel in which the dough is mixed, and the spoon with which it is stirred, should be warm. There is a vast difference in the quality of corn-bread made with scalded meal and that made with meal which has been merely soaked with warm water. Almost every kind of corn-bread is better for being cooked from forty to sixty minutes, and if the meal is not thoroughly scalded when mixed it should be baked considerably longer. Granulated meal makes much lighter, drier, sweeter, and more delicious bread than bolted meal, and is preferable for all culinary purposes. But it should be always thoroughly scalded with boiling water or milk before it is made into bread or cakes, and whenever cold milk is used it should be added gradually. There are several grades of granulated meal—some being quite coarse and some very fine—and as the coarse will absorb fully twice as much water as the fine in the process of scalding, it requires the exercise of judgment to have the dough of the proper consistency—neither too soft nor too stiff. The formulas here given are for meal of medium fineness. If the meal used is very coarse more liquid will be required, if very fine less liquid.

Corn Dodgers.—One cup of granulated corn-meal, three fourths of a cup of boiling water, half a cup of cold sweet milk, one heaping teaspoon sugar, one level teaspoon salt. Mix the salt and sugar with the meal, pour the boiling water over the mixture, and when thoroughly scalded add the cold milk gradually, and stir well. The dough should be sufficiently stiff to retain its shape without spreading, when placed upon the griddle. Put a piece of butter about the size of a pea upon the griddle, where the cake is to be placed, and as soon as it melts drop a spoonful of the dough upon it. Fill the griddle in this manner with cakes, and when they are browned on the under side, place a bit of butter upon each of them, turn them over, and gently press as close to the griddle as possible, with a knife or cake paddle. After being turned on the griddle and browned on both sides, the cakes can be transferred to a baking pan, and finished in a hot oven; or if more convenient they can be baked, without the griddle being used, on a baking pan in the oven. Such cakes or dodgers can be baked in thirty minutes, but are sweeter and nicer when baked a longer time. The heat should be moderate so as not to burn the cakes, and if necessary they can be turned several times while baking.

Corn Crusts.—One cup of granulated meal, three fourths of a cup of boiling water, half a cup of cold sweet milk, one heaping teaspoon of sugar, one level teaspoon of salt, one tablespoonful of butter, one egg. Mix the salt and sugar with the meal, scald the mixture with the boiling water, add the butter, then the cold milk gradually, and stir well. When the dough is sufficiently cool beat in the egg, spread thin in a greased pan, and bake in a quick oven. If the dough should be too stiff to shape smooth in the pan, it can be thinned to the proper consistency with a little more milk or water.

Corn-Bread.—One cup of granulated corn-meal, one and one quarter cups boiling milk, one tablespoonful of butter, one heaping teaspoonful of sugar, one level teaspoonful of salt, two eggs. Mix the meal, salt, and sugar together, scald with boiling milk, add the butter, and, when the mixture is sufficiently cool, stir in the yolks and whites of the eggs, beaten separately. Bake in loaves.

Corn Muffins No. 1.—One cup of granulated corn-meal, three fourths cup of boiling water, one half cup cold sweet milk, one heaping teaspoonful of sugar, one level teaspoon of salt, one egg. Mix the sugar and salt with the meal, scald with the boiling water, add the cold milk gradually, stir in the egg, and bake in muffin cups, or in shallow pie pans.

Corn Muffins No. 2.—One cup granulated corn-meal, three fourths of a cup of boiling water, one half of a cup of cold sweet milk, one cup of boiled rice, one heaping teaspoonful of sugar, one level teaspoonful of salt, one tablespoonful of butter, one teaspoonful of baking powder, two eggs. Mix the salt and sugar with the meal, scald with the boiling water, add the butter, then the milk, then the eggs, then stir in the rice, then lastly add the baking powder. Bake in muffin cups or pie pans.

Corn Griddle Cakes No. 1.—One cup of granulated corn-meal, three fourths of a cup of boiling water, half a cup of cold sweet milk, one heaping teaspoonful of sugar, one level teaspoonful of salt, one tablespoonful of flour, one teaspoonful of baking powder, one egg. Mix the sugar and salt with the meal, scald with the boiling water, stir in the egg, add the flour and baking powder, beat well, and bake in small cakes on the griddle.

Corn Griddle Cakes No. 2.—One cup of granulated corn-meal, one cup of boiling water, three fourths of a cup of sweet milk, half a cup of flour, one teaspoonful of sugar, one teaspoonful of salt, one teaspoonful of butter, one teaspoonful of baking powder, one egg. Put together and bake the same as Griddle Cakes No. 1.

Corn-meal Mush.—Three cups of boiling water, one cup of corn-meal, half a cup of cold water, one teaspoonful of salt. Moisten the meal with the cold water, and stir the mixture gradually into the boiling water, to which the salt has been added. Cook thirty minutes, stirring occasionally to keep it from sticking to the kettle and burning, then move to the back of the stove, and let simmer gently an hour, or until ready to serve.

If the mush is to be used for frying, moisten the meal with cold milk instead of water—as it will brown easier—and after it has cooked half an hour turn it into a pan or mold that has been wet with cold water, and let cool.

Hominy Rolls.—To four cups of boiled, granulated hominy, add, while hot, one cup of corn-meal, mix thoroughly, form into cakes or rolls, and bake on a griddle like corn dodgers.

Hominy Muffins.—To four cups of boiled, granulated hominy, add, while hot, one cup of corn-meal, one cup of cold sweet milk, two tablespoonfuls of melted butter, and the yolks of two eggs. Mix thoroughly, then add the whites of the eggs beaten stiff, and bake in muffin cups, or shallow pie pans.

CHAPTER XVI.

PASTRY AND PIE.

Pie, when properly made, is perhaps as healthful an l nutritious as any of the ordinary articles of food. And if properly-made pie ever produces indigestion it is because it is eaten between meals, or at the close of a meal when the stomach is overloaded with food. There are several varieties of pastry or pie crust, some of them especially adapted to certain kinds of pies, but any of which can be used whenever pastry or paste is required, and none of which need be indigestible.

Puff Paste.—For each pound of flour use a pound of butter. Spread a napkin in a pan of cold water. Put the butter in the napkin and work with a wooden spoon, carefully keeping the napkin between the butter and the spoon, until the butter becomes pliable and waxy. Shape the butter into a compact roll, and flatten until not more than an inch thick. Mix the flour, an eighth of the butter, and an egg with sufficient water to form a stiff, smooth paste. Work the paste well with the tips of the fingers. Beat five or ten minutes with the rolling pin, doubling and folding frequently, and using flour to keep it from sticking to the molding board or rolling pin. When the paste becomes light and puffy, roll it out, circular in shape, until about an inch thick. Lay the flattened lump of butter in the center of the rolled-out paste. Fold the paste over from each side, so as to cover the butter and leave the paste oblong in shape, and twice as long as wide. Press the rolling pin on it in three or four places, to hold the folded paste together, roll out gently with a light, even pressure until about an inch in thickness, then wrap it toward you, over the rolling pin, lift from the table, turn the upper surface downward, and again roll out till not more than three fourths of an inch in thickness, and about three times as long as wide. Fold this oblong strip over toward the middle twice, using a third of its length in each fold, then turn it at right angles on the table. Press the rolling pin on it three or four times, as before, roll down to an inch in thickness, turn over on the table, upper side downward, and roll out exactly as before, until the paste again assumes an oblong shape. Perform this operation six times, then brush the upper surface of the paste with lemon juice, fold over twice as at first, lay in a shallow pan, and place on ice for several hours. After it becomes thoroughly chilled it can be rolled out to the required thickness, cut in the form desired, and baked in an oven at 375 degrees, or about the same temperature as for bread.

As it is necessary to keep puff paste cold it should be made in a cold room, at an open window, and after each turn of the paste it should be laid carefully in a shallow pan and placed on ice until chilled, but not frozen. During the entire process of making puff paste, flour—in addition to that allowed for making the paste—should be sprinkled freely on the molding board and rolling pin whenever they are used; but each time the paste is to be folded, all adhering flour should be carefully brushed from the upper surface with a pastry brush, before the rolling is begun.

To make *vol-au-vents*, or small patty cases, cut them, from the rolled-out paste, in circular or diamond shapes, with a tin cutter or a sharp knife, lift to a baking sheet with a broad-bladed knife, cut lightly into the top of each with a small cutter, and, when baked, remove the cut top, pick out the unbaked paste, and replace the little covers. Fill the cases with any mixture desired and serve.

Flaky Pie Crust.—Three cups of flour, half a cup of butter, half a cup of lard, three fourths of a cup of ice water.

Sift the flour into a chopping bowl, add the butter and lard, and chop with a hash knife until no pieces of the shortening larger than a pea can be seen. Then sprinkle the ice water here and there through the flour, and mix with a fork into a rather soft dough or paste. Pile upon a well-floured kneading board, dust lightly with flour, press down with the rolling pin, and roll gently back and forth until the paste becomes an oblong sheet not more than half an inch in thickness. Slip a broad-bladed knife under each end of this sheet, and fold over toward the center, thus forming three layers of the paste. Lift, with the knife, from the board—which dust with fresh flour—lay it at right angles with the position it occupied when lifted, dust with flour, roll out, and again fold over as before. Repeat the operation, and the paste is ready to lay aside for future use, or to roll into form and use at once.

When the ice water is added to the flour and shortening, the shortening becomes distributed through the flour in small balls, and if the mixing is done lightly it remains as balls and is not packed together in a mass, and when the dough is drawn together and lightly pressed with the rolling pin these balls flatten into flakes, which, by repeated foldings, are piled one upon another, and by gentle rolling become thinner and more delicate. Three rollings and foldings are as much as these flakes will bear. Rolling and folding a greater number of times causes them to become broken and packed, so that the paste will not rise and puff up, as it should, in baking.

It is well to let the paste lie on ice, or in a cold place, for an hour before rolling it out for pies, as its quality is improved by so doing; and if the weather is warm it may advantageously be placed on ice ten minutes between each rolling out. If a teaspoonful of baking powder be sifted with the flour, less shortening can be used, but the pastry will not be as crisp and delicate.

Suet Pastry.—To three cups of flour add one cup of finely shredded beef suet, three teaspoonfuls of baking powder, and one teaspoonful of salt. Mix, with cold water, or cold sweet milk, to a soft dough.

Egg Pastry.—To one egg, slightly beaten, add a pinch of salt, a tablespoonful of melted butter, and flour sufficient to make a soft dough. Knead in the flour with the finger-tips until the dough is smooth and very elastic, and can be kneaded without flour and without sticking to the molding board. When properly made, egg paste can be rolled as thin as a sheet of paper.

Potato Pastry.—To two cups of finely mashed boiled potato add a tablespoonful of melted butter, half a teaspoonful of salt, and half a cup of flour. Work together into a smooth dough.

Apple Pie No. 1.—Roll a piece of flaky pie crust to the thickness desired. Place upon a pie pan or dish, shaping it carefully to the dish, and cut off around the edges with a sharp knife. Cover the bottom of the crust with a thin layer of sugar, dust with flour, then fill the crust with quarters of pared and cored apples. Dust them lightly with salt, and generously with sugar—especially if they are very tart—roll an upper crust and lay over them, trim around the edges as before, press the upper and lower crusts together lightly, and bake half an hour, or until the apples are soft, and the top and bottom crusts are both nicely browned.

Apple Pie No. 2.—Roll the paste and fill with apples as above. Dust lightly with salt only, fit on the upper crust, but do not press the crusts together at the edges, and bake until the apples are cooked and the crusts nicely browned. Take from the oven, slip from the tin or pan in which it was baked to a warm plate on which it is to be served. Remove the upper crust carefully, season the apples to taste with sugar, replace the upper crust, and serve warm.

Apple Pie No. 3.—Make and bake like Pie No. 2. Take from the oven, remove the upper crust, pour over the apple a dressing made by cooking together two tablespoonfuls of orange juice, a quarter of the peel of an orange, grated, and enough sugar to sweeten the pie. Replace the upper crust and serve warm.

English Apple Pie No. 1.—Butter lightly an earthen or granite-ware pie or pudding dish, and sprinkle sugar over the bottom. Rinse the quarters of pared and cored apples in cold water, put them in the dish, dust lightly with salt, sweeten to taste with sugar, cover with a sheet of paste, and bake until well done.

English Apple Pie No. 2.—Lay halves of pared and cored apples, inside down, on an earthen or granite-ware dish, buttered and sprinkled with sugar. Season like English Apple Pie No. 1, cover with a paste, rolled somewhat thicker than ordinary pie crust, and bake till well done. Serve as apple dumpling, with sweet cream. Or omit the seasoning in the pie and serve with a sweet sauce, either hard or liquid.

New England Apple Pie.—Cover a deep earthen or granite-ware pie pan or a shallow pudding dish with paste, dust flour over the bottom, fill with quarters of apples pared and cored, and cover generously with New Orleans molasses. Fit on an upper crust, and make a few slits in it to allow the steam to escape, and bake slowly until brown and crisp. Serve with sweet cream. Or the bottom crust may be omitted, and the top crust made twice as thick as ordinary pie crust. This is a very delicious pie peculiar to New England, and is frequently called "pan-dowdy."

Apple Strudels.—Roll out a piece of egg pastry until it is large enough to cover a pie pan, but only half as thick as flaky pie crust. Cover it nearly to the edge with sour apples sliced very thin and seasoned to taste with sugar and ground cinnamon. Roll up like a roly-poly, pinch the edges securely together, lay upon a greased pan, and bake half an hour, or until cooked. Serve warm.

Strudels may be made in a similar manner of other fruit.

Raspberry Pie No. 1.—To two cups of raspberries add one cup of ripe currants and one heaping cup of granulated sugar, with which a tablespoonful of flour has been mixed, and stir all well together. Line the sides of a shallow pudding dish with flaky pie crust, put in the fruit, cover with a tolerably thick sheet of the paste, make several incisions for the escape of steam, and bake till the crusts are nicely browned. Serve cool.

Raspberry Pie No. 2.—Prepare the fruit as in Raspberry Pie No. 1 and bake between two crusts in pie pans.

Strawberry Pie No. 1.—Two cups of strawberries, three fourths of a cup of granulated sugar, one tablespoonful of flour. Mix the sugar with the flour, then with the berries, and bake between two crusts in pie pans.

Strawberry Pie No. 2.—Line a pie pan with paste, fill with white tissue paper, cover carefully with a sheet of paste, being careful not to press the edges of the upper and under crusts together, and bake till a nice brown. Take from the oven, slip to a warm plate, remove the top crust, take out the paper, fill the pie with fruit prepared as for Strawberry Pie No. 1, and cooked in a sauce-pan while the crusts were baking, replace the top crust, and serve when cool.

Blackberry Pie.—Blackberry pie can be made in the same manner as strawberry pie. If the berries are very acid the same quantity of sugar will be necessary; if **very sweet** only half as much will be required.

Huckleberry Pie.—Huckleberry pie may be made in the same manner as blackberry pie, but will be improved by adding to the huckleberries one third as many ripe currants as are to be used of huckleberries.

Gooseberry Pie.—Cover the gooseberries with cold water, and heat to boiling point, then drain off the water, and make the gooseberries into pies after either of the methods given for making strawberry pies.

Pie-plant Pie.—Wash the pie-plant and cut in pieces half an inch long. Put it in a sauce-pan, cover with cold water, heat to boiling point, then drain. To two cups of the drained pie-plant add three fourths of a cup of sugar with which a tablespoonful of flour has been mixed. Roll out the under crust, fit it to the pie pan, and fill with the prepared plant. Cover with a layer of paste, make an incision for the escape of steam, and bake until the crust is brown and crisp.

Cherry Pie.—Pick over and wash two cups of sour cherries, add to them one cup of granulated sugar and a tablespoonful of flour, mixed together. Line the sides of an earthen or granite-ware pudding dish with paste, fill with the prepared cherries, and cover with a sheet of paste, rolled twice as thick as ordinary pie crust. Make several incisions near the center for the escape of steam, and bake till the crust is a nice brown. If the cherries are sweet use less sugar.

Damson Pie.—Pies may be made of damsons or other varieties of plums by following the method given for cherry pie. The sugar must be proportioned to suit the acidity of the damsons or plums used.

Grape Pie.—To two cups of grapes, add half a cup of

sugar and a tablespoonful of flour, mixed together—unless the grapes are very sour, when more sugar must be used—and bake between two crusts in a deep pie pan.

Peach Pie.—Line the sides of a granite or earthenware pudding dish with paste, fill with medium-sized ripe, but not soft, peaches, that have been pared, add to each quart of peaches a cup of granulated sugar and a tablespoonful of flour, mixed together, and cover with a thick sheet of paste. Bake till well done, and when cool serve with sweet cream.

Pumpkin Pie.—To two cups of stewed pumpkin add one cup of rich sweet milk, half a cup of New Orleans molasses, half a cup of granulated sugar, one tablespoonful of melted butter, one tablespoonful of ginger, one even teaspoonful of salt, and two eggs beaten very light. Stir well together, line a deep tin pie pan with paste rolled moderately thick, sift a little flour evenly over the bottom, and fill about three quarters full with the prepared mixture. Bake until the pie is brown in the center, serve cool or cold. The quality of pumpkin pie depends largely upon the manner of cooking the pumpkin. In preparing the pumpkin use very little water. Cover the kettle, in which it is cooking, closely, and stew until the pumpkin is perfectly soft, then remove the cover and continue the stewing, stirring frequently until the moisture evaporates and the pumpkin becomes a smooth paste. Rub through a fine sieve and use for filling the pie crust or paste.

Sweet Potato Pie.—To two cups of boiled sweet potato, rubbed through a sieve, add two tablespoonfuls each of butter and lemon juice, a cup of sugar in which have been mixed half the grated rind of a lemon, a tablespoonful each of ginger and cinnamon, a level teaspoonful of salt, and a fourth of a nutmeg grated. Stir all well together, add gradually two cups of milk and the beaten yolks of three eggs, and lastly add the whites of the eggs beaten stiff. Fit the paste to the pie pan, dust it with flour, fill, and bake as directed for pumpkin pie.

White potato may be used in the same manner as sweet potato for making pie.

Squash Pie.—To two cups of steamed squash, rubbed through a sieve, add one tablespoonful each of butter, ginger, and cinnamon, half a teaspoonful of salt, a fourth of a grated nutmeg, one cup of sugar, two cups of hot milk, and three eggs, beaten light. Make, bake, and serve like pumpkin pie.

Custard Pie.—To half a cup granulated sugar add one tablespoonful of cornstarch, mix well, stir it into two cups of milk, boiling hot, and simmer five minutes. When cool add three well-beaten eggs and a pinch of salt. Line a deep pie pan with paste, dust with flour, and fill three quarters full with the mixture. Bake in a moderate oven until firm in the center. Grate nutmeg over the top and serve cool.

Lemon Pie No. 1.—Half a cup of lemon juice, a cup and a half of granulated sugar, quarter of a cup of butter, three eggs, grated peel of a lemon, one cup of Bread Crumbs No. 2, or stale sponge cake crumbs. Strain the lemon juice over the crumbs and soak half an hour, cream the butter, add gradually half the sugar, then, one at a time, the yolks of the eggs, then the balance of the sugar, with the lemon peel, and a pinch of salt. With a fork mix the crumbs well with the lemon juice, and stir them into the butter and sugar, beating them well, then add the whites of the eggs, beaten stiff. Bake and serve like custard pie.

Lemon Pie No. 2.—Two cups of boiling water, a cup and a half of sugar, half a cup of lemon juice, a tablespoonful of butter, a tablespoonful of cornstarch, grated peel of a lemon, three eggs. Mix the sugar and cornstarch well together, add them to the boiling water, and cook five minutes. Remove from the fire, add the butter, lemon juice, and peel, and lastly the eggs, beaten very light. Line a deep pie pan with paste, dust with flour, fill three fourths full with the mixture, and bake in a moderate oven till firm in the center. When cold sift powdered sugar over it and serve.

Orange Pie.—Follow the directions given for lemon pie, substituting orange peel for lemon peel.

Vanilla Cream Pie.—Mix together a tablespoonful of cornstarch and half a cup of granulated sugar, and add two cups of boiling milk. Cook five minutes, then add slowly, stirring rapidly while adding, three well-beaten eggs. Continue the cooking about half a minute, or until the egg is delicately cooked but not curdled, then remove from the fire and stir into the mixture a tablespoonful of butter. When the butter is perfectly mixed with the custard add a teaspoonful of vanilla, and pour into a freshly baked tart shell.

Orange cream pie and lemon cream pie may be made by using orange or lemon extract in place of vanilla, and following in all other respects the formula for vanilla cream pie.

Tart Shells.—Line a deep pie pan with flaky pie crust, cover it with paraffine paper, fill with bread, cut in dice, or with almond shells, to keep the paper and crust in place, and bake. Lift out the paper, and fill the shell with any cream or tart mixture desired. The diced bread after being browned in the tart shell can be used in soups, or stewed tomatoes, or may be rolled into crumbs.

Cranberry Tart.—To a quart of cranberries add a pint of boiling water, cover closely, and boil rapidly for about five minutes, or until the berries burst. Rub through a sieve, return the pulp to the sauce-pan, add two cups of granulated sugar and a pinch of salt, cook two minutes after it boils, pour into hot tart shells, and serve when cool.

Apple Tart.—Cook the apples as directed in stewing, page 95, rub through a sieve, return to the sauce-pan, add sugar to taste, a pinch of salt, and such flavoring as liked, fill hot tart shells, and serve when cool. Orange, lemon, and pine-apple are excellent combined with apples for making tarts. And tarts from nearly all kinds of fruits may be prepared after the formulas for cranberry and apple tarts, merely varying the quantity of water and sugar to suit the conditions of the different fruits.

Beefsteak Pie.—Line the sides of a pudding dish with suet pastry, and fill three fourths full with beefsteak, diced, minced, or hashed, and seasoned to taste. With every cup of prepared meat mix a level teaspoonful of flour. Bake until the pie is cooked.

Scrap Meat Pie.—Line the sides of a baking dish with paste, and fill three quarters full with odds and ends of cold cooked meat—chicken, beef, veal, lamb, etc.—from which the skin, gristle, and objectionable bones have been removed. Cook together in a sauce-pan one tablespoonful of butter and two tablespoonfuls of flour, add two cups of mixed stock, simmer five minutes or until smooth, season to taste, and pour over the prepared scrap meat in the pie. Cover with paste, and bake until the crust is cooked. Thinly sliced uncooked, or thickly sliced cooked, potato may be added to the meat, if desired.

Baked Chicken Pie.—Cover the bottom and sides of a baking dish with flaky pie crust, or with Baking Powder Biscuit Dough No. 2. Fill with white tissue paper, or with clean white rags, and cover with crust. Do not pinch the edges together. Bake until well cooked. Lift off the top crust, take out the paper or rags, fill the shell with stewed chicken, replace the top crust, and serve.

Oyster Pie.—Prepare and bake the crust as for chicken pie, and fill with stewed or creamed oysters.

Sweetbread and Mushroom Pie.—Prepare and bake the crust as for chicken pie, and fill with stewed sweetbreads and mushrooms.

In a similar manner pies may be made and filled with any meat, poultry, game, fish, or shell fish mixture suitable for filling patty cases or timbales, or for serving as entrées.

Fish Pie.—Line the sides of a buttered baking dish with mashed potato, half an inch thick, and fill the dish three fourths full with any cold fresh fish, either boiled or baked, freed from skin and bones, and pour over the fish enough drawn butter, parsley, or White Sauce No. 4 to moisten and enrich it. Bake in a moderate oven half an hour, or until thoroughly heated.

English Meat Pie.—Line a baking dish with Baking Powder Biscuit Dough No. 2. Fill it with thin strips of cold meat, either turkey, chicken, game, veal, or lamb, or with a combination of these meats. Use also a small portion of boiled ham or tongue for flavor and decorative effect. Lay the meat in the pie in such position that in cutting the pie the cuts will be across the strips of meat, and not parallel with them, and lay a strip of dark meat beside and upon a strip of white meat. Fill the interstices with cooked mushrooms, sweetbreads, and hard-boiled eggs, cut in dice. Minced parsley or a few capers, if liked, may also be used. Roll the top crust twice the thickness of ordinary pie crust, and cut from the center, but do not remove until the pie is baked, a piece of the paste about an inch square. Bake in a moderate oven until the crust is thoroughly cooked and nicely browned. When cold remove the square piece of crust cut from the center, and fill the pie with aspic jelly, which is liquid, but not warm. Set on ice, or in a cold place, ten or twelve hours. Cut in slices an inch thick, and serve for breakfast, luncheon, or picnics.

Chicken Patties.—Warm puff paste patty cases and fill with creamed chicken.

Oyster Patties.—Warm puff paste patty cases and fill with creamed oyster.

Sweetbread patties are made by filling patty cases with creamed sweetbreads, mushroom patties by filling them with stewed mushrooms, and mock terrapin patties by filling them with mock terrapin. Creamed celery, creamed asparagus, and green peas may also be used for filling patty cases.

CHAPTER XVII.

PUDDINGS.

Puddings can be classified as legitimately as soups, salads, or sauces, and the subject of pudding-making is materially simplified when puddings are divided into three classes, quite different in character, and arranged in the following order:

Class 1.—Junkets and Blanc-Manges.

Class 2.—Custards, Soufflés, Batter, Rice, Sago, Tapioca, and Bread Puddings.

Class 3.—Roly-Polies, Dumplings, Fruit and Mixed Puddings.

But even with the aid of such classification one may find difficulty in determining what puddings require the addition of a sauce, and what the character of the sauce should be. This must be decided by the nature and composition of the pudding. If a pudding seems perfect in flavor and complete in itself, it needs no sauce of any kind; but if it lacks flavor or sweetness or moisture, a spicy, a sweet, or a liquid sauce should be served with it. A pudding sauce should always be in contrast to the pudding. It should either enrich the pudding or relieve it from over-sweetness. A sweet pudding may be improved by a plain cream sauce, or by one composed largely of orange or some other slightly acid fruit juice.

This law of contrast may be illustrated by a simple

batter pudding, which being a plain pudding with no decided flavor, needs a rich, highly flavored sauce. And as it is neither very dry nor very soft, either a hard or liquid sauce is suitable to serve with it. Such a pudding will also admit of a great variety of flavors.

CLASS I.

Junket No. 1.—Set sweet milk at a temperature of seventy-five degrees until it thickens or becomes "clabber." Then place on ice until perfectly chilled. Serve with sugar, or mace sugar, and thin cream. Junket is frequently called "curds and whey."

Junket No. 2.—Sweeten and flavor to taste a quart of sweet milk. Heat until lukewarm and then add to it the quantity directed on the package of either liquid or powdered rennet. Let the mixture stand in a moderately warm place until it stiffens or "sets," then place on ice till chilled, and serve like Junket No. 1.

If only the whey is wanted, cut the curds into dice, with a silver knife, and strain off the liquid.

Cottage Cheese.—Heat clabber very gently to ninety-eight or 100 degrees, put in a cheese-cloth bag, and hang to drain over night, or for several hours. When well drained season to taste with salt, and enrich with sweet cream, or a little butter, mixing it thoroughly with the curds. Serve cold. Cottage cheese is known in some sections as "smear-case."

Sea Moss Blanc-Mange.—Wash a small handful of sea moss, Irish moss, or Iceland moss, free from sand and dust. Soak in cold water for half an hour, then put it in a quart of boiling milk, and let steep at boiling heat for twenty or thirty minutes. Test it by putting a spoonful to cool, and if it stiffens like jelly it has steeped long enough. When sufficiently steeped drain off the liquid, and sweeten and flavor to taste. Serve cold, with or without cream.

Cornstarch Blanc-Mange No. 1.—To two cups of boiling milk add half a cup of cornstarch, wet with half a cup of cold milk. Season to taste with salt, cook for ten minutes, and cool in cups or molds wet with cold water. Serve cold with sweet cream, boiled custard, or crushed or preserved fruit.

Cornstarch Blanc-Mange No. 2.—To two cups of boiling milk add one fourth of a cup of cornstarch mixed with the same quantity of granulated sugar, and salt to taste. Cook ten minutes, add the well-beaten yolks of two eggs, continue the cooking a couple of minutes, then remove from the fire, beat into the mixture the whites of the eggs beaten stiff, and lastly add a teaspoonful of extract of vanilla. Cool in molds wet with cold water, and serve with cream.

Arrow-root Blanc-Mange.—Use arrow-root in place of cornstarch, and follow either recipe for making cornstarch blanc-mange.

Farina Blanc-Mange.—To five cups of boiling milk add half a cup of farina—sprinkling it in slowly and stirring to prevent the formation of lumps—and a level teaspoonful of salt. Simmer gently half an hour, put in molds, and let cool. Serve with sugar and cream, or with fruit or boiled custard.

Rolled Wheat Blanc-Mange.—To four cups of boiling milk or water, or two cups of each mixed together, add one cup of rolled wheat and one level teaspoonful of salt. Sprinkle in the wheat and stir till well mixed, then cover closely and cook gently for an hour and a half. Serve cold with sugar and cream.

Farinose Blanc-Mange.—To four cups of boiling milk add half a cup of farinose, and proceed as in making farina blanc-mange.

CLASS 2.

Boiled Custard No. 1.—Heat to boiling point two cups of sweet milk, to which have been added half a cup of caramel and a pinch of salt. Stir into it the yolks of four eggs beaten very light with one tablespoonful of cold milk. As soon as the egg is cooked remove from the fire, pour into a cold bowl, and stir for a minute to prevent curdling. When quite cold whip the whites of the eggs stiff, and beat into the custard.

Boiled Custard No. 2.—To two cups of boiling milk add a pinch of salt and the yolks of four eggs, beaten very light with one tablespoonful of cold milk. As soon as the egg stiffens pour it into a cold bowl and stir a minute to prevent curdling. Beat the whites of the eggs stiff, add gradually four tablespoonfuls of pulverized sugar, and a teaspoonful of vanilla extract. When the custard is cold add the beaten eggs and sugar, whip all well together, and set on ice until ready to serve.

Boiled Custard No. 3.—To two cups of boiling milk add a pinch of salt and a tablespoonful of flour mixed with four tablespoonfuls of granulated sugar. Cook ten minutes, add the yolks of three eggs beaten light with one tablespoonful of cold milk, and as soon as the egg stiffens pour out, flavor to taste with vanilla, orange, lemon, pistachio, almond, mace, or nutmeg, and when cold add the whites of the eggs beaten to a stiff froth.

Boiled Custard No. 4.—To three cups of boiling milk add two tablespoonfuls of flour, four tablespoonfuls of granulated sugar, and a pinch of salt, well mixed together. Simmer ten minutes, then add slowly—stirring rapidly meanwhile—the yolks of three eggs beaten light with one tablespoonful of cold milk. As soon as the egg is cooked to a creamy consistency pour out, and when cool flavor to taste and pour into a glass or china bowl. Beat the whites of the eggs to a stiff froth, drop it, in large spoonfuls, upon boiling water in a shallow pan, and when cooked lift with a skimmer to a sieve, and place upon the boiled custard. This preparation, which is sometimes called "floating island," is frequently made by putting the beaten whites of the eggs in a china dish and pouring the boiling custard over them.

There is a decided advantage in using more or less flour in making a boiled custard. But whenever flour, cornstarch, or arrow-root is used in conjunction with egg, it should be well cooked before the egg is added, and the mixture should be removed from the fire as soon as the egg is cooked to a creamy consistency. Flour has a richer flavor than cornstarch or arrow-root, and is preferable to either in all liquid or semi-liquid sauces or custards. But in mixtures for lemon, cream, or custard pies it is better to use cornstarch or arrow-root, as they cause them to stiffen like jelly when cold.

Baked Custard.—To two cups of rich milk add a pinch of salt and four eggs beaten with four tablespoonfuls of sugar. Stir well together, pour into cups brushed with melted butter, or into a pudding dish, bake in a pan of water, in a slow oven, or cook in a steamer. As soon as the custard becomes stiff in the center it is sufficiently done, and should be removed from the oven, as over-cooking will harden the egg and produce whey.

Caramel Custard.—Use half a cup of caramel to four eggs, instead of sugar, and follow the recipe for baked custard.

Baked Sago Custard.—Sprinkle carefully into two cups of boiling milk one fourth of a cup of sago. Simmer ten minutes, add a fourth of a teaspoonful of salt, and half a cup of granulated sugar. Let it cool slightly, add two well-beaten eggs, flavor with lemon or orange extract, pour into a buttered baking dish, and bake, like custard, in a moderate oven. Serve cold, with or without cream.

Baked Tapioca Custard.—To three cups of boiling milk add half a cup of tapioca that has been soaked several hours in cold water and drained. Cook until the tapioca is transparent, then add half a cup of sugar and half a teaspoonful of salt. Let stand until it becomes lukewarm, add three eggs, well beaten, flavor with lemon or orange extract, and bake, like custard, in a buttered pudding dish. Serve cold with sweet cream.

Baked Corn-meal Pudding No. 1.—To one cup of well-boiled corn-meal mush add one teaspoonful of butter, and one teaspoonful of ginger mixed with two tablespoonfuls of granulated sugar. Stir in gradually one cup of sweet milk, then add two well-beaten eggs. Bake in a buttered pudding dish until it is firm in the center, and remove from the oven before it is wheyed. Serve warm, with sweet cream.

Baked Corn-meal Pudding No. 2.—To one cup of granulated white corn-meal add one cup of boiling milk or water, one tablespoonful of butter, half a teaspoonful of salt, and, gradually, one cup of cold milk. Butter a shallow pudding dish with apples pared, cored, and sliced thin, pour the batter over them, and bake slowly for an hour. Serve warm, with sugar and sweet cream.

Souffle Pudding.—To two cups of milk add one tablespoonful of cornstarch, mixed with one tablespoonful of granulated sugar. Cook ten minutes, remove from the fire, add a tablespoonful of butter and a pinch of salt, and, when cool, the well-beaten yolks of four eggs, and lastly fold into the mixture the whites of the eggs beaten stiff. Half fill cups that have been brushed with clarified butter, or olive oil, and bake like custard, in water, in a moderate oven, until stiff in the center. Serve hot with caramel sauce, liquid sauce, or Foamy Sauce No. 1 or No. 2.

Steamed Batter Pudding.—Stir one third of a cup of butter to a cream, add gradually half a cup of sugar, then one egg, and another half cup of sugar with a pinch of salt, then alternately, a little at a time, one cup of milk and two cups of flour, and lastly sift in a third of a cup of flour into which two teaspoonfuls of baking powder have been mixed. Beat all well together, and steam in pudding molds two hours, or in small cups half an hour. The molds should not be more than two thirds full when put in the steamer. Serve with liquid, lemon, or strawberry sauce.

French Pudding.—To one cup of Bread Crumbs No. 1 add one cup of sweet milk. Stir well together and let soak an hour. Mash smooth with a fork, add two eggs beaten together, half a teaspoonful of salt, and gradually one cup of milk. Bake in a moderate oven, in a buttered pudding dish, or in cups, until firm in the center. Serve with liquid, orange, or strawberry sauce.

Creamed Rice.—To two cups of boiling milk add two cups of well-boiled rice which has been drained. Add salt, if necessary, and sugar to taste. While boiling add the yolks of two eggs beaten with a tablespoonful of milk, and, as soon as the egg is lightly cooked, remove from the fire. When cold flavor with vanilla, orange, lemon, mace, or nutmeg. Whip the whites of the eggs stiff, add a tablespoonful of sugar, and pile on top of the rice. Serve in a bowl, or in individual dishes.

Creamed Sago.—To two cups of boiling milk add half a cup of sago by sprinkling in slowly and stirring it smooth. Add half a teaspoonful of salt and half a cup of sugar, and cook gently fifteen or twenty minutes. Beat the whites of two eggs to a stiff froth and put in a china bowl or dish. Beat the yolks with a tablespoonful of milk, and add to the pudding, and when cooked to a creamy consistency pour the boiling mixture over the beaten whites in the bowl, which will rise to the surface, slightly cooked. Dust with mace or grated nutmeg, and serve cold.

Creamed Tapioca.—Soak a cup of tapioca in two cups of cold water for several hours. Drain, and put it into two cups of boiling milk, with a cup of sugar and half a teaspoonful of salt. Simmer gently for fifteen minutes, or until the tapioca is transparent, then add two eggs beaten very light, cook until creamy, and when cold flavor with vanilla.

Suet Pudding.—Prepare like suet pastry, and mold with the tips of the fingers into an oval-shaped loaf, about three times as long as wide. Wring a napkin from hot water, dust with flour, lay the loaf upon it, fold the napkin up over the loaf, place in a steamer, and cook an hour and a half. Serve with liquid or transparent sauce, from which the butter has been omitted, or with raisin or cherry sauce.

Steamed Pudding No. 1.—Sift together two teaspoonfuls of baking powder, half a teaspoonful of salt, and two cups of flour. Rub into it two tablespoonfuls of butter. Add three fourths of a cup of milk, or enough to make a soft dough. Dust the molding board with flour, form into an oval-shaped loaf with the finger-tips, and steam, like suet pudding, for an hour and a half. Serve hot, with any pudding sauce preferred.

Steamed Pudding No. 2.—Omit the butter, use thin cream for wetting, and make in all other respects like Steamed Pudding No. 1.

Steamed Pudding No. 3.—Sift together two cups of flour, one even teaspoonful of soda, and half a teaspoonful of salt. Add a cup of sour cream, stir until perfectly mixed, then fill a buttered pudding bowl about two thirds full of the batter, and steam an hour and a half. Serve hot, with liquid, foamy, or fruit sauce. Sour milk can be used instead of cream for making this pudding, if a spoonful of butter be mixed with the flour.

Steamed Pudding No. 4.—Sift together two cups of

flour, two teaspoonfuls of baking powder, and half a teaspoonful of salt. Mix with it three tablespoonfuls of butter, three eggs, well beaten, and sufficient milk to make a dough soft enough to drop from the spoon. Fill a buttered pudding mold three fourths full of the dough and steam an hour and a half. Serve with any pudding sauce desired.

CLASS 3.

Steamed Fruit Pudding.—Prepare like batter pudding or Steamed Pudding No. 4, and add one cup of seeded raisins, or minced citron, or dried currants, or one cup of a mixture of all three, well dusted with flour. Steam two hours.

Steamed Apple Pudding No. 1.—Sift together two cups of flour, two teaspoonfuls of baking powder, and half a teaspoonful of salt. Cream three tablespoonfuls of butter, add two tablespoonfuls of sugar, and two eggs, then add the prepared flour and one cup of milk, alternately, a little at a time—lastly stir in two cups of apples, pared, quartered, cored, and sliced thin. Steam an hour and a half. Serve with creamed butter and sugar, or with liquid sauce.

Steamed Apple Pudding No. 2.—Prepare like Steamed Pudding No. 3, and stir into it two cups of apples pared, quartered, cored, and sliced thin. Steam an hour and a half.

Steamed Cherry Pudding.—Prepare the batter as for Steamed Pudding No. 1. Stir into it one cup of unseeded cherries, mixed with a fourth of a cup of flour, and the same of granulated sugar. Steam an hour and a half, and serve with creamed butter and sugar, or with liquid sauce.

Steamed blackberry pudding can be made, cooked, and served like steamed cherry pudding.

Steamed Huckleberry Pudding.—Prepare the batter as for Steamed Apple Pudding No. 1, and add in place of apples one cup of huckleberries, picked over, washed, and mixed with a quarter of a cup of flour.

Apple Roly-Poly.—Prepare the paste as for suet pudding, or for Steamed Pudding No. 1. Lay on a molding board well dusted with flour. Dust the paste with flour, and roll down until not more than a third of an inch in thickness. Cover it thickly with apples prepared as for Steamed Apple Pudding No. 1, and dust generously with flour and sugar mixed together in equal proportions. Begin at one end and roll into an oval-shaped loaf. Pinch the paste securely together at the ends and over the top, place in a napkin, and steam an hour and a half.

Roly-poly can be made of any kind of fruit—cooked or uncooked—in a similar manner, care being taken to use more or less flour and sugar with the fruit, according to its juiciness and acidity.

Bread and Butter Pudding No. 1.—Butter slices of stale bread thinly on both sides, and cover the bottom of a shallow baking dish with them. Pour as much sweet milk over the bread as it will absorb, then pour over it a custard, prepared like Baked Custard No. 1. Bake in a moderate oven until firm in the center, and nicely browned over the surface. Dust with mace or nutmeg, and serve cold.

Bread and Butter Pudding No. 2.—Prepare and bake like Bread and Butter Pudding No. 1, but omit the sugar from the custard, and the mace or nutmeg from the baked pudding. Serve hot, with creamed butter and sugar, or liquid or foamy sauce.

Baked Tapioca Pudding.—Butter a quart pudding dish, cover the bottom with tart apples, pared and cored, and pour over them a cup of tapioca that has been soaked for several hours and drained. Add a dust of salt and a cup of boiling water. Sift a tablespoonful of granulated sugar over the top of the pudding, and bake until the tapioca is transparent and the apples are cooked and a light brown color. Serve warm or cold, as preferred, with sugar and cream.

Baked sago pudding can be made in a similar manner, using sago instead of tapioca.

Peach or apricot tapioca pudding can be made like apple tapioca pudding, by using peaches or apricots, in place of apples.

Fruit and Rice Puddings.—Rice is frequently baked with eggs and fruit in a variety of puddings; but the best and most palatable preparations of rice and fruit are those where the rice is perfectly cooked, without any fruit being added, and the fruit, either baked, stewed, or preserved, is served with the rice, with or without a sauce.

Fruit and Bread Puddings.—A great number of puddings can be made by combining bread in various forms with many varieties of fruit. The principle involved is illustrated in the following formulas:

Huckleberry Pudding.—Butter enough thin slices of

bread to half fill a china bowl or dish. Stew enough huckleberries to half fill the same and sweeten to taste. Place a layer of the buttered bread in the bottom of the dish and cover it with berries, and so add bread and berries alternately, until all the bread is used. Let the last layer of berries be thicker than any of the other layers, and pour over it whatever juice remains, or enough of it to fill the dish or bowl. Cover the pudding, and set away to cool. Serve with sweet cream.

Any fresh or dried fruit of fine flavor, that is abundantly juicy, can be made into simple, palatable puddings in a similar manner.

Baked Apple Pudding No. 1.—Cover the bottom of a buttered pudding dish with quarters of sour apples that have been pared and cored. Dust lightly with salt, and lay over them slices of stale bread that have been soaked in cold water until thoroughly saturated. Place a layer of quarters of apples upon the moist bread and cover thickly with Bread Crumbs No. 2, moistened lightly with melted butter. Sift two tablespoonfuls of granulated sugar over the apples, cover with a buttered pie pan or tin cover, and bake in a moderate oven for half an hour, or until the apples are soft, then remove the cover, let the pudding brown, and serve warm with creamed butter and sugar, foamy, or liquid sauce.

Baked Apple Pudding No. 2.—Cover the bottom of a buttered, quart pudding dish with quarters of apples. Dust lightly with salt, cover with Bread Crumbs No. 2, moistened with melted butter, and dust with cinnamon and ginger. Add another layer of apples, dust as before with cinnamon and ginger, pour over the pudding half a cup of New Orleans molasses mixed with an equal quantity of warm water, cover with the bread crumbs, place a buttered pie pan over the top, and bake until the apples are soft, then remove the pie pan, brown the pudding, and serve with any sauce preferred.

Fig Pudding.—Mix together two cups of flour, two teaspoonfuls each of baking powder, cinnamon, and ginger, and half a teaspoonful each of salt, cloves, and mace. Add one cup of minced beef suet, and one cup of chopped figs, rubbing them well through the prepared flour, then add one cup of sweet milk, one cup of New Orleans molasses, and three eggs. Stir the mixture well, pour into a pudding mold, and steam three hours.

Plum Pudding No. 1.—Prepare like fig pudding, but instead of adding figs add one cup of seeded raisins, half a cup of English currants, half a cup of candied citron sliced thin, and a teaspoonful each of grated orange and lemon peel. Serve with liquid or foamy sauce.

Plum Pudding No. 2.—Cream three quarters of a cup of butter, add to it one cup of granulated sugar, then the yolks of five eggs, and one cup of flour with which two teaspoonfuls of cinnamon and half a teaspoonful each of cloves, nutmeg, and salt have been mixed. Add a teaspoonful of lemon juice, one cup each of currants and seeded raisins, half a cup of thinly sliced citron peel, and a cup of flour with which two teaspoonfuls of baking powder have been sifted. Add lastly the whites of five eggs, beaten stiff, to which half a cup of granulated sugar has been added. Pour in a pudding mold, steam five hours, and serve with Foamy Sauce No. 2.

Plum Pudding No. 3.—To half a cup of creamed butter add one cup each of granulated sugar, seeded raisins, and English currants, half a cup of sliced citron peel, two cups of Bread Crumbs No. 2, and five unbeaten eggs. Stir in the eggs one at a time, alternating them with the fruit and bread crumbs, add half a teaspoonful each of salt and grated lemon or orange peel, and half a cup of orange juice, beat all well together, and add two teaspoonfuls of baking powder mixed with a quarter of a cup of flour. Pour into a pudding mold, steam five hours, and serve with any sauce preferred.

PUDDING SAUCES.

The sauces used for puddings may be varied in their mixing and seasoning so as seemingly to constitute a great number, but the distinct varieties are very few, and may be classified as : plain cream, whipped cream, mock cream, boiled custard, syrup, mock syrup, creamed butter and sugar, foamy sauce, liquid sauce, fruit sauce, and mixed sauce.

Plain Cream.—When plain cream is used as a pudding sauce it should be of medium richness, and not more than twelve hours old. If not of uniform consistency it should be rendered so by straining through a sieve.

Whipped Cream.—The most perfect whipped cream is obtained from cream of medium richness. If the cream used for whipping is too thin, a froth will be produced upon the surface by whipping, but the whole mass will not become, as it should, a thick, light mixture ; and if too thick and rich it will stiffen by whipping, but will lack lightness and delicacy. A Dover beater and an ordinary tin bucket about four inches in diameter make a convenient, cheap, and excellent whipping machine. But in order to whip cream successfully it must be ice cold. Put the cream in the bucket, pack the bucket in broken ice, nearly to the top, and add water to the ice, that it may chill quickly and uniformly. Put the beater also in ice water. When the cream is ice cold whip rapidly until it is stiff all through, then remove the beater, cover the bucket, and put it in a cold place until the cream is wanted for use. A small quantity of sugar, and any flavoring desired, can be added to the cream before it is whipped. The white of an egg can also be added to every cup of cream if it is desired to have it very light and frothy when whipped. One cup of plain cream should make three cups of the best whipped cream.

Mock Cream.—Cook together until well mixed one teaspoonful of butter and two teaspoonfuls of flour. Add a pint of sweet milk, simmer five minutes, add the yolk of a fresh egg beaten light with a tablespoonful of milk, and cook one minute. Beat the white of the egg stiff, add a tablespoonful of pulverized sugar, and add to mock cream when it is quite cold. Flavor to taste, and serve in place of plain cream.

Boiled Custard No. 5.—Mix together half a cup of granulated sugar, a pinch of salt, and a tablespoonful of flour. Add to a pint of boiling milk, let simmer five minutes, then add three eggs, beaten very light—adding the eggs slowly, and stirring the mixture rapidly, while adding. As soon as the eggs stiffen the mixture, remove from the fire, pour from the sauce-pan, and continue stirring two or three minutes to prevent curdling. When nearly cold flavor to taste. Vanilla is the most delicate flavoring for creams and custards.

Boiled Custard No. 6.—To a pint of boiling water add three fourths of a cup of granulated sugar, two tablespoonfuls of flour, and a quarter of a teaspoonful of salt, well mixed together.. Simmer five minutes, add slowly the yolks of six eggs, beaten with two tablespoonfuls of cold water—stirring the mixture rapidly while adding the eggs—and as soon as it is delicately cooked, remove from the fire and pour from the sauce-pan. When cold add a teaspoonful of vanilla and a cup of whipped cream. Pile in glasses, and serve as a dessert; or serve as a sauce with snow, rice, or cold apple pudding.

Syrup.—Add one cup of white, brown, or maple sugar to half a cup of water. Boil five minutes—removing any scum that appears upon the surface—add a pinch of salt, flavor, if desired, and serve either hot or cold.

Caramel Sauce.—To one cup of granulated sugar add half a cup of water, and boil until the mixture begins to color, then cook slowly, and stir, if necessary, to produce an even or uniform coloring. When of a bright chestnut brown, add half a cup of hot water, cook five minutes, and serve either hot or cold.

Creamed Butter and Sugar.—Put half a cup of butter into a pint bowl, slightly warmed, and stir with a wooden spoon until it is soft and creamy, then add, a tablespoonful at a time, one cup of pulverized sugar—stirring the mixture after adding each spoonful of sugar. Flavor with vanilla, orange, lemon, pistachio, or any flavoring liked, and add also, if desired, two or three tablespoonfuls of sweet cream—a tablespoonful at a time, beating well before adding more. The white of an egg, beaten to a stiff froth, may also be added to give the mixture lightness. By using strawberry, raspberry, or pine-apple juice, instead of cream, a fruit flavor may be given to this sauce.

Foamy Sauce No. 1.—To butter and sugar creamed as directed add two or three tablespoonfuls of boiling milk or water—a spoonful at a time—and beat while adding the boiling liquid.

Foamy Sauce No. 2.—Mix together a tablespoonful of flour and a cup of granulated sugar, add a cup of boiling water, and simmer five minutes. Heat a pint bowl and a Dover beater. Break a fresh egg into the bowl, beat very light, and pour the liquid sauce over the beaten egg—beating while adding the sauce, then add half a cup of butter beaten to a cream, and flavor to taste.

Transparent Liquid Sauce.—Follow the directions given for making liquid sauce, but use arrow-root or cornstarch instead of flour, and add the butter without having it beaten to a cream. If transparent sauce is to be served with a rich pudding, omit the butter, if with an apple, or an acid fruit, pudding, omit the lemon juice.

Orange Sauce.—Mix together a cup of granulated sugar, a tablespoonful of flour, and a teaspoonful of grated orange peel. Add a cup of hot water, simmer five minutes, remove from the fire, and add the juice of an orange and half a cup of butter, beaten to a cream.

Lemon Sauce.—Make the same as orange sauce, using lemon peel in place of orange peel, and a teaspoonful of lemon juice in place of the juice of an orange.

Strawberry Sauce.—Mix a tablespoonful of flour with a cup of granulated sugar, add a cup of hot water, simmer five minutes, remove from the fire, and stir into the mixture a cup of crushed strawberries and half a cup of creamed butter.

Pine-Apple Sauce.—Make the same as strawberry sauce, using grated pine-apple in place of strawberries.

Banana Sauce.—Make the same as strawberry sauce, using a cup of thinly sliced bananas in place of strawberries.

Raisin Sauce.—To a cup of seedless or sultana raisins add four cups of water, cover closely, and cook slowly for two hours. Add a pinch of salt, a teaspoonful of cornstarch, and a cup of granulated sugar mixed together, and simmer five minutes. Remove from the fire, add a tablespoonful of lemon juice, and serve with either plain suet pudding, cottage, or bread and butter pudding, or with boiled rice.

Sauces for puddings may be made in a similar manner from fresh or dried cherries, and from some other fruits.

Mace Sugar.—Mix together one cup of pulverized sugar and one teaspoonful of ground mace. Serve with boiled rice, clabber, junket, or any simple blanc-mange.

Liquid Sauce.—Mix together a tablespoonful of flour

and a cup of granulated sugar, add a cup of boiling water, and simmer five minutes. Add a teaspoonful of lemon juice, half a teaspoonful of grated lemon peel, a fourth of a teaspoonful of grated nutmeg, and ten drops of extract of ginger mixed together, and lastly whip into the mixture half a cup of butter, beaten to a cream.

CHAPTER XVIII.

CAKE-MAKING.

CAKE-MAKING is so universally practiced that any one who understands the elementary principles of mixing can, with the aid of a few formulas, make an unlimited variety of the different classes of cake.

All pans in which thick loaves of cake are baked should have a center tube as large at top as bottom, and extending an inch or an inch and a half above the top edges of the pan. A pan made of tin seven inches square and three inches in depth, with a center tube two inches square and four and a half inches deep, is excellent for baking cake of all kinds—angel cake included—in loaves. And the tube extending an inch and a half above the pan furnishes the best possible rest for the tin cover which should be used to protect the top of the cake from browning until the cake is perfectly risen. Use buttered paper on the bottom of cake pans, and for all cakes containing butter, sift over the paper a small quantity of flour before putting the cake mixture in the pan. To test whether or not the cake is done, press with the finger lightly upon its surface. If it rebounds when the pressure is removed the cake is sufficiently baked; if it does not, let it remain in the oven until it is baked.

Angel Cake.—One cup of white of egg, one heaping

cup of winter wheat flour, one and a half cups of fine granulated sugar, one level teaspoonful cream of tartar, one teaspoonful of almond extract. Eggs vary so much in size that it is better to take a certain measure of the white than a certain number of the eggs. Put the measured whites in an earthen bowl, break lightly with an egg whip, sift in the cream of tartar, and beat until the egg will cling to the bowl and not slip out if the bowl is turned upside down, then beat the sugar into the egg, sifting it in gradually, add the flavoring, and lastly sift in the flour, stirring only enough to combine it with the egg and sugar. Put the mixture in an ungreased pan, the bottom of which has been covered with white paper, place carefully in an oven of moderate temperature, and cover with a baking sheet or tin, so as to protect the top of the cake but not exclude the air. Remove the cover in half an hour—when the cake should be perfectly risen—and bake half an hour longer. When taken from the oven turn the pan bottom upwards, and if it has no center tube rest it upon cups or bowls until the cake is perfectly cold, then remove by slipping a thin-bladed knife between the cake and the sides of the pan. Success in making angel cake depends largely upon having an oven of the proper temperature. If the oven is too warm the cake will be tough.

Sunshine Cake.—Add the yolks of two or more eggs to the mixture for angel cake, just before sifting in the flour.

Sponge Cake.—Ten eggs, their weight in fine granulated sugar, half their weight in flour, juice and grated rind of a lemon. Break the eggs, separate the whites from the yolks, and reject two of the yolks. Put the eight yolks, with the lemon juice and grated peel, into a bowl and whip very light, with a Dover beater, then beat in gradually two thirds of the sugar. Beat the whites of the eggs stiff, and whip into them the remaining third of the sugar. Add the yolks to the whites, folding in carefully, then add the flour, sifting it in a little at a time, and mixing it carefully, by folding rather than by beating. Bake in a moderate oven from twenty minutes to an hour, according to the depth of the pans.

Pound Cake.—One pound each of eggs, butter, sugar, and flour, juice of one lemon, two teaspoonfuls of almond extract. Cream the butter, add gradually two thirds of the sugar, then the yolks of the eggs well beaten with the lemon juice, then the flour, gradually, and stir and beat thoroughly. Whip the whites of the eggs stiff, gradually add the other third of the sugar, and fold into the cake. If baked in a thick cake, cover the pan for half an hour, and bake in a very moderate oven until perfectly risen, then increase the heat slightly for fifteen or twenty minutes, then lessen it until the cake is done. For baking this cake an hour—perhaps a longer time—will be required.

Rich Fruit Cake.—Make as directed for pound cake, adding a heaping teaspoonful of baking powder to the flour, a pound of raisins, seeded and torn in pieces, a pound of English currants, and half a pound of citron sliced very thin, before folding in the whites of the eggs. Bake in a slow oven two and a half or three hours.

Delicate Cake.—Three fourths of a cup of butter, one

cup of white of egg, measured before beating, three cups of flour, two cups of fine granulated sugar, two teaspoonfuls of baking powder, one teaspoonful of orange, lemon, almond, or any flavoring extract liked, and one cup of cold water. Cream the butter, add two thirds of the sugar, then the water and flour into which the baking powder has been sifted, a little at a time, alternating, then the flavoring, and beat well. Whip the whites of the eggs stiff, add the remaining third of the sugar, and fold into the cake lightly. Bake in thick or medium cakes in a moderate oven. If baked in thick loaves cover for half an hour until fully risen, then bake until done.

Citron Cake.—Add one cup of thinly sliced citron, cut in small pieces, to the delicate cake mixture just before the whites of the eggs are added.

Nut Cake.—Add a cup of chopped nuts to the cake mixture, or sprinkle chopped nuts thickly over the top of the cake before baking it.

Ginger Wafers.—One cup of butter, two cups of pulverized sugar, one cup of cold water, four cups of flour, ginger to taste. Cream the butter, add the sugar and ginger, then stir in the water and flour gradually and alternately. Spread the mixture as thin as possible on a greased baking sheet, and bake in a moderate oven. As soon as done cut quickly, and while hot, into squares or diamonds, and roll, if desired.

Soft Ginger Cake.—Quarter of a cup of butter, half a cup of sugar, half a cup of sour milk, one cup of New Orleans molasses, one tablespoonful of ginger, one teaspoonful of cinnamon, one teaspoonful of soda, half a teaspoonful of salt, and three cups of flour. Sift the soda, salt, and spices with the flour. Cream the butter, add the sugar, then the milk, then the flour and molasses alternately. Beat well and bake in shallow pans in a moderate oven.

Frosting for Cake.—Cake frosting is often less ornamental and attractive than the beautiful brown crust of the cake. Still, frostings have their uses—especially in preserving the texture and flavor of cake that is to be kept for several days.

White frosting may be ornamented by scattering over its surface, while soft, finely chopped nuts and the green portions of finely chopped candied citron; or in any manner liked, with sliced or chopped candied fruits. Boiled Frosting No. 3 may be ornamented with either whole or chopped walnut meats.

Uncooked Frosting.—To one cup of the unbeaten white of egg add four cups of the finest pulverized confectioner's sugar. Sift the sugar before measuring, and stroke the measuring cup each time. Beat the mixture with a strong whip, until, as it falls back upon itself, it will remain in a pile until forced to settle by shaking. Flavor with any extract desired, pour upon the cake, and allow it to run over the edges. If sufficiently beaten it will run very slowly, and if spread over the sides with a limber knife, will remain where it is placed. If an ordinary teacup be used this quantity of white of egg and sugar will make sufficient frosting for four medium-sized cakes. A smaller quantity of frosting can be made by using a smaller cup or measure, but care must be taken to preserve these proportions of white of egg and **sugar.**

Cocoa or grated or melted chocolate can be added to the frosting, if desired, just before spreading upon the cake.

If the atmosphere is dry, in two or three hours the frosting will cease to stick to the fingers when touched, and will remain soft and creamy below the surface for days—sometimes for weeks. If dried by artificial heat it may be rendered brittle and ruined.

Boiled Frosting No. 1.—To one cup of granulated sugar add half a cup of water, and cook until a spoonful of the syrup, when dropped in cold water, can be rolled into a ball of soft candy, then pour it gradually, beating meanwhile, upon the white of an egg beaten stiff. Continue the beating until the frosting is so stiff it will not run off the cake when poured over it. Flavor to taste.

Boiled Frosting No. 2.—Make a syrup as in Boiled Frosting No. 1. Set the sauce-pan containing it into a large pan of cold water, and let it remain there, covered, until the surface, if touched with the finger, will not adhere to it. Then pour into an earthen bowl, but do not scrape from the sides or bottom of the sauce-pan, and stir with a wooden spoon until it grains and is stiff enough to be formed into a ball. Work and knead until smooth, fine-grained, and ready for use. If covered closely, this frosting will keep an indefinite length of time, and when needed can be softened by setting the bowl containing it in a pan of warm water, and stirring it continually, until it becomes soft enough to spread and settle smooth when poured upon the cake. It can be flavored just before being used.

Boiled Frosting No. 3.—Put into a sauce-pan one cup of brown sugar, half a cup of water, and a tablespoonful of butter. Boil until a little of the syrup when dropped into cold water can be rolled into a ball, then remove from the fire, stir until it begins to grain, add a teaspoonful of vanilla, and continue stirring until the frosting becomes stiff enough to be poured upon the cake and not run off.

Chocolate Frosting.—Add to Boiled Frosting No. 1, while hot, two or three tablespoonfuls of cocoa or grated chocolate and a teaspoonful of vanilla.

CHAPTER XIX.

DELICATE DESSERTS.

A GREAT variety of delicate desserts have gelatine as a base, and are made by combining fruits and fruit juices of different kinds with a certain proportion of gelatine. The principle underlying their preparation is fully illustrated in the following formulas:

Grape Jelly.—To one third of a box of gelatine add one cup of cold water and let soak an hour. Then add one cup of hot water, one and a half cups of granulated sugar, strain into a bowl, set in ice water, surrounded with bits of broken ice, and, when slightly cooled, add a cup of Concord grape juice and the juice of a lemon. Let stand until the mixture is jellied, then set on ice until ready to serve.

Lemon Jelly.—To one third of a box of gelatine add one cup of cold water, soak an hour, add a cup of hot water, half a cup of lemon juice, a teaspoonful of lemon extract, and two cups of granulated sugar. Stir until the sugar is dissolved, then set on ice until jellied and ready to serve.

When phosphated or acidulated gelatine is used in making lemon jelly or snow pudding omit the juice of one lemon; when it is used in making jellies, puddings, creams, etc., of other fruits omit the lemon juice entirely.

Orange Jelly.—To one third of a box of gelatine add

one cup of cold water, let soak an hour, add half a cup of boiling water, one cup of granulated sugar, one cup of orange juice, the juice of one lemon, and a teaspoonful of orange extract. Stir until the sugar is dissolved, then set on ice until jellied and ready to serve.

Pine-Apple Jelly.—Prepare the gelatine as above directed, add one cup of pine-apple juice, the juice of one lemon, and one and a half cups of granulated sugar. Stir until the sugar is dissolved, strain, set on ice until jellied, and then serve.

Strawberry Jelly.—Prepare one third of a box of gelatine as before directed, add one cup of strawberry juice, the juice of a lemon, and one and a half cups of granulated sugar. Stir until the sugar is dissolved, strain, set on ice until jellied, then serve.

In a similar manner jellies may be prepared from the juice of raspberries, nectarines, peaches, plums, and numerous other berries and fruits.

Mock Peach Jelly.—Prepare the gelatine as before directed, add the juice of a lemon, two tablespoonfuls of sugar caramel, four drops of almond or peach extract, and one cup of granulated sugar, stir until the sugar is dissolved, strain, set on ice until jellied, then serve.

Charlotte Russe No. 1.—Whipped cream, slightly sweetened and flavored to taste, may be served as Charlotte Russe—without the addition of gelatine—in shells of cake, baked for the purpose; or slices of cake may be arranged on the inside of a mold of any desired form, and the mold filled with whipped cream and put on ice till ready to serve. Lady-finger cakes separated, and cut in two, make attractive individual molds when arranged in a prettily shaped cup. The pieces of cake can be made to adhere to the cup and retain their position by being slightly moistened with syrup.

Charlotte Russe No. 2.—To one fourth of a box of gelatine add half a cup of cold water and soak an hour, then add half a cup of hot milk and a tablespoonful of granulated sugar. Stir until the sugar is dissolved, strain into a two-quart bowl, surrounded with ice and water, and add a cup of cold cream and a teaspoonful of vanilla extract. When the liquid begins to jelly beat vigorously with a Dover egg-beater until it is very light, then add the whites of two eggs beaten light, to which has been added a pinch of salt and two tablespoonfuls of granulated sugar. Remove the beater, and, with a strong whip or a wooden spoon, beat into the mixture a pint of whipped cream. Pour into molds, and set on ice till ready to serve.

Bavarian Cream.—Prepare like Charlotte Russe No. 2, omitting the whipped cream.

Bavarian Cream with Eggs.—Soak a quarter of a box of gelatine in half a cup of cold water for half an hour. Make a pint of Boiled Custard No. 2. Remove from the fire, and stir the soaked gelatine into it. When cool flavor to taste with vanilla extract, set in ice water, surrounded with broken ice, and when it begins to stiffen whip until very light. Add the whites of two eggs beaten stiff, and set on ice until ready to serve.

Chocolate Bavarian Cream.—Prepare like Charlotte Russe No. 2, but before mixing the hot milk with the soaked gelatine add to it half a cup of grated chocolate, and let simmer until smooth.

Chopped candies, fruits, and nuts, and stale cake, or macaroons rolled fine, may be mixed with Bavarian creams at pleasure, and thus a great variety of them may be readily prepared.

Snow Pudding.—Prepare lemon jelly as directed, and when it begins to jelly and is slightly thickened all through, whip with a Dover beater until perfectly light, then add the whites of three eggs beaten stiff, to which has been added a pinch of salt and three tablespoonfuls of granulated sugar. Whip all well together, and set on ice until firm. Serve with Boiled Custard No. 2.

Orange Pudding.—Prepare as directed for snow pudding, using orange jelly in place of lemon jelly. After whipping the whites of the eggs into the mixture, pour it into a mold lined with sections or slices of oranges, arranged according to taste, and set on ice for several hours. Serve with or without cream.

Banana Pudding.—Prepare a snow pudding from lemon jelly, as directed, omitting the lemon extract, and, when ready to mold, whip into it two cups of thinly sliced bananas. Serve with plain cream.

Other fruit jellies can be converted into fruit puddings by following the formula given for snow pudding. But most fruit puddings made in this manner, of oranges, strawberries, raspberries, grapes, etc., are better served with cream, either plain or whipped, than with custard.

Orange Cream.—Prepare as directed for orange pudding, and after adding the whites of the eggs, whip into the mixture two cups of whipped cream and two tablespoonfuls of granulated sugar.

Pine-Apple Cream.—Prepare a pine-apple pudding as

directed for snow pudding, using pine-apple jelly in place of lemon jelly, and after adding the whites of the eggs, whip into the mixture two cups of whipped cream and two tablespoonfuls of granulated sugar.

Strawberry Cream.—Prepare as directed for orange cream, using strawberry jelly in place of orange jelly, and after adding the cream mix lightly with it large strawberries, or scatter some berries in the mold, add a covering of cream, scatter more berries, cover again with cream, and so alternate until the mold is filled.

Various fruit creams can be garnished with fruit in a similar manner—provided the fruit is of the same kind of which the cream is made and is really decorative.

Banana Cream.—Prepare a banana pudding as directed, and after adding the sliced bananas, beat into it two cups of whipped cream.

Peaches in Jelly.—Prepare a mock peach jelly as directed, and when cold and just beginning to stiffen pour it over freshly cut peaches, in a glass bowl, and, with a silver fork, lightly separate the peaches so that the jelly may be distributed uniformly among them. Set the dish on ice, and, when the jelly is firm, serve with plain or whipped cream.

Fancy Fruits in Jelly.—Select a mold to correspond in shape with the dish in which the fruit is to be served, and put into it jelly to the depth of a quarter of an inch. Set the mold on ice, and when the jelly becomes firm place on it candied fruit, arranged in some pretty design. Cherries may be cut in halves, limes sliced and cut in the shape of leaves, etc., and each piece of fruit fastened in place with a few drops of liquid jelly. When firm, cover the fruit with jelly and let stiffen, and so continue to add fruit and jelly alternately until the mold is filled. Let stand on ice for several hours, and, when ready to serve, dip the mold in warm water, turn out the jelly on a glass dish, and garnish with a border of whipped cream.

CHAPTER XX.

SHERBETS, WATER ICES, AND ICE CREAMS.

SHERBETS and water ices are similar in character and are generally considered the same. But ices are always frozen, sherbets are not. Sherbets are prepared by mixing broken ice with fruit juice and adding sugar to taste. They are usually served in glasses, with the meat or game course at dinner.

Mixed Fruit Sherbet.—To half a cup of lemon juice add two cups of granulated sugar, one cup each of pineapple and strawberry juice, and two cups of water. Serve in glasses half filled with broken ice.

Lemon Sherbet.—To half a cup of lemon juice add two cups of granulated sugar, and three cups of ice water. Stir until the sugar is dissolved, then serve in glasses half filled with broken ice.

Orange Sherbet.—To two cups of orange juice add three tablespoonfuls of lemon juice and a cup of granulated sugar. Stir until the sugar is dissolved, then serve in glasses half filled with broken ice.

To either lemon or orange sherbet a small quantity of the grated peel, or of the extract of lemon or orange may be added, if liked; or, if preferred, a few drops of cinnamon or ginger may be used in either sherbet.

Strawberry Sherbet.—To two cups of strawberry juice add two tablespoonfuls of lemon juice, and two cups of ice water. Sweeten to taste, and serve in glasses half filled with broken ice. Or add a pint of crushed ice to a quart of crushed strawberries, and sweeten to taste.

Pine-Apple Sherbet.—To two cups of pine-apple juice or pine-apple syrup add two tablespoonfuls of lemon juice, two cups of ice water, and sugar to taste. Stir until the sugar is dissolved, then serve in glasses half filled with broken ice. Or, to two cups of grated pine-apple add two tablespoonfuls of lemon juice and two cups of crushed ice. Sweeten to taste and serve in glasses.

Lemon Ice.—To four cups of boiling water add two cups of sugar, boil five minutes, remove from the fire, add half a cup of lemon juice and a teaspoonful and a half of lemon extract. Strain, pour into a freezer, and freeze.

Orange Ice.—To two cups of boiling water add a cup and a half of granulated sugar, boil five minutes, remove from the fire, add two cups of orange juice, the juice of a lemon, and a teaspoonful and a half of orange extract. Strain, pour into a freezer, and freeze.

Banana Ice.—To half a cup of lemon juice add two cups of sugar, four cups of water, and a dust of salt. Stir until the sugar is dissolved, then add six bananas sliced very thin. Pour the mixture into a freezer, add the unbeaten whites of two eggs, and freeze. This mixture increases in bulk considerably, and sufficient space should be given it to swell in the freezer.

Strawberry Ice.—To one cup of strawberry juice or strawberry syrup add the juice of a lemon, and sweeten to taste. Strain, pour into a freezer, and freeze.

A variety of other fruit juices may be prepared and frozen in a similar way, and served as ices.

Ice Cream No. 1.—To one quart of thin cream add three quarters of a cup of granulated sugar and one tablespoonful of vanilla extract. Strain and freeze.

Ice Cream No. 2.—To one pint of boiling milk add three quarters of a cup of granulated sugar and one tablespoonful of flour, sifted together. Cook five minutes, add a pint of thin cream, let boil, and remove from the fire. When cold flavor to taste with vanilla or lemon extract, add the unbeaten whites of two eggs, and freeze.

Ice Cream No. 3.—To one quart of boiling milk add two tablespoonfuls of flour mixed with three quarters of a cup of sugar, and cook five minutes. Add the well-beaten yolks of three eggs, and as soon as the eggs are lightly cooked remove from the fire, add a tablespoonful of butter, and stir until the latter is melted and mixed uniformly with the cream. Flavor to taste, when cold add the whites of the eggs unbeaten, and freeze.

Strawberry Ice Cream.—Scatter a cup of granulated sugar over two cups of strawberries, and mash and strain them. Add a cup of the strained juice to three cups of ice cold cream, and freeze at once. More sugar can be added to the mixture, if needed, before freezing it.

Pine-Apple Ice Cream.—To three cups of thin cream, ice cold, add one cup of pine-apple juice or pine-apple syrup, sweeten to taste, and freeze.

Coffee Ice Cream.—To half a cup of strong coffee add one cup of sugar caramel and four cups of thin cream. Sweeten to taste and freeze.

The unbeaten whites of eggs may be added to any cream or mixture that is to be frozen, if it is desired to have it lighter.

PART V.—SEASONING.

INTRODUCTION.

Some edibles are improved in flavor by having salt cooked with them, while others should only be salted when served. It is safe to say that all delicately flavored food is, as a general rule, salted too highly and seasoned too heavily. The more delicate the flavor of an article of food, the more careful one should be not to disguise or destroy it by the use of too liberal a quantity of sugar or salt. Delicately flavored fruits and cereals are often ruined with sugar and salt, as are also white flour bread, graham bread, and corn-bread. Pepper, spices, and other flavoring condiments and extracts are used principally in three capacities—to stimulate and strengthen, to soften and tone down, or to modify and change, the flavor of an article or dish. There is a seeming affinity between certain foods which makes it appropriate to serve them together. They are so like they blend harmoniously; or so unlike that one seems the complement of the other, and when mingled produce the best results.

The fact should never be lost sight of that we season food to render it more palatable, digestible, and nutritious—not to give the taste of the seasoning to the food, but to render finer and more potent the flavors of the edible seasoned. Each edible, whether fish, flesh, fowl, vegetable, fruit, or cereal, should be so cooked and seasoned as to develop its flavor in the greatest degree. Each should be so cooked and seasoned that a first taste would enable one, though blind, by the clear, distinctive flavor, to discover its legitimate place in the animal or vegetable kingdom. The palatability of food—its appetizing quality—is of vital importance in rendering it digestible. Food, no matter how simple or nutritious it may be, never perfectly digests and assimilates unless it can be eaten with a relish, and is appetizing and pleasing to the taste.

Many people are sick because they fail, in a greater or less degree, to assimilate their food, and it ceases to nourish them. An eminent physician when asked, "What is disease?" replied, "It is the lack of nutrition." And his brief reply covers the entire question. Lack of nutrition causes starvation—a disease that may be local or general in its effect—but a disease the only remedy for which is food that can be digested and assimilated.

But as perplexing and puzzling as may be the problem of nutrition, considered hygienically, it is pretty definitely settled that the flavor of food is of vital importance in aiding its digestion and assimilation. A writer who has given the subject much careful consideration tells us that all edible things are in the most perfect condition for human food when their flavors are finest, and that whether foods should be eaten cooked or uncooked, and also the exact amount of cooking they require, should be determined by the flavor. In other words, no edible whose flavor is not improved by cooking should ever be subjected to such process, as to cook such edible renders it less digestible and nutritious. The taste for certain articles of diet is very much a matter of education and habit. Our tastes become coarse and vitiated, or cultured and discriminating, in eating and drinking, as they do in other things, by the training they receive. Most people would probably become fond of all food that is wholesome and nutritious, if it were properly cooked and seasoned, and when we are educated in these respects we shall no doubt have the keenest relish for food best adapted to our special needs. We season food mainly to increase or modify its flavor, and as the natural flavor of most foods is exceedingly delicate and very easily destroyed, a tablespoonful of sugar or salt often proves so complete an extinguisher of all flavor as to leave in the mouth only a sweet or a briny taste.

Salt is the most common of all seasonings and undoubtedly the most essential. A small quantity of salt added to the water in which meats, vegetables, etc., are boiled is supposed to prevent the fiber or texture of the edible being cooked from breaking down or disintegrating too rapidly. It is also supposed that less of the flavor of the article passes off with the steam when salt is present in boiling water. But the main reason that salt is so universally used in the preparation of food, or added to it when eaten, is, no doubt, because it possesses the power of developing the richest and finest flavors of the edible. When used in this capacity it should be used only to the extent required to induce the edible to yield the flavor that would otherwise remain latent and undiscovered, and the proper quantity required for different articles can be determined only by a correct, discriminating taste.

Next to salt, sugar is perhaps most useful in developing flavors; and many meats, fish, and shell fish, as well as fruits and vegetables, have their flavors improved by its judicious use. In many made dishes, rich soups, and elaborate sauces a great number of things are mixed together, and sometimes twenty or thirty different flavoring principles are in one dish. Yet, like the colors in the rainbow, or the lights and shades in a picture, each one of them is necessary for its completeness. In these complex culinary mixtures, in order that even a moderate degree of excellence may be achieved, three important rules must be observed:

First, the various ingredients must be so chosen as to be harmonious in flavor, or to present only a spicy and piquant contrast.

Second, they must be introduced into the mixture in a certain specific order.

Third, the method of combining or mixing the various ingredients must be that best suited to their nature. They must be sliced, mashed, broken, grated, pounded in a mortar, or manipulated in such other ways as experience has proved will cause them to yield the most satisfactory results.

Nearly all foods have a finer and more intense flavor when freshly cooked and warm. This is true of fruits, as well as of meats, vegetables, etc., and baked and stewed fruits of nearly all kinds, notably apples, damsons, prunes, and cranberries are much richer and more delicate in flavor when freshly cooked and warm, than when they have been cooked and allowed to become cold. In cooling the flavor is thrown off and dissipated. And for this reason some few articles of food, the flavor of which is very marked, are relished better cold than warm—their flavor when cold being less pronounced and more delicate.

CHAPTER XXI.

SALAD-MAKING.

Salad-making, although one of the most important branches of the preparation of food, is, perhaps, less perfectly understood than any other culinary operation.

Salads, when skilfully made and artistically arranged, are grateful to the taste and pleasing to the sight, and should therefore have a prominent place on bills of fare. The hygienic value of salads can scarcely be over-estimated, while their decorative possibilities are almost illimitable.

A salad should always be appetizing in a high degree. It should always be refreshing, also. And, whenever possible, attractiveness should be added to these two essentials, so that the useful and ornamental may be combined in its preparation. A salad can be made so beautiful as to lend a charm and grace to its surroundings, and so delicious that, when daintily served, it will go far, of itself, to redeem from utter failure a very ordinary dinner.

There are numberless incongruous mixtures—compounded of a variety of things stirred together—that are served, and pass current, in some sections, as salads. But as such compounds are violations of all the laws that govern the mixing and seasoning of food, and set at defiance every principle of the culinary art, they cannot be classed among legitimate salads. Any one who wishes can make them, but no one of cultured taste will care to do so.

A dinner salad should rarely, if ever, be heavy or complex. It should be of fresh fruits or vegetables, simply dressed, and delicately served. And the heavy and more complex salads should be served alone, or at a less hearty meal.

In no department of cookery is a more analytical study of relative flavors needed than in that of salad-making. And the greatest care should be observed in handling salad materials, not to destroy their natural flavors by mixing together those which do not make a harmonious combination, or by using with them an inappropriate, or too highly seasoned, dressing. Each kind of fruit, vegetable, meat, or fish designed for salad-making should be regarded as belonging to a distinct class; and its peculiar requirements in that direction should be considered, and only such things be mingled, or served, with it as will best develop its especial flavor and render it most appetizing and attractive.

The dressing of a salad should invariably be suited to the peculiar flavor and condition of that particular salad, and whenever two or more edibles are mingled together in a mixed salad, they should be selected with especial reference to the effect each will have upon the other.

CLASS I.—FRUIT SALADS.

Many fruits served at breakfast as a relish, and after dinner in the form of dessert, are also frequently served at dinner as a salad, notably among such being strawberries, currants, and oranges.

A great variety of salads may be prepared in the same manner from different fruits, but in their preparation it should be borne in mind that when two or more fruits are so mingled, one of them should be chosen with especial reference to giving the mixture flavor, and the others mainly to give it bulk. Pine-apples, bananas, and a dozen other fruits that readily suggest themselves, possess flavor enough to make palatable twice the bulk of less sapid fruit. The distinctive character of finely flavored food-stuffs should not be destroyed or obscured by mingling them together indiscriminately. And there can be no grosser culinary blunder than to combine two highly flavored fruits in one dish. Such a combination is opposed to the principles that govern salad-making, and is a direct violation of the laws of harmony that should control all food preparations.

Strawberry Salad.—Select large strawberries with long stems. Serve two or three to each guest, on a fancy dish, and place beside each dish a tiny cup containing pulverized sugar.

Currant Salad.—Select perfect stems of large currants, and serve like strawberries.

Orange Salad.—Select perfect, medium-sized oranges. Wash and wipe them. Divide the peel into rather small sections, at the blossom end, and loosen from the orange about three fourths of its length. Curl in, bend out, or partly cut away, according to fancy, these sections of peel. Carefully remove the thick white covering, leaving the delicate skin of the orange pulp unbroken. Separate the sections of orange at the end from which the peel has been removed, and with a fork twist out the core. Pick out the seeds, and serve the prepared orange with a spoonful of whipped cream, sweetened, or oil or cooked mayonnaise dressing, placed in the opening from which the core has been removed.

Banana Salad No. 1.—To half a cup of lemon juice add a cup of granulated sugar. Put six or eight thinly sliced bananas into a glass or china bowl. Pour over them the lemon syrup. Cover closely, and stand the salad in a cold place for an hour before serving.

Banana Salad No. 2.—To the juice of three oranges and one lemon add a fourth of a box of gelatine soaked an hour in cold water. Warm the mixture until the gelatine is dissolved, add a cup of granulated sugar, and when perfectly cold pour over six thinly sliced bananas. Set the salad on ice until stiff, then serve.

Banana Salad No. 3.—Skin, cut in halves, and seed half a pound of white grapes. Scoop the pulp from four oranges, keeping it in distinct pieces. Pare and slice four bananas. Put the grapes, orange pulp, and bananas in alternate layers in a glass or china bowl. Squeeze the juice of a lemon into a cup, add to it the orange juice obtained by squeezing the skins after the pulp has been scooped from them, and fill up the cup with water. Pour the liquid over a quarter of a box of gelatine which has soaked for an hour in half a cup of cold water, and warm until the gelatine dissolves, then add a cup of sugar. When cold pour over the mixed fruit in the bowl, and place on ice till stiff enough to serve.

Pine-Apple Salad.—Skin, cut in halves, and seed half a pound of Malaga grapes. Scoop four oranges. Prepare a cup of pine-apple, or use a cup of shredded canned pine-apple. Drain the juice from the fruit, and add to it the juice of a lemon, and a fourth of a box of gelatine soaked an hour in half a cup of cold water. Warm the mixture just enough to melt the gelatine, then strain, and add to it a cup of granulated sugar. Mix the pine-apple, orange pulp, and grapes together in a bowl, and when the jelly is cold mix with the fruit and set the bowl on ice. When it jellies it is ready to serve.

Apple Salad No. 1.—Select mellow, sour apples, pare, core, and slice very thin. To two cups of sliced apples add one cup of chopped walnut meats, and cover with cooked mayonnaise dressing to which has been added one cup of whipped cream, seasoned to taste with sugar and salt.

Apple Salad No. 2.—Prepare the apples as for Apple Salad No. 1, and to three cups of sliced apples add one cup of cream dressing to which has been added a tablespoonful of minced onion. Season to taste with Seasoning No. 2.

Apple Salad No. 3.—Prepare the apples as in No. 1 and cover with a cup of whipped cream seasoned with a teaspoonful of sugar and a pinch of salt.

CLASS 2.—VEGETABLE SALADS.

Lettuce Salad.—Place the prepared lettuce in the salad bowl and sprinkle over it French Dressing No. 1 or No. 2, according to taste. Turn it over and about carefully, until each leaf is covered with dressing. Serve on cold plates. Half a cup of dressing will dress lettuce enough for six people. Chicory or endive, and water cress are prepared and served like lettuce.

Cucumber Salad.—Select cucumbers of medium size, remove a thick paring, and cut away all green portions. Slice, not too thin, on broken ice, cover closely, let stand half an hour, or until chilled and crisp, then drain the water from the cucumbers and serve them with French dressing. A small quantity of minced onion may be served with them, if liked.

Cucumbers sprinkled with salt and allowed to stand become tough and indigestible.

Onion Salad.—Remove the skin from onions, slice as thin as possible, on broken ice, and when chilled and crisp serve with a dressing of vinegar, sugar, salt, and pepper; or with French dressing, if preferred.

Some hygienists think sugar assists the digestion of onions, and prevents their imparting an unpleasant odor to the breath.

Cabbage Salad.—Soak the prepared cabbage in cold water till crisp. Shave thin, and dress with cooked mayonnaise, or with vinegar, seasoned with Seasoning No. 3.

Celery Salad.—Soak the prepared celery in ice water until chilled and crisp, then dice the white tender portions, and dress with oil mayonnaise dressing.

Tomato Salad No. 1.—Select medium-sized, ripe tomatoes, and with a sharp knife cut off about one third of each tomato. Cut the pulp loose from the skin, and scoop it out, with a teaspoon, without breaking the outside skin. Fill the cup or shell of each scooped tomato with broken ice. Put the pulp on a plate and, with a silver knife, cut it into large dice. Sprinkle lightly with salt, drain in a sieve, add a teaspoonful each of minced onion and oil mayonnaise to each cup of drained tomato, and mix well together. Empty the ice and water from the tomato cups, and fill each cup with the prepared salad. Place on a plate on the crossed stems of two large nasturtium leaves, or on lettuce leaves. Lettuce leaves make a very nice garnish for tomato cups, but are not nearly so dainty as nasturtium leaves.

Tomato Salad No. 2.—Skin and slice ripe tomatoes in thick slices. Lay on ice till chilled. Serve on cold plates, with French or mayonnaise dressing, or without dressing. Salt, pepper, sugar, and vinegar, as a dressing for tomatoes, is preferred by many.

Potato Salad No. 1.—To one cup of cooked mayonnaise dressing seasoned with Seasoning No. 2, add a tablespoonful each of minced onion and parsley, and a cup of thin cream or milk, stirred in gradually. Pour the mixture over thinly sliced, cold boiled potatoes, and serve with cold meats or boiled fish.

Potato Salad No. 2.—Dice two or three slices of breakfast bacon, cook in a spider until transparent, add a tablespoonful of minced onion, and cook slowly until it turns yellow. Add two cups of cold boiled potato cut in dice, seasoned with salt and pepper, and with which a tablespoonful of minced parsley has been mixed. Stir lightly together with a fork, cover closely, let simmer for ten minutes, or until the potato is well heated, then add a tablespoonful of vinegar, shake well together, and serve hot.

Beet Salad No. 1.—Boil the beets until very tender, skin, slice thin, put in a sauce-pan, and to each cup of sliced beet add a tablespoonful each of butter and vinegar, with salt and pepper to taste. Heat, shake well together, and serve.

Carrots, parsnips, and salsify may be prepared and served as salads in precisely the same manner.

Beet Salad No. 2.—Boil the beets till very tender, remove the skins, and when cold, hash, or cut into dice, and serve with cream dressing, seasoned with salt and pepper.

Beet and Potato Salad.—Mix together, with a fork, equal portions of cold boiled beet and potato cut in dice. Serve with cream dressing seasoned with salt and pepper.

Cooked spinach, asparagus, and many other green vegetables may be dressed with cream dressing, seasoned with salt and pepper, and served cold as salads.

CLASS 3.—MIXED SALADS.

Oysters and clams, when served raw as relishes, can scarcely be called salads with strict propriety, but for the sake of convenience they are placed among mixed salads, as are also various other relishes and salads that cannot be legitimately classified as either fruit or vegetable salads.

Raw Oysters.—Wash the shells of the oysters in cold water, then pack in broken ice till well chilled. Serve on the half shell—from three to five grouped on a plate—and garnish with two or three lemon points.

Clams and other shell fish that are eaten raw should be served in the same manner.

Raw oysters are sometimes cut in pieces, mixed with celery, dressed with mayonnaise or French dressing, and served as a salad. But as neither the oyster nor celery is improved by such inharmonious combination, an oyster salad is not likely to commend itself to popular favor.

Shrimp Salad.—Put the prepared shrimps—either fresh or canned—in a bowl of broken ice until chilled. Remove the ice and water, put over the shrimps about two tablespoonfuls of French Dressing No. 2 to each cup of shrimps, and place on ice until ready to serve. Arrange dainty cups of crisp lettuce leaves by placing together in the form of a cup three or four medium-sized lettuce leaves. Place from three to five shrimps in each lettuce cup, and serve with French Dressing No. 1.

Lobster Salad.—Prepare and serve lobster in every respect like shrimps, mixing in each lettuce cup some of the different portions of the lobster.

Mayonnaise dressing may be served instead of French, if preferred, with either shrimp or lobster salad, and water cress may be used in place of lettuce.

Salmon Salad.—Pick the cooked salmon in pieces suitable for serving. With two cups of prepared salmon mix two cold, hard-boiled eggs chopped fine. Dress with mayonnaise dressing, and serve in lettuce cups or garnished with cresses.

Any cold boiled, baked, or broiled fish may, with an admixture of hard-boiled eggs, be served in a similar manner as a salad. And, if lacking in flavor, a spoonful of capers, or a little finely minced pickle, may be added.

Lettuce, cucumbers, tomatoes, and cress can be indiscriminately mixed with fish and shell fish of all kinds in the preparation of salads, and are admirably adapted to the purpose. Celery and fish are so inharmonious in flavors that they should not be used in that connection.

Chicken Salad No. 1.—Put four cups of cooked chicken, freed from skin, bones, and coarse pieces, and cut into dice, in an earthen bowl, and pour over it half a cup of French Dressing No. 2. Set in a cold place for an hour, drain through a sieve, mix with it three cups of white, tender celery cut in dice, and add, and mix lightly through it, a cup of oil mayonnaise dressing. Place in the salad bowl—heaping in the center—spread half a cup of mayonnaise dressing over it, sprinkle a spoonful of capers upon the dressing, and garnish with curled celery and water cress ; or with olives, lemon points, hard-boiled eggs, or lettuce.

Nothing should be used in garnishing a salad that cannot be eaten in conjunction with the salad without disguising or detracting from the delicacy of its flavor. Therefore chicken salad made with celery should not be garnished with beets, radishes, or parsley.

Chicken Salad No. 2.—To four cups of prepared chicken cut in dice add two cups of white, tender celery also cut in dice, mix well together, and add a cup of cooked mayonnaise. Place in a salad bowl, spread more dressing over the top, and garnish according to taste.

Chicken Salad No. 3.—Mix well together two cups each of prepared chicken, sweetbreads, or veal tongue, and tender white celery, all diced, and add one cup of oil mayonnaise, cooked mayonnaise, or the oil and cooked mixed in equal quantities. Put in a salad bowl, cover with dressing, and garnish according to taste with curled celery, cress, lettuce, lemon points, hard-boiled eggs, capers, olives, or pickles.

Chicken Salad with Lettuce.—Strip the green from the white stems of well-grown, crisp lettuce leaves. Throw the stems into ice water for half an hour, then break or cut them into dice. To two cups of the diced lettuce add a teaspoonful of celery seed, scattering it over the lettuce as evenly as possible. Use, the same as celery, for chicken salad. It makes an excellent substitute, and is much preferable to entire lettuce leaves or to cabbage.

Sweetbread Salad No. 1.—Prepare and cook the sweetbreads as directed on page 38, and, when perfectly cold, free from skin, cut into dice, and put in a bowl. To two cups of sweetbreads add half a cup of French Dressing No. 2 and set on ice for half an hour. Pare and cut into dice two cups of cucumber, and put into a covered dish with broken ice for half an hour. Remove the ice, drain the cucumber, also the sweetbreads, and mix them together, adding half a cup of French Dressing No. 1, in an iced salad bowl. Serve at once, or set on ice and keep cold.

Sweetbread Salad No. 2.—Prepare the sweetbreads as directed in last formula. Drain and mix with an equal portion of celery cut in dice. Mix with oil mayonnaise dressing and serve. Whenever the cooked mayonnaise dressing is used alone, or whenever it is used in connection with oil mayonnaise dressing, the French dressing can be omitted, as it is used with oil mayonnaise—which contains but little acid—simply to increase the acidity of the salad.

Cucumber and Fish Salad.—Pick into pieces suitable for serving any cold cooked fresh fish, freed from skin and bones. With two cups of the prepared fish mix half a cup of French Dressing No. 2.

Prepare cucumber as for sweetbread salad and let stand for half an hour on broken ice. Drain the cucumber, also the fish, mix in equal quantities, and pour over the mixture half a cup of French Dressing No. 1.

Tomato and Fish Salad.—Prepare cold cooked fish as before directed. Skin and cut the tomatoes in dice, and put on ice as directed for cucumbers. Mix two cups of each, and a tablespoonful of finely minced onion together, and dress with three fourths of a cup of oil mayonnaise dressing.

Mixed Fish Salad.—To four cups of prepared cold cooked fish add one cup of chopped hard-boiled eggs, and half a cup of chopped pickle. Mix well together, add one cup of either oil or cooked mayonnaise dressing. Serve in lettuce cups, or garnished with cress, or nasturtium leaves.

Egg Salad No. 1.—Divide six hard-boiled eggs in halves. Remove the yolks, mash fine, and add a teaspoonful of Seasoning No. 1, a tablespoonful of olive oil, butter, or cream, and a tablespoonful of lemon juice or vinegar. Mix all well together, fill the halves of eggs with the mixture, arrange them on a bed of lettuce, nasturtium leaves, or cress, and serve.

Egg Salad No. 2.—Hash the whites and yolks of hard-boiled eggs separately. Mix lightly together, and to two cups of egg add one cup of celery, or one cup of white stems of lettuce cut fine. Cresses or nasturtium leaves may be used instead of celery or lettuce. Serve with either oil or cooked mayonnaise dressing.

SALAD DRESSINGS.

French Dressing No. 1.—Put a tablespoonful of very sharp vinegar into a cup which has been iced or made cold, add salt and white pepper to taste, then add gradually, stirring meanwhile, three tablespoonfuls of olive oil. The salt should be almost as plain to the taste in the mixture as the vinegar.

These proportions mixed in this manner will produce the best French dressing.

French Dressing No. 2.—Season to taste with salt and pepper three tablespoonfuls of vinegar, then add one tablespoonful of olive oil.

Mayonnaise Dressing.—In making this dressing select for use a Dover egg-beater and a large bowl-shaped coffee cup, or a pint bowl with straight sides. Have both well cooled with ice, also a fresh egg and the oil to be used for the dressing. Put the yolk of the egg into the cup and beat it for a few seconds before adding any oil. Beat in the oil, a few drops at a time, until it shows that it is combining perfectly with the egg, then add more freely. When the mixture becomes too stiff to beat easily add, one at a time, two teaspoonfuls of lemon juice or vinegar, which will thin it. Beat in more oil until again very stiff, when thin with acid as before. By thus alternating the oil and acid, a quart or more of oil may be made into a light, thick, cream-colored dressing with only one egg yolk. With an assistant to pour the oil, very slowly at first and more freely afterward, one can convert a large bottle of oil into a deliciously smooth, thick mayonnaise dressing in five minutes. To each cup of dressing add a teaspoonful of Seasoning No. 1.

Cooked Mayonnaise Dressing.—Pour four tablespoonfuls of boiling vinegar over two whole eggs, or the yolks of four eggs, which have been well beaten, stirring the mixture while adding the vinegar. Put in a small saucepan over the fire, and cook slowly, stirring constantly, until the mixture is thick and creamy. Remove from the fire, add a tablespoonful of butter, and stir until perfectly mixed. To each cup of dressing add two teaspoonfuls of Seasoning No. 2. When cold add an equal quantity of whipped cream, and use wherever oil mayonnaise dressing would be suitable, or mix together equal portions of the two dressings, and use wherever either would be suitable.

This cooked dressing may be put in glass jars or tumblers and kept an indefinite length of time. The whipped cream should be added just before the dressing is used.

Cream Dressing.—To one cup of White Sauce No. 2 add gradually four tablespoonfuls of vinegar or lemon juice, and, when perfectly cold, beat into it one cup of whipped cream, or half a cup of thin cream.

SEASONINGS FOR SALAD DRESSINGS.

Different salads require, in their preparation, different dressings; and those different dressings require different kinds and quantities of seasoning. Hence the seasonings required for various kinds of salad dressings are given below:

Seasoning No. 1.—Mix together two teaspoonfuls of salt, one teaspoonful of mustard flour, and half a teaspoonful of mixed pepper.

Seasoning No. 2.—Mix together three teaspoonfuls of salt, one teaspoonful of mustard flour, and one third of a teaspoonful of mixed pepper.

Seasoning No. 3.—Mix together one teaspoonful of salt, two teaspoonfuls of granulated sugar, and a third of a teaspoonful of mixed pepper.

CHAPTER XXII.

ENTRÉES AND SIDE DISHES.

Almost everything broiled, fried, stewed, scalloped, or deviled may be served as an entrée or side dish. But the things that should be, and most usually are, served as such are made dishes, or dishes prepared from left-overs, odds and ends, and broken bits of former meals. And in these made dishes it is quite legitimate to introduce foreign sauces and seasonings, in order to give flavor to the food in lieu of that which it has lost by cooling and exposure.

It is somewhat difficult to draw the line which ought to separate dishes alike in many respects, but quite different in others. The whole subject of made dishes can, however, be pretty well illustrated under the following classes, viz.: creamed dishes, scalloped dishes, deviled dishes, fricassees, hashes, croquettes, jellied meats, and boned meats.

Creamed Chicken.—Free the cold chicken—either roasted, boiled, broiled, or fried—from skin and tough or sinewy bits, and cut in small pieces. To two cups of prepared chicken add one cup of White Sauce No. 2 or No. 3, mix well together, season to taste, simmer five minutes in a covered sauce-pan, and serve.

Creamed Fish.—Free the cold fish—either baked, broiled, boiled, or fried—from skin and bones, and separate in pieces. To each cup of prepared fish add half a cup of White Sauce No. 4, egg sauce, or drawn butter, to any of which may be added a teaspoonful of minced onion or parsley, with salt and pepper to taste. Mix carefully with a fork, simmer five minutes in a covered sauce-pan, and serve.

Creamed Sweetbreads.—Free the cooked sweetbreads from skin and separate them into small pieces. To each cup of sweetbreads add half a cup of White Sauce No. 4 and an eighth of a teaspoonful of grated lemon peel, mixed with half its bulk of ground mace. Simmer five minutes in a covered sauce-pan, season, and serve.

Creamed Oysters No. 1.—To one cup of hot White Sauce No. 2 add a pint of oysters drained in a colander. Stir with a wooden spoon while heating, and as soon as the mixture boils and the thin edges of the oysters wrinkle and separate, remove from the fire, season, and serve in patty cases, *vol-au-vents*, or pies.

Creamed Oysters No. 2.—To one cup of White Sauce No. 4, boiling hot, add one pint of drained oysters, cook until the edges curl and separate, then season and serve on toast, or as stewed oysters.

Creamed Shrimps.—If canned shrimps are used, cover them for half an hour with broken ice and water, then drain, and to a can of shrimps add a cup of White Sauce No. 4. Simmer five minutes in a sauce-pan, season to taste, and serve.

Creamed Lobster.—To one cup of White Sauce No. 4 add two cups of cooked lobster, picked in small pieces, season to taste with Seasoning No. 1, simmer five minutes in a covered sauce-pan, and serve.

Salmon may be prepared and creamed like lobster. A teaspoonful of lemon juice or vinegar may be added to either dish when liked.

Creamed Potatoes.—Cut cold boiled or baked potatoes into dice or slices. To each pint of potato add a teaspoonful of minced parsley, if liked, and a cup of White Sauce No. 4. Season to taste, simmer five minutes in a covered sauce-pan, and serve with cold meats, or with broiled or fried meats, fish, or birds.

Creamed Macaroni.—To about a quart of boiled and drained macaroni add a cup of White Sauce No. 4. Season to taste, simmer five minutes in a covered sauce-pan, and serve with grated cheese, or mix a tablespoonful of grated cheese with the white sauce when added.

Spaghetti and vermicelli may be creamed in the same manner.

Creamed Codfish.—Soak two cups of salt codfish, freed from skin and bones and cut into dice, for fifteen minutes, in a quart of cold water. Drain off the water, put the fish in a sauce-pan, add to it a cup of White Sauce No. 1, and pepper to taste, cover, and simmer five minutes. Serve with boiled or baked potatoes, or on dipped toast. Black or white pepper should be used in creamed codfish, and cayenne or mixed pepper in codfish balls or cakes.

Creamed Toast.—Put in a shallow pan or basin on the back of the stove a cup of milk, a tablespoonful of butter, and a fourth of a teaspoonful of salt. Mix well together and dip the toasted bread, by laying a slice at a time in the hot mixture. With a fork and a limber-bladed knife turn it over, press under the milk, and lift at once into a warm tureen. After all the toast wanted has been dipped and lifted to the tureen in this manner, pour over it a cup of White Sauce No. 4.

Dipped Toast.—Put a cup of boiling water, a tablespoonful of butter, and a fourth of a teaspoonful of salt, in a shallow basin, on the back of the stove. Dip the toasted bread, a slice at a time, into the mixture, turn it over with a knife and fork, and lift on to a heated platter before it becomes too soft. If the toast is required richer more butter may be used. Hot milk may also be used in place of water, if preferred.

Curried Toast.—To a cup of White Sauce No. 4 add curry powder to taste, and serve with dipped toast.

Curried Rice.—To one cup of White Sauce No. 3 add curry powder to taste, and serve with boiled rice. Curried rice is appropriately served with stewed chicken or stewed veal.

Scalloped Potatoes No. 1.—Pare and slice the potatoes of a uniform thickness. Butter a baking dish and fill three quarters full with the prepared potatoes. Add new milk, seasoned to taste with salt and pepper, until the potatoes are nearly covered, then sprinkle Bread Crumbs No. 3 generously over them, and bake in a moderate oven for half an hour, or until the potatoes are cooked and the crumbs browned.

For scalloping potatoes a simple broth or any made gravy or meat sauce combined with water may be substituted for milk, and a tablespoonful of minced parsley, or minced onion, may be added to two or three cups of the prepared potatoes to give variety to the dish.

Scalloped Potatoes No. 2.—To three or four cups of

cold boiled or baked potatoes cut into dice, sliced, or hashed, add a teaspoonful of minced parsley and a cup and a half of White Sauce No. 4. Put in a buttered baking dish, cover with Crumbs No. 3, and cook in a moderate oven until the mixture is well heated and the crumbs are brown.

Scalloped Fish No. 1.—Cut uncooked fish in pieces suitable for serving, free from skin and bones, and season with salt, pepper, and parsley, if liked. Fill a buttered baking dish three fourths full with the prepared fish, cover with sweet milk, sprinkle Bread Crumbs No. 3 over the top, and bake in a moderate oven for half an hour, or until the fish is thoroughly cooked and the crumbs are brown.

Fish and potatoes may be scalloped together in this manner by putting in the baking dish alternate layers of uncooked fish and potatoes.

Scalloped Fish No. 2.—Free from skin and bones and cut in small pieces cold cooked fish. Slice or hash cold boiled or baked potatoes and cold boiled eggs. Fill a buttered baking dish three fourths full of the prepared material—placing the fish, potato, and eggs in alternate layers—and scattering, if liked, minced parsley over the layers of fish. Cover with White Sauce No. 4, sprinkle the top with Bread Crumbs No. 3, and bake twenty or twenty-five minutes in a moderate oven.

Scalloped Salt Codfish.—Prepare as for creamed codfish, put in a buttered baking dish, cover with White Sauce No. 4, sprinkle Bread Crumbs No. 3 over the top, and bake twenty or thirty minutes, according to the size of the dish, in a moderate oven.

Scalloped Fresh Codfish and Oysters.—Free cold boiled codfish of skin and bones, cut it in pieces suitable for serving, and with each pint of prepared fish use a pint of oysters, rinsed in cold water and drained. Put the fish and oysters in a shallow, buttered baking dish in alternate layers, add half a cup of drawn butter, left over with the fish, or made with water, sprinkle Bread Crumbs No. 3 over the top, and bake in a quick oven until the crumbs are a nice brown.

Panned Oysters.—Put in a spider a tablespoonful of butter, half a teaspoonful of salt, and a dust of pepper. When the butter is melted and hot, add a pint of oysters that have been washed and drained. Cover and cook over a hot fire about two minutes, shaking the spider occasionally while cooking. Serve in a warm dish, on thin slices of buttered toast—or without the toast, if preferred.

Curried Oysters.—Add curry powder to taste to oysters that have been washed and drained, and then pan, stew, or cream them.

Scalloped **Eggs No. 1.**—Slice or dice cold boiled eggs, put them in a buttered baking dish, cover with White Sauce No. 4, and heat to boiling point in a moderate oven.

Scalloped Eggs No. 2.—Put into a shallow, buttered baking dish one tablespoonful of White Sauce No. 4 for each egg. Break the eggs separately and slip carefully into the baking dish, sprinkle half a teaspoonful of grated cheese, or minced parsley, or cold boiled ham minced fine, over each egg, cover each with another tablespoonful of white sauce, and cook to taste in a moderate oven. If preferred, use only white sauce. The eggs can be scalloped in individual dishes, and the same proportion of white sauce allowed each egg as in the large dish.

Scalloped Lobster.—Cut the cooked lobster into pieces suitable for serving, put in a buttered baking dish, and to four cups of lobster add one cup of white sauce, and half a teaspoonful of mustard flour. Cover lightly with Bread Crumbs No. 3, and cook in a moderate oven twenty or twenty-five minutes. Salmon can be scalloped like lobster.

Deviled Clams.—Chop two dozen clams very fine, season with a teaspoonful each of minced parsley and onion, and salt and cayenne or mixed pepper to taste, and moisten with half a cup of sweet milk. Sprinkle a light covering of Bread Crumbs No. 3 in a buttered baking dish, or in buttered shells, place upon them a layer of prepared clams, sprinkle with bread crumbs, place upon them another layer of clams, cover the top generously with bread crumbs, and bake in a moderate oven fifteen or twenty minutes.

Deviled Crabs.—To two cups of hard-shell crab meat picked into small pieces add a teaspoonful of mustard flour, salt and pepper to taste, and half a cup of milk or thin cream. Sprinkle a buttered baking dish, or buttered shells, lightly with Bread Crumbs No. 3, place upon them a layer of crab meat, sprinkle again with crumbs, place another layer of crab meat upon the crumbs, and finish with a covering of crumbs. Bake fifteen or twenty minutes, or until the crumbs are nicely browned. Serve, with lemon points, either hot or cold.

Lobster and various kinds of fish may be deviled in a similar manner, and the seasoning may be varied to suit the taste. Hard-boiled eggs chopped fine may also be added at pleasure, to deviled fish, clams, lobster, or crabs.

Deviled Eggs.—To five hard-boiled eggs, minced fine, add two tablespoonfuls of grated cheese, salt, and cayenne or mixed pepper to taste, and half a cup of White Sauce No. 4. Put in a sauce-pan, simmer five minutes, and serve on toasted bread, or on heated snowflake crackers.

Scalloped and deviled dishes are much alike in many respects, but there are some quite marked differences. In scalloped dishes there is usually a greater preponderance of liquid than in deviled dishes—the latter being invariably dry, while the former are usually quite the reverse. In deviled dishes the food is always cut or divided into pieces small enough to be eaten with a fork. And in deviled dishes bread or cracker crumbs are always used, while in scalloped dishes they may or may not be used. The idea used to obtain that deviled dishes must be intensely hot with seasoning, but that idea has been abandoned, and deviled and scalloped dishes are now alike in that respect, both being seasoned to taste.

Fricasseed Oysters.—Select large oysters and wrap about each oyster a thin slice of salt pork or breakfast bacon. Lay on a very hot griddle or spider, and cook over a quick fire until the wrapping is brown and crisp, and the oyster delicately cooked. Serve on thin slices of toast, with lemon points.

Fricasseed oysters are sometimes absurdly called "little pigs in blankets."

Fricasseed Salt Pork.—Slice half a pound of salt pork in thin slices, and remove the rind. Lay the slices upon a hot spider and cook over a quick fire until the under side is brown, then turn and brown the other side in a similar manner. Lift the brown slices to a warm platter and drain the grease from the spider, until only two or three tablespoonfuls remain. Place the spider over the fire, put in it two tablespoonfuls of flour, mix well with the fat in the spider, add two cups of sweet milk, simmer five minutes, season to taste, and pour over the slices of meat on the platter. Serve with it boiled or baked potatoes.

Fricasseed Chicken.—In frying chicken, quail, and other birds it is economy to use only the breast and second joints, and to reserve the wings, legs, back, and giblets for stewing or fricasseeing. To fricassee these portions sauté them in clarified butter until nicely browned, then remove to a sauce-pan. To the butter in the spider where they were sautéd add a teaspoonful of flour and mix well, then pour in two cups of hot water, stir all the browning from the spider and mix with the liquid, season lightly with salt, strain, and pour over the chicken in the sauce-pan. Cover and simmer gently for an hour and a half, or until very tender, add a tablespoonful of flour stirred to a smooth paste with two tablespoonfuls of cold water, simmer five minutes, season to taste, and serve. A cup of fresh or canned mushrooms, cut in thin slices, can be added to this fricassee five or ten minutes before it is served.

Frizzled Beef.—Put two tablespoonfuls of butter in a spider over a quick fire, and when hot add two cups of thinly shaved dried beef, from which the rind has been removed, and stir constantly with a fork, to keep from burning, until it curls and looks cooked. Then remove the spider to a cooler part of the stove, sift in two tablespoonfuls of flour, mix well with the meat, pour in two cups of sweet milk, and simmer and stir till the sauce or gravy is smooth. Serve on a hot platter. Beef will frizzle in about two minutes.

Dried mutton, veal, and venison can be cooked in the same manner. A little dried liver shaved thin can be added to the beef or mutton, if liked.

Stewed Giblets with Mushrooms.—Cut the giblets of a fowl in pieces suitable for serving, put them in a saucepan, add two cups of hot water and a pinch of salt, cover closely, and cook gently for two hours, or until they are tender. Cook together until a light brown color two tablespoonfuls each of flour and butter, add to it the water from the giblets, also half a can of mushrooms sliced, with half the water from the can. Simmer five minutes, season to taste, pour over the giblets, shake well together, and serve. A teaspoonful of lemon juice or vinegar may be added to the mixture, if liked.

Fish Hash.—Melt a tablespoonful of butter in a sauce-pan, add a cup of water or milk and two cups of any kind of cold fresh fish, freed from skin and bones, and picked into small pieces. Season to taste, simmer five minutes, and serve on slices of dipped toast.

Hard-boiled eggs may always be added to hashed fish, also a flavoring of minced parsley, if liked; and any fish sauce left over from a previous meal may be used, instead of milk or water, for moistening the hash.

Turkey Hash.—Remove the skin and fat from left-over portions of turkey, and chop the meat fine, or cut it in dice. Put the bones, skin, and refuse bits in a sauce-pan with some trimmings of celery, add a teaspoonful of salt, and sufficient water to cover the bones, simmer for three hours, strain, and remove the grease. Cook together a tablespoonful each of butter and flour, add to it two cups of the turkey broth, cook until smooth, then add two or more cups of the prepared turkey meat, simmer five minutes, season, and serve on toast, or with baked or boiled potatoes.

Turkey and Oyster Hash.—Cut cold roast or boiled turkey into pieces as large as a medium-sized oyster. Prepare a broth as for turkey hash. Put two or more cups of the prepared meat into a sauce-pan, add enough of the broth to cover it, set on the back of the range, and let simmer until tender. Cook together in another sauce-pan two tablespoonfuls each of butter and flour until well mixed but not brown, add two cups of the turkey broth, simmer five minutes, add a pint of oysters, rinsed and drained, stir gently with a wooden spoon, and as soon as the edges separate and curl add the turkey meat, season to taste, and serve with or without toast.

This dish may be served at breakfast or lunch, or as an entrée at dinner—in the latter case on a triangular slice of toast.

Chicken and oyster hash may be prepared and served in the same manner. The proportions of fowl and oysters in these hashes may be the same, or either may predominate according to circumstances. Boiled fresh codfish combined with oysters in a similar manner makes a very delicious dish. In such combination the fish should be heated in a few spoonfuls of butter, and the oysters cooked in a white sauce or drawn butter before they are mixed together.

Veal Hash.—Cold roast or stewed veal, when freed from skin and bones and minced fine, makes excellent hash. Prepare the broth the same as for turkey hash. Cook together in a sauce-pan one tablespoonful each of butter and flour, add one cup of veal broth, cook until smooth, add two cups of minced veal, simmer five minutes, season to taste, and serve on toast. Finely chopped mushrooms may be added to turkey, chicken, or veal hash if desired, or two or more of these meats may be mixed together in one hash.

Veal Terrapin.—Cut cold roast or stewed veal, freed from bones and tough portions, into irregular sized pieces—some as large, others twice as large, as dice. The fat and skin can both be used, unless the skin is hard. Cook together in a sauce-pan, until a light brown, two tablespoonfuls each of butter and flour, add two cups of veal broth, and the water from a can of mushrooms, and season with mixed pepper and half a level teaspoonful of grated lemon peel mixed with half its bulk of ground mace or grated nutmeg. Add two or more cups of the prepared veal, the can of mushrooms sliced, three hard-boiled eggs chopped fine, and a cup of cooked sweetbreads, prepared as for creaming, or a cup of calf's brains cooked in salted water and cut in dice. Simmer gently five minutes, or until the mixture is well heated, add a tablespoonful of lemon juice mixed with a teaspoonful of sugar, and serve.

Mock Terrapin.—Cook in a sauce-pan, until brown, four tablespoonfuls of butter, add one cup of veal broth, two tablespoonfuls of lemon juice, half a teaspoonful of grated lemon peel, half as much grated nutmeg or ground mace, and a teaspoonful of sugar. Mix lightly together with a fork two cups of veal, one cup of veal kidneys, one cup of sweetbreads or calf's brains, prepared as for veal terrapin, and a cup of hard-boiled eggs minced fine. Add them to the broth, cover closely, simmer five or ten minutes until well heated, season, and serve.

In a similar manner various kinds of delicate meats may be combined in a dish, and such ingredients as mushrooms, eggs, brains, sweetbreads, and kidneys may be omitted. The advantage of using such articles in this connection is, that without them there would frequently be an insufficient quantity of odds and ends to make a family dish, and with one or more of them added the richness and flavor of the dish are improved.

Mutton Hash.—Prepare cold boiled or roast mutton in pieces suitable for serving. Put in a sauce-pan, cover with Jelly Sauce No. 3, simmer ten minutes, or until heated, season, and serve. Slices of cold duck or venison may be heated in the same manner.

Cold sliced beef or veal may be served with cold Tomato Sauce No. 1, or with cold tomato or cucumber catsup; or may be re-warmed in slices, dice, or cubes, in any brown or tomato sauce.

Breakfast Hash.—To one cup of coarsely hashed cold boiled or baked potato add one cup of finely hashed cold meat, either beef, veal, lamb, chicken, or a mixture of any or all of them, season to taste with salt and pepper, add two or three tablespoonfuls of broth, gravy, milk, or cream, and brown in a buttered pan on the range, or in the oven. Or heat thoroughly, without browning, if preferred. For an occasional change flavor the hash with minced onion or sweet herbs, or serve with fried or broiled breakfast bacon, baked apples, apple sauce, or some acid stewed fruit.

Scrapple.—To three cups of simple beef stock, or of Mixed Stock No. 1, add one cup of granulated cornmeal wet with one cup of cold water. Season sharply with salt and pepper, cook half an hour, and turn into a brick-shaped bread pan. When perfectly cold cut in slices and sauté on a griddle with clarified butter or drippings, or crumb and fry in deep fat, like mush.

Calf's Head.—Prepare and cook a calf's head as for mock turtle soup. Serve as in mock turtle soup, making the sauce thicker than the soup; or serve the head and brains in Brown Sauce No. 2 or No. 3, in Jelly Sauce No. 3, or in Tomato Sauce No. 5.

Hashed Potato.—Cook together one tablespoonful of butter and one teaspoonful of flour. Add half a cup of cream or sweet milk. Season with salt and pepper. Stir until the mixture boils and is smooth. Add two cups of cold boiled or baked potato—cut in dice or hashed—cover, and let simmer ten or fifteen minutes. Serve in a heated dish.

Browned Hashed Potato.—Prepare a sauce as for hashed potato. Mix the potato carefully with it. Put the mixture in a well-buttered skillet or pan, and cook slowly until nicely browned. Serve hot.

Lyonnaise Potato.—Put two tablespoonfuls of clarified butter in a skillet or frying pan, and when melted add to it two tablespoonfuls of minced onion. Cook till the onion turns yellow, then add two cups of diced or hashed cold potato, with which a tablespoonful of minced parsley has been mixed, and which has been seasoned with salt and pepper. Cover and cook slowly until nicely browned on the under side, then fold like an omelet, and serve on a heated dish. If the cold potato is very dry two or three spoonfuls of sweet milk may be mixed with it before the parsley and seasoning are added.

Browned Potato Cakes.—Mix one egg and one tablespoonful of cream or milk with two cups of cold mashed potato. Roll the mixture into balls. Flatten the balls into cakes about half an inch thick. Dust with flour and brown on a griddle, with just sufficient clarified butter, or beef drippings, to keep them from sticking.

Potato and Fish Cakes.—Prepare cold mashed potato as for potato cakes. Mix with it an equal quantity of cold boiled, baked, broiled, or fried fish, freed from skin and bones and picked up fine ; add a teaspoonful of melted butter, form into cakes, and brown on a griddle.

Browned Sliced Potatoes.—Slice cold boiled potatoes into tolerably thick slices. Season with salt and pepper, and dust with flour. Lay on a griddle, well greased with drippings or clarified butter, over a quick fire. When brown on the under side, pour a few drops of melted butter on each slice of potato, turn over, and brown. Serve hot.

Creamy Chicken Croquettes.—Cook together in a

sauce-pan until well mixed a tablespoonful each of flour and butter, add a cup of jellied chicken, or veal stock, and two cups of finely minced chicken, with or without sweetbreads, mushrooms, etc., and seasoned like Chicken Croquettes No. 1, 2, 3, or 4. Simmer five minutes, spread to cool on oiled plates, and, when cold, shape in any form desired by rolling lightly under the hand on a smooth board. When shaped, roll in Crumbs No. 2, cover with egg batter by laying the croquettes, one at a time, on a plate and dipping the batter over them with a spoon until every portion is covered, then slip a limber knife under the end of each croquette its full length, and lift to a plate covered thickly with Bread Crumbs No. 4. Pile the crumbs all over the croquette with a spoon, pressing them gently upon the ends, and lay it on several folds of cheese-cloth, the croquette being so soft that if laid upon a plate or board the under side will be flattened and its form rendered imperfect. When all the croquettes are prepared, place in a frying basket and fry in deep fat.

To make chicken or veal croquettes that will be very soft and creamy when fried, rich chicken or veal stock, or a combination of both, should be used. Any meat or fresh fish croquettes can be made soft and creamy in a similar manner by using stiff veal stock with which to make the sauce.

Lobster Cutlets.—Prepare the lobster as for croquettes. Place a spoonful of the mixture on a board or plate well covered with Crumbs No. 2. With a spoon in the left hand, its back toward the mixture, and a limber knife in the right hand, press it into the form of a cutlet or neatly trimmed lamb chop, half an inch in thickness. Level up the sides of the cutlet by pressure with the spoon and knife, and when perfect in shape, cover all over with Crumbs No. 2, then with egg batter, as in creamy chicken croquettes. With a broad spatula or pancake ladle lift to a plate, cover again with Crumbs No. 2, and sauté in clarified butter, until a rich brown color. Serve, garnished with lemon points, cress, curled celery, or thick slices of tomato.

Fish Turbans.—Prepare and press into the required form, as directed for lobster cutlets, any kind of cold fresh fish. Season to taste, crumb, and sauté in like manner.

Potato Croquettes No. 1.—Mash cold boiled potatoes. Season with salt, pepper, and a little butter. Add a teaspoonful of minced parsley and the unbeaten white of an egg to each cup of mashed potato. Stir well together. Drop by spoonfuls into a frying basket in deep fat of the proper temperature. Remove when sufficiently brown. Drain on several folds of cheese-cloth. Serve hot.

Potato Croquettes No. 2.—Peel and boil one medium-sized onion and three potatoes. Drain, dry off, mash fine, add a tablespoonful of rich cream and a teaspoonful of butter, or a tablespoonful each of butter and milk—an additional spoonful of milk may be added if necessary to make the mixture sufficiently soft—season with salt and pepper, and beat with a wooden spoon till light. When slightly stiffened by cooling, form into croquettes as directed for creamy chicken croquettes, cover with crumbs, then with egg batter, then again with crumbs, and fry in deep fat. Serve with broiled or cold meats, or with boiled ham or tongue.

Potato Croquettes No. 3.—Prepare the potatoes as in last formula—with or without onion—flatten to thickness of a sixteenth of an inch enough of it for one croquette. Have the croquette rectangular in shape, place upon the center of it a teaspoonful of minced boiled ham, or any highly seasoned meat, cooked and seasoned as for croquettes or sandwiches, spread the minced meat lengthwise on the potato, fold up the sides, and pinch the sides and ends carefully together. Cover with crumbs, then with egg batter, then again with crumbs, and fry in a basket in deep fat.

Rice Croquettes No. 2.—Boil and enrich the rice as in Rice Croquettes No. 1 (page 143), omitting the sugar. Put a tablespoonful of rice on an oiled plate, flatten to a sixteenth of an inch, in rectangular shape, and place upon the center a teaspoonful of thick jam, a piece of preserved fruit, a teaspoonful of grated pine-apple from which the juice has been drained, or of preserved ginger, citron, or limes minced fine. Spread slightly lengthwise, fold the rice carefully over the fruit with a limber knife, and pinch it well and smoothly together at the top and ends. Lift the croquette carefully with the knife, cover it with Bread Crumbs No. 2, then with egg batter, then again with Bread Crumbs No. 2, and so proceed until the croquettes are all prepared, when place in a basket and fry in deep fat. Serve with pulverized sugar sifted over them, or with the syrup of the fruit used in making them.

Timbales.—Put into a large cup or small bowl one egg, a fourth of a cup of cold water or milk, a pinch of salt, and half a cup of flour. Stir with a fork till mixed, then beat very light with a Dover beater. Put the timbale iron in the kettle of hot fat until heated, lift out, shake off the fat, wipe lightly, lower into the prepared batter about half its length, hold it there half a minute, then dip into the kettle of hot fat and cook until the timbale cup drops off. Lift the cup from the kettle and turn over on cheese-cloth to drain. Repeat the operation until all the batter is used. These cups are suitable for any purpose where puff paste patties are used, and the quantity of batter given will make a dozen cups.

Timbales of Rice.—Line a buttered baking dish with rice prepared as for croquettes—but without sugar or flavoring—by pressing it over the bottom and sides of the dish, leaving it an eighth of an inch thick, brush the inside surface with white of egg slightly beaten, and dry ten minutes in a warm oven, then fill the dish three fourths full of creamed or hashed chicken, turkey, or veal. Bake in the oven half an hour, or until well heated through, and serve in the dish in which it was cooked.

Timbales of Potato.—Press potato, prepared as for croquettes, over the inside of a buttered baking dish, until it forms a smooth coating a fourth of an inch thick, then fill the dish three fourths full of creamed, hashed, or otherwise prepared meats, poultry, fish, or eggs, or a combination of such, and bake for half an hour, or until heated through. If it is desired to serve some very soft preparation, in either rice or potato timbales, brush the inner surface of the rice or potato with a brush dipped in white of egg slightly beaten, and dry in the oven a few minutes before filling with the mixture.

Chicken Souffle.—To one cup of White Sauce No. 2 add two cups of very finely chopped breast of chicken, a tablespoonful of minced parsley, half a teaspoonful of grated lemon peel, and half as much mace. Simmer five minutes, remove from the fire, and when lukewarm add the whites of four eggs beaten stiff. Put the mixture into a buttered dish or mold, and steam or bake for half an hour, or until stiff in the center, then turn out on a warm dish, and garnish lightly with cress or endive.

Veal, sweetbreads, or any delicate fish can be used in place of chicken, and the same formula as for chicken be followed.

Cheese Souffle No. 1.—To two cups of rich American cheese grated add a fourth of a teaspoonful of mustard flour, and the same of salt, and pepper to taste. Beat the yolks of two eggs very light, mix with half a cup of sweet milk, and stir in the cheese. Melt a tablespoonful of butter in a sauce-pan, pour in the cheese mixture, and stir constantly over a slow fire until the cheese melts, and the mixture becomes smooth and hot—not boiling. Remove from the fire, add the well-beaten whites of three eggs, pour into a buttered baking dish, and bake in a very slow oven about twenty minutes.

Cheese Souffle No. 2.—To one cup of White Sauce No. 1 add two cups of grated cheese, season to taste, add the yolks of three eggs well beaten, and lastly the whites beaten stiff. Bake in a very moderate oven, in a dish, or in six individual molds. If in the latter, serve in the molds in which they are baked.

Potato Souffle.—To two cups of boiled potato mashed fine add one cup of sweet cream, or one tablespoonful of butter, and one cup of sweet milk, salt and white pepper to taste, and a tablespoonful of minced parsley. Mash and beat with a wooden spoon until very light and smooth, and when slightly cool whip into the mixture the whites of four eggs beaten stiff, or whip the whites in, one at a time, unbeaten. Cook, and serve like chicken soufflé.

There are omelet soufflés, pudding soufflés, and a variety of fruit, fish, chicken, potato, and rice soufflés. But a soufflé is simply a mixture containing a large proportion of the white of egg beaten stiff and mixed with it just before it is put to cook, and when this principle is understood, soufflés can be multiplied indefinitely, if desired, by using the various edibles that are adapted to their preparation.

Welsh Rarebit No. 1.—To two cups of grated American cheese add mustard, pepper, and salt to taste, and half a cup of sweet milk with which the well-beaten yolk of an egg has been mixed. Put a tablespoonful of butter in a sauce-pan over the fire, and when melted add the cheese mixture. Heat slowly, stirring constantly, until the cheese is melted and the mixture becomes a smooth paste, then spread on thin slices of buttered or dipped toast, and serve hot.

Golden buck is the same as Welsh rarebit, with the addition of a poached egg, served on each slice of toast.

Welsh Rarebit No. 2.—Cover slices of dipped toast very thickly with grated cheese, seasoned to taste. Place on a buttered pan, and put in a hot oven where the greatest heat will be at the top. Remove from the oven when the cheese is melted and slightly scorched, and serve on small plates.

Welsh Rarebit No. 3.—Prepare bread as for French toast, but, instead of sautéing, lay the slices upon a well-buttered pan, cover with grated cheese seasoned with salt and pepper, and cook in the oven until the cheese is toasted.

Cheese Straws No. 1.—If the cheese straws are to be made of puff paste, roll the paste very thin—if they are to be made of flaky pie crust, roll the same thickness as for pies. When rolled, cut in strips from six to ten inches wide, and cut the strips into straws or sticks a fourth of an inch in width. Lay upon baking sheets or shallow pans, leaving a space between the straws about a third as wide as the straws. Grate rich American cheese, season to taste with salt and red pepper, and scatter quite thickly over the straws, and over the spaces between them also. Place in the oven where the greatest heat will be at the top, and bake ten or fifteen minutes, or until cooked. Remove from the oven, cut the cheese in the center of the spaces between the straws, and pile the straws on a plate in the form of a log cabin.

Cheese Straws No. 2.—To a cup of grated cheese add salt and pepper to taste, two tablespoonfuls of melted butter, three tablespoonfuls of cold water, and flour enough to make a soft dough. Mix with a fork until stiff enough to cleave from the sides of the mixing bowl. Lay upon a molding board dusted with flour, sift flour over the dough, roll gently until as thin as pie crust, cut in strips a fourth of an inch wide, and bake.

French Toast.—Beat one egg very light, gradually

beat into it a cup of sweet milk, and add a generous pinch of salt. Remove the crust from half a dozen slices of bread about a quarter of an inch thick, lay them upon a platter, and pour part of the egg and milk mixture over them. After they have soaked a minute turn them over carefully, add the balance of the mixture, and after they have soaked another minute coat each slice with prepared Crumbs No. 2, and sauté in clarified butter until richly browned; or sauté in butter, without crumbing, if preferred. Serve hot with a liquid, a raisin, or a cherry sauce, in place of a pudding, or as a sweet entrée at dinner; or serve at breakfast, without a sauce.

Tropical Toast.—Prepare and cook the slices of bread as for French toast. To one cup of raisin sauce add half a cup of flaked pine-apple, and half a cup of orange pulp cut in small pieces. Heat all together and serve a spoonful of fruit on each slice of toast. Or the pine-apple may be omitted, and half a cup of thinly sliced bananas used in its place.

Aspic Jelly.—To three pints of veal or chicken broth, or a mixture of the two, rich enough to form a jelly when cold, add the slightly beaten whites of two eggs, half a cup of celery roots and trimmings cut in small pieces, a slice of onion, the thin rind of a lemon, a small blade of mace, six cloves, and salt and pepper to taste. Put all together in a sauce-pan, and heat slowly until the mixture boils, then let simmer for fifteen minutes, add a tablespoonful of lemon juice, and strain through two or three folds of cheese-cloth. If the jelly is wanted more acid a larger quantity of lemon juice can be used. Aspic jelly when cold becomes clear and stiff, and is served suitably with boned turkey or chicken. It is often poured, in liquid form, over prepared meats, in the preparation of jellied meats, etc.

If a dark jelly is wanted beef or mixed stock can be used in making it, and, in such case, carrots, bay leaf, and allspice may be added to the flavoring, and a tablespoonful of tarragon vinegar may be used instead of lemon juice.

Jellied Chicken.—Boil the chicken whole, and, when cool, free the best portions from skin and bones. Cut the larger pieces of meat into strips half an inch in width, and the same thickness, if convenient, and lay these strips in an oval or rectangular dish, placing the light and dark meat in alternate layers. When the dish is full pour in aspic jelly made from the chicken broth, cover so as to keep the chicken under the jelly, and set in a cold place until firm. Serve for breakfast, luncheon, tea, or picnics.

Pressed Corned Beef.—Arrange the cooked beef in a pan or mold as directed for jellied chicken, and pour over it the broth in which it cooked, freed from grease, and seasoned to taste, or, if preferred, use plain beef soup stock in place of the water in which the corned beef cooked, cover, put a light weight upon the meat, and set in a cold place till firm.

Pressed Veal.—Stew a piece of veal, free it from skin and bones, arrange as directed for corned beef, pour over it the broth in which it cooked, press it, and set in a cold place till firm.

CHAPTER XXIII.

BONED MEATS.

The bones can be removed easily from all kinds of meats, poultry, game, and fish by inserting a small, sharp knife-blade close to the bone, at the point where it is most exposed, or nearest the surface, and cutting away and separating from the bone all the flesh, skin, ligaments, etc., that are attached to it, until it can be removed from its surroundings.

To Bone and Stuff a Turkey.—Singe, wash, and wipe dry the skin of the turkey. Cut, from head to tail, down the center of the back, through the skin and flesh, to the bone. Beginning at the head, scrape the flesh from the bones, with a dull-bladed knife, working from the back toward the breast, and removing, when reached, the shoulder blades and the bones from the upper joints of the wings, and also those from the upper joints of the legs. Be careful not to cut or break the skin, and when it clings to the bone, loosen it carefully with the fingers. The flesh should be left adhering to the skin, and as intact as possible. If the turkey has not been drawn, cut the skin around the vent, lift off the skeleton, and remove its contents. Separate the skeleton into pieces, and wash them, then cook three or four hours in slightly salted water, so as to extract the gelatine and flavor from the bones. After the turkey has been boned the carcass may be filled with quail, grouse, prairie chicken, chicken, veal, or fresh pork, or with a combination of part, or all, of these things. Sweetbreads, mushrooms, and truffles can also be used in conjunction with other articles, and lean ham, beef tongue, and hard-boiled eggs are very desirable as part of the filling, because of their color and flavor. For a seven or eight-pound turkey three and a half or four pounds of filling will be needed, also a pint of poultry or veal broth, sufficiently strong to become a stiff jelly when cold. The main portion of the material to be used for filling should be minced fine, like meat for croquettes, seasoned sharply with salt and pepper, and mixed with the broth, after it has been warmed until liquid. All the filling material must be cooked before it is put in the turkey.

After all the material has been prepared stuff the boned fowl in this manner: Lay the turkey, skin side down, on a large platter. Remove some portions of the breast, and lay in the places of the removed portions long cubes of lean boiled ham or tongue, and place upon these strips a layer of chopped meat. Stuff the wings and second joints from which the bones were removed with the chopped meat. Sprinkle with whole allspice. Place through the center lengthwise a row of hard-boiled eggs, from which the shells have been peeled. Cover the eggs with a layer of the chopped meat, some cubes of tongue or ham, and the displaced portions of the breast. Add mushrooms, truffles, or sweetbreads, if desired, and when full enough, draw up over the filling, the back of the turkey, and sew the edges of the carcass together. Wet the seam with water, and dust flour over it. Lay the stuffed fowl upon its back, tie the legs and wings in position, place it upon a piece of muslin, wrap tightly and fasten the muslin securely together along the back. Put it, back up, in a steamer and cook for two hours, then lay in a roasting pan and cook slowly in the oven, until well browned. Baste frequently, while roasting, with turkey, chicken, or veal broth, well seasoned with salt and pepper. After it is done, place in an earthen tureen, breast down, to cool, and strain over it the broth used for basting.

Chickens and all kinds of fowls and birds can be boned in the same way that a turkey is boned.

To Bone and Stuff a Leg of Lamb.—Insert the boning knife close to the bone at the upper end of the leg. Cut the sinews, and scrape the flesh from the bone, half way through the leg, then cut and scrape in the same manner, from the other end of the leg, until the bone can be slipped from the meat. After removing the bone, fill the cavity from which it has been taken with bread crumbs prepared and seasoned as for roast turkey. Fasten with skewers, wrap and tie securely, and cook the same as boned turkey. Serve cold, with currant, grape, plum, or cranberry jelly.

To Bone and Stuff a Leg of Veal.—Follow the directions given for boning a leg of lamb. After the bone has been removed stuff the veal with rich sausage meat, highly seasoned with salt and pepper, wrap and tie up securely, steam for an hour, then roast for two and a half hours—basting frequently with water highly seasoned with salt and pepper and enriched with a spoonful of butter.

To Bone and Stuff a Leg of Pork.—Select a small leg of pork for boning, and follow the directions given for boning a leg of lamb. After the bone has been removed fill the opening with bread crumbs, prepared as for stuffing roast turkey, and seasoned with salt, pepper, and pulverized sage. Skewer, wrap up, fasten securely, and cook as directed for cooking a boned leg of veal.

CHAPTER XXIV.

EGGS AND OMELETS.

Eggs, in whatever form cooked, should be cooked gently, and at as low a temperature as possible. Too high a temperature in cooking toughens the white of the egg and renders it indigestible.

To Boil an Egg.—See under the title Boiling, page 70.

To Poach an Egg.—Break the egg into a cup, from which slip it carefully into water at boiling temperature, but not actively boiling. Let it remain until cooked as desired, then lift from the water with a spatula or skimmer, and serve on dipped or buttered toast. The water in which eggs are poached should be well salted. Egg poachers, which hold the eggs in shallow tin cups over a pan of boiling water, where they are cooked by the steam, are easily handled and very convenient.

To Saute Eggs.—Break into separate cups as many eggs as are to be cooked. Have, smoking hot, in the sauté pan or spider a teaspoonful of bacon or ham drippings, or clarified butter for each egg. Put the eggs, one at a time, into the pan, and as soon as they are all in add two tablespoonfuls of hot water, cover the pan with a close-fitting lid, and cook over a quick fire one minute, when it will be seen upon lifting the lid that the steam has drawn the white neatly over the yolk of each egg. Continue the cooking more slowly until done as desired.

Scrambled Eggs No. 1.—Put in an omelet pan half a teaspoonful of butter for each egg. When the butter is hot pour in the eggs, without beating, and when set on the bottom of the pan mix or scramble them lightly with a fork or spoon. Cook as desired, season to taste, and serve. Minced parsley is an excellent flavoring for scrambled eggs.

Scrambled Eggs No. 2.—Put a teaspoonful of butter in a sauce-pan, add half a cup of sweet milk or cream, and when boiling hot pour in three well-beaten eggs. Stir and beat the mixture with a wooden spoon until sufficiently cooked, season to taste, and serve.

Shirred Eggs No. 1.—Put in a shirred egg dish a teaspoonful of melted butter for each egg. Break the eggs separately, slip carefully into the dish, bake to taste in a moderate oven, season with salt and pepper, and serve.

Shirred Eggs No. 2.—Separate the yolks from the whites of two eggs, and preserve them unbroken. Beat the whites very light, put into a shirred egg dish, and, with the back of a spoon, make two small cavities or nests, in the beaten white, by packing, at equal distances from each other and from the edges of the dish. Put the yolks in these cavities, and set the dish in a moderately hot oven until the yolks are cooked and the ragged points of white nicely browned, then remove, season with salt, pepper, and butter, and serve. The whites and yolks should be cut up and mixed together before they are eaten. Eggs shirred in this manner have the flavor of roasted eggs.

Creamy Omelet.—Beat together lightly four eggs and four teaspoonfuls of water, milk, or cream, just enough to break and mix sufficient to allow a spoonful of the mixture to be dipped up. Heat, but be careful not to brown, a tablespoonful of butter in an omelet pan. Have a pan that will correspond in size to the number of eggs used, so that the beaten mixture will cover the bottom to the depth of at least half an inch. Pour in the mixture and place the pan over a quick heat, add salt and pepper to taste, and as soon as the egg "sets" or stiffens slightly upon the bottom of the pan, lift it up lightly and carefully with a fork, so the uncooked egg can take the place of that which is cooked. Continue this lifting process as long as there is any uncooked egg in the pan, and until all the mixture lies in a soft creamy pile of a delicate golden hue. Permit the bottom to set quite firmly, then tip the pan slightly, loosen the edges with a broad-bladed, limber knife, or spatula, slip it under one side of the omelet, and fold over, tipping the pan at the same time to facilitate the folding. Then, by still further tipping the pan, turn the omelet, nicely folded, on a platter and serve hot.

If minced parsley is desired for flavoring, it should be sprinkled over the omelet just before beginning the lifting operation.

Ham Omelet.—Prepare and cook like a creamy omelet, and, just before folding, cover the surface of the omelet with boiled ham finely minced and warmed. Serve hot.

Oysters, shrimps, mushrooms, or any admixture liked, may, after they are cooked, be added in a similar manner. Grated cheese may also be scattered thickly over the omelet, when first put in the pan, or the omelet may be covered lightly with it just before folding.

Omelet with Breakfast Bacon.—Broil or sauté thin strips of breakfast bacon, and garnish a creamy or plain omelet with them.

Light Omelet.—To the yolks of two eggs beaten light add two tablespoonfuls of water, milk, or cream, beat until well mixed, then fold in the whites of the eggs, seasoned to taste with salt and pepper, and well beaten. Grease the omelet pan with olive oil or clarified butter, heat it, pour in the omelet, and cook for a minute— lifting the pan so as to relieve the bottom from too great heat, and turning it around on its sides. Then place in a moderate oven for about five minutes, or until the omelet is firm and lightly cooked to the center—which can be ascertained by running a knife into it. Fold, and turn out like a creamy omelet.

Orange Omelet.—To the yolks of two eggs beaten light add two tablespoonfuls of orange juice, half a teaspoonful of grated orange peel, and two teaspoonfuls of sugar. Beat all well together, fold in lightly the whites of the eggs, beaten stiff, cook, fold, and turn out like light omelet.

Omelet Souffle.—To the well-beaten yolks of two eggs add three teaspoonfuls of sugar, one teaspoonful of lemon juice, and half a teaspoonful of lemon, orange, vanilla, or any flavoring extract liked. Beat very light and fold in the whites of four eggs beaten stiff. Put in a hot omelet pan, well greased, and cook ten or twelve minutes, in a very moderate oven. Slip on to a warm dish, without folding. A pinch of cream of tartar added to the whites of the eggs improves all omelets containing no other acid.

PART VI.—SERVING AND GARNISHING.

INTRODUCTION.

The rules that should govern the serving and garnishing of food are founded upon common sense, and can be compressed into a few words: Use platters larger than are necessary for merely holding the food to be served, so there may be space on them for garnishing material, without having to place it against the food, or at the extreme edge of the platter.

In garnishing aim to produce some distinctive effect—either of harmony or contrast—and be careful to garnish lightly. Edibles alone should be used for garnishing material, and only such edibles as are palatable with the food they are used to garnish.

Elaborate decoration of food, like elaborate decoration in any direction, is indicative of an uncultured taste; and ribbons or paper, in such connection, are out of place and have a cheap and tawdry appearance.

CHAPTER XXV.

CARVING.

A DULL knife and a platter of insufficient size are the dread of a skilled carver. To insure success in carving, the carving knife must be sharp and the platter upon which a fish, fowl, or joint of meat is sent to table large enough to hold the article served upon it and leave sufficient space besides for the different portions when carved.

It is in accordance with common sense to either sit or stand at table while carving and serving, and is therefore good form for one so engaged to take whichever position may be most conducive to comfort and effective work.

To Carve a Turkey.—Place the turkey on its back on the platter with the head at the left. Stick the fork firmly into the flesh astride the breast-bone. Separate the wings from the body at the shoulders. Cut off the legs or drumsticks at the lower joint. Insert the point of the carving knife close to the thigh joint and cut through the flesh of the thigh or second joint, parallel with the bone, its entire length on both sides of the bone, leaving a strip of flesh not much wider than the bone, attached to it. Put the point of the knife under the end of this bone and turn it back, thus separating it from the body at the joint. After the wings and legs and the bones from the second joint have been removed, carve the meat from the breast and sides of the fowl in thin slices, cutting across the grain as long as well-shaped slices can be obtained. Take off the wish-bone by putting the knife under it at the front of the breast-bone and turning it back. Slip the knife under the end of the shoulder blade, tip the bone over, and remove it. Cut through the cartilage which divides the ribs, and separate the back from the breast. Turn the back, skin side upward. Lay the edge of the knife across it just below the ribs, lift up the tail end with the fork, and thus divide the back into two pieces. Place the fork in the middle of the back-bone and free the side-bone by cutting close to the back-bone from one end to the other. This completes the carving, and leaves the turkey in such condition that the different portions can be served as desired. If the entire turkey is not needed at a meal, only such part of it as is wanted should be carved.

The method of carving other fowls is similar in most respects to that of carving a turkey.

To Carve a Joint or Roast. — In carving a sirloin roast cut out the tenderloin, slice it across the grain, and serve before carving the balance of the roast—unless the whole roast should be needed. Where a roast is too large to be eaten at a single meal it is both wise and economical to serve the best portions while hot, and before their finest flavors and richest juices have escaped. In carving a leg of lamb or mutton cut several slices crosswise through the thickest part of the leg, then slip the knife under, separate them from the bone, and serve. If more be required, cut them from the thickest and juiciest part of the joint in the same manner.

As a general rule, all joints of meat, whether roasted or boiled, should be carved essentially in the same manner, that is, they should be cut in thin slices and across the grain of the meat. And whenever practicable the joint should be so placed and held by the carver that the juice will remain upon the surface of the meat, and not run out upon the platter.

CHAPTER XXVI.

BILLS OF FARE.

A DINNER of five courses is sufficiently elaborate to meet the requirements of a cultured taste, and is always enjoyable and satisfactory when the dishes composing it are judiciously selected and properly served. In such a dinner there should be a soup, fish, shell fish, or game, poultry or one of the staple meats, a salad, an acid vegetable or fruit, and a simple dessert, with salted almonds, cheese, or some sort of relish, and also the proper accompaniments of the leading dish of each course. As great a variety of articles may be presented as can be selected within a certain range and grouped harmoniously. Yet no article in any one of the courses must trench upon the province, or interfere with the mission, of any article in any of the other courses of the dinner. In other words, no articles that are similar in character or flavor must be permitted to appear in different courses, except those privileged by established custom to remain on the table during the entire meal. To illustrate the principle that governs the selection of such a dinner a few bills of fare are given.

If a four-course dinner is desired, it is only necessary to drop from any of these bills of fare the fish course. If only a three-course dinner is wanted the fish course and the salad course can be dropped; or, if preferred, the salad course can be retained and the fish course and dessert omitted.

These bills of fare are not arranged with a view of their being taken up consecutively, in the order in which they are given. Each dinner is complete in itself, without any reference to the dinner that precedes or the dinner that follows, and the housekeeper is at liberty to select from the list the dinner that is best adapted to the special occasion. Care must be observed, however, not to have dinners on two successive days that correspond too nearly in their prominent characteristics.

BILLS OF FARE FOR DINNER.

No. 1.

Cream of Celery.

Pickles.   Olives.

Bread.   Butter.

———

Broiled Birds.   Currant Jelly.

———

Boiled Mutton.   Caper Sauce.

Mashed Potato.   Stewed Turnip.

———

Fish and Tomato Salad.
Saltines.

———

Orange Pudding.   Cake.

Fruit.   Nuts.   Cheese.

Coffee.

No. 2.

Mutton Broth.　　Barley.
Celery.　　Pickles.　　Olives.
Bread.　　Butter.

Scalloped Oysters.　　Cabbage Salad.

Roast Turkey.　　Cranberry Sauce.
Boiled Potatoes.　　Sweet Corn.

Fruit Salad.

Ice Cream.　　Cake.
Fruit.　　Nuts.　　Cheese.
Coffee.

No. 3.

Clear Soup.
Celery.　　Pickles.
Bread.　　Butter.

Broiled Fish.
Creamed Potatoes.　　Cucumbers.　　French Dressing.

Roast Beef.
Browned Sweet Potatoes.　　Lima Beans.

Egg Salad.
Crackers.　　Cheese.

Strawberry Jelly.　　Whipped Cream.
Cake.　　Fruit.　　Nuts.
Coffee.

No. 4.

Oysters on the Half Shell.
Lemon Points.   Olives.   Celery.
Bread.   Butter.

Mixed Soup.

Roast Chicken.   Giblet Gravy.
Boiled Potato.   Spaghetti with Cheese.
Fruit Sherbet.

Lettuce.   French Dressing.
Toasted Crackers.

Steamed Pudding.   Foamy Sauce.
Fruit.   Nuts.   Cheese.
Coffee.

No. 5.

Boiled Cod.   Oyster Sauce.
Boiled Potatoes.
Olives.   Pickles.
Bread.   Butter.

Mushroom Patties.

Roast Lamb.   Mint Sauce.
Green Peas.   Cauliflower.

Chicken Salad.

Ice Cream.   Cake.
Fruit.   Nuts.   Cheese.
Coffee.

Oyster Soup.

Celery.   Olives.

Bread.   Butter.

Broiled Sweetbreads.   Breakfast Bacon.

Stewed Potatoes.

Roast Fillet of Beef.   Mushroom Sauce.

Hubbard Squash.   Sliced Tomatoes.

Lettuce Salad.

Cheese Straws.   Salted Almonds.

Caramel Custard.

Fruit.   Nuts.   Cheese.

Coffee.

No. 7.

Vegetable Soup.

Olives.   Celery.   Pickles.

Bread.   Butter.

Chicken Croquettes.   Mock Bisque Sauce.

Roast Veal with Dressing.

Scalloped Tomatoes.   Boiled Potatoes.

Stewed Onions.

Broiled Birds.

Chicory.   French Dressing.

Corn-Meal Pudding.

Fruit.   Nuts.   Cheese.

Coffee.

No. 8.

Chicken Soup with Macaroni.

Olives.   Celery.   Salted Almonds.
Bread.   Butter.

Fish Cutlets.
Sliced Tomatoes.

Roast Beef.   Yorkshire Pudding.
Stewed Corn.   Mashed Potato.
Prune and Apricot Sauce.

Water Cress Salad.

Fig Pudding.   Transparent Sauce.
Fruit.   Nuts.   Cheese.
Coffee.

No. 9.

Clear Soup.

Celery.   Olives.
Bread.   Butter.

Boiled Tongue.   Tomato Sauce.

Stewed Chicken.
Mashed Turnips.   Boiled Rice.

Mixed Fruit Salad.

Chocolate Cream.   Cake.
Fruit.   Nuts.   Cheese.
Coffee.

No. 10.

Beef Broth.

Olives.   Celery.

Bread.   Butter.

Chicken Croquettes.   Creamed Potatoes.

Roast Pork.   Apple Sauce.

Boiled Onions.   Fried Parsnips.

Lettuce Salad.

French Pudding.   Fruit Sauce.

Fruit.   Nuts.   Cheese.

Coffee.

No. 11.

Salsify Soup.

Olives.   Pickles.

Bread.   Butter.

Boiled Fish.   Hollandaise Sauce.

Boiled Carrots.

Broiled Chicken.

Stewed Peas.   Asparagus.

Creamed Potatoes.

Tomato Salad.

Strawberry Shortcake.

Fruit.   Nuts.   Cheese.

Coffee.

No. 12.

Asparagus Soup.

Olives.   Pickles.

Bread.   Butter.

Boston Baked Beans.
Brown Bread.

Roast Beef.

Browned Potatoes.   Stewed Tomatoes.

Boiled Hominy.

Broiled Birds.   Chicory Salad.

Bread and Butter Pudding.

Fruit.   Nuts.   Cheese.

Coffee.

No. 13.

Oxtail Soup.

Celery.   Olives.

Bread.   Butter.

Fish Croquettes.   Tomato Sauce.

Boiled Lamb.   Egg Sauce.

Mashed Potato.   Spinach.

Orange Salad.

Apple Tapioca.

Fruit.   Nuts.   Cheese.

Coffee.

No. 14.

Mock Bisque.

Olives.   Celery.   Pickles.

Bread.   Butter.

Creamed Chicken on Toast.

Roast Beef.

Browned Sweet Potatoes.   Boiled Potatoes.

Stewed Onions.

Celery Salad.

Cheese Straws.   Salted Almonds.

Custard Pie.

Fruit.   Nuts.   Cheese.

Coffee.

No. 15.

Clear Soup.

Olives.   Celery.

Bread.   Butter.

Boiled Trout.   Drawn Butter.

Stewed Carrots.   Boiled Potatoes.

Roast Mutton.   Jelly.

Baked Sweet Potatoes.   Mashed Turnips.

Lettuce Salad.   French Dressing.

Cheese Straws.   Salted Almonds.

Ice Cream.   Cake.

Fruit.   Nuts.   Cheese.

Coffee.

No. 16.

Cream of Potato.

Olives.   Pickles.

Bread.   Butter.

Broiled Chicken.

Asparagus on Toast.

Corned Beef.

Boiled Carrots.   Boiled Turnips.

Boiled Potatoes.

Lettuce Salad.   French Dressing.

Rice Pudding.

Fruit.   Nuts.   Cheese.

Coffee.

No. 17.

Gumbo Soup.

Olives.   Celery.

Bread.   Butter.

Baked Fish.   Brown Butter.   Sliced Tomatoes.

Boiled Ham.

Mashed Potatoes.   Spinach.   Macaroni.

Apple Salad.

Steamed Fruit Pudding.

Fruit.   Nuts.   Cheese.

Coffee.

No. 18.

Tomato Soup.

Celery.   Olives.

Bread.   Butter.

Sweetbread Timbales.

Boiled Fowl.   White Sauce.
Cauliflower.   Sauce Hollandaise.
Mashed Potato.   Boiled Hominy.

Lobster Salad.

Charlotte Russe.

Crackers.   Cheese.
Fruit.   Nuts.
Coffee.

No. 19.

Fish Chowder.

Olives.   Pickles.

Bread.   Butter.

Broiled Chicken.   Creamed Potato.
Water Cress.

Baked Ham.   Sliced Tomatoes.
Baked Sweet Potatoes.   Boiled Rice.

Fruit Salad.

Apple Pie.   Edam Cheese.
Fruit.   Wafers.   Nuts.
Coffee.

No. 20.

Mock Turtle Soup.

Celery.   Olives.

Bread.   Butter.

Broiled Oysters on Toast.

Roast Turkey.   Cranberry Sauce.

Mashed Potato.   Browned Sweet Potato.

Curried Rice.

Sweetbread Salad.

Cheese Straws.   Salted Almonds.

Plum Pudding.

Pumpkin Pie.   Cheese.

Nuts.   Fruit.

Coffee.

No. 21.

Green Turtle Soup.

Celery.   Olives.

Bread.   Butter.

Broiled Quail on Toast.

Asparagus.   Hollandaise Sauce.

Roast Venison.   Jelly.

Mashed Potato.   Stewed Carrots.

Boiled Macaroni.

Lettuce.   French Dressing.

Crackers.   Cheese.

Pine-Apple Jelly.

Fruit.   Nuts.

Coffee.

The foregoing bills of fare were prepared upon the presumption that a five-course dinner is usually served in the evening, and is preceded by breakfast and luncheon. But as a majority of people adhere to a noon-day dinner and as the other meals of the day should correspond with, and depend largely upon, the structure of the dinner, the bills of fare that follow for breakfast, luncheon, and supper are appropriate with either evening or mid-day dinners and can be used for that purpose without modification, or with such slight variations—when any are desired—as will readily suggest themselves to the mind of the busiest housekeeper. Like the dinner bills of fare any of those given for breakfast, luncheon, or supper can be used without regard to the order in which they are arranged.

BILLS OF FARE FOR BREAKFAST.

No. 1.

Grapes.

Cracked Wheat.   Cream.

Bread.   Butter.

Beefsteak.   Fried Potatoes.   French Rolls.

Coffee.

No. 2.

Apples.

Oatmeal.   Cream.
         Bread.   Butter.

Broiled Fish.   Creamed Potatoes.
            Buttered Toast.
               Coffee.

No. 3.

Bananas.

Farinose.   Cream.
         Bread.   Butter.

Lamb Chops.   Baked Potatoes.   Corn Griddle Cakes.
                  Coffee.

No. 4.

Melons.

Rolled Wheat.   Cream.
         Bread.   Butter.

Baked Hash.   Hot Apple Sauce.
      Boiled Eggs.   Rice Muffins.
                Coffee.

No. 5.

Grapes.

Hominy Grits.   Cream.

                 Bread.   Butter.

Broiled Chicken.   Stewed Potatoes.   Vienna Rolls.

                                  Coffee.

No. 6.

Oranges.

Rolled Oats.   Cream.

                  Bread.   Butter.

Codfish Balls.   Poached Eggs on Toast.

                         French Rolls.

                               Coffee.

No. 7.

Mixed Fruits.

Boiled Rice.   Cream.

                  Bread.   Butter.

Veal Chops.   Brown Hashed Potato.

                       Buttered Toast.

                              Coffee.

No. 8.

Oranges.

Oatmeal. Cream.
Bread. Butter.

Fried Oysters. Breakfast Bacon.
Creamed Hashed Potato. Corn-Bread.
Coffee.

No. 9.

Grapes and Apples.

Graham Mush. Cream.
Bread. Butter.

Beefsteak. Lyonnaise Potato.
Whole Wheat Rolls.
Coffee.

No. 10.

Blackberry Mush. Cream.
Bread. Butter.

Broiled Ham. Creamy Omelet.
Baked Potatoes. Federal Bread.
Coffee.

No. 11.

Strawberry Shortcake.

Bread.   Butter.

Broiled Chicken.   Creamed Hashed Potato.

Vienna Rolls.

Coffee.

No. 12.

Raspberries.   Cream.

Bread.   Butter.

Mutton Chops.   Fried Potatoes.

Rice Muffins.

Coffee.

No. 13.

Blackberries.   Cream.

Bread.   Butter.

Broiled Tripe.   Breakfast Bacon.

Creamed Potatoes.   Sliced Tomatoes

Waffles.

Coffee.

No. 14.

Strawberries.   Cream.
             Bread.   Butter.

Broiled Beefsteak.   Baked Potatoes.
    Graham Muffins.   Sliced Tomatoes.
                  Coffee.

No. 15.

Melon.

Oatmeal.   Cream.
             Bread.   Butter.

Poached Eggs.   Creamed Codfish.
       Boiled Potatoes.   French Rolls.
                  Coffee.

No. 16.

Peaches.

Barley Grits.   Cream.
             Bread.   Butter.

Sweetbreads Sautéd.   Breakfast Bacon.
       Stewed Potatoes.   Graham Muffins.
                  Coffee.

No. 17.

Mixed Fruits.

Farina.   Cream.
         Bread.   Butter.

Broiled Mackerel.   Plain Omelet.
    Sliced Tomatoes.   Brown Hashed Potato.
                Vienna Rolls.
                   Coffee.

No. 18.

Peaches.

Cracked Wheat.   Cream.
  Bread.   Butter.

Frizzled Beef.   Scrambled Eggs.
  Baked Potatoes.   Dry Toast.
             Coffee.

No. 19.

Oranges.

Corn-Meal Mush.   Cream.
    Bread.   Butter.

Pork Chops.   Apples Sautéd.
   Boiled Potatoes.   Egg-Plant.
              Coffee.

No. 20.

Grapes.

Boiled Rice.   Cream.

Bread.   Butter.

Liver and Bacon.   Lyonnaise Potato.

Boiled Eggs.   Flannel Cakes.

Coffee.

No. 21.

Mixed Fruits.

Rolled Barley.   Cream.

Bread.   Butter.

Panned Oysters.   Broiled Quail.

Fried Potatoes.   Currant Jelly.

Rice Waffles.

Coffee.

BILLS OF FARE FOR LUNCHEON.

No. 1.

Cream of Celery.

Bread.   Butter.

Broiled Chicken.   Mashed Potato.

Sliced Tomatoes.

Vanilla Cream Pie.

Wafers.   American Cheese.

Tea or Cocoa.

No. 2.

Oyster Soup.

Bread. Butter.

Boiled Tongue. Tomato Sauce.
Spinach. Boiled Potatoes.

Ice Cream. Cake.
Tea or Cocoa.

No. 3.

Cream of Corn.

Bread. Butter.

Broiled Fish. Sliced Cucumbers.
Creamed Potatoes.

Apple Pie. Edam Cheese.
Tea or Cocoa.

No. 4.

Cream of Chicken.

Bread. Butter.

Broiled Lamb Chops. Currant Jelly.
Fried Potatoes.

Ice Cream. Cake.
Tea or Cocoa.

No. 5.

Cream of Salsify.

Bread.   Butter.

Chicken Salad.   Cold Boiled Ham.

Potato Croquettes.

Strawberry Shortcake.
Tea or Cocoa.

No. 6.

Rice Soup.

Bread.   Butter.

Fried Chicken.   Creamed Potatoes.

Cresses.   French Dressing.

Orange Cream Pie.   Pine-Apple Cheese.

Tea or Cocoa.

No. 7.

Okra Soup.

Bread.   Butter.

Scalloped Oysters.   Cabbage Salad.
Cold Boiled Ham.   Browned Sweet Potatoes.

Orange Pudding.
Tea or Cocoa.

No. 8.

Bisque of Tomato.

Bread.   Butter.

Cold Roast Veal.

Spiced Peaches.   Brown Hashed Potato.

Soft Ginger Cake.   Saltines.   Cheese.

Tea or Cocoa.

No. 9.

Barley Soup.

Bread.   Butter.

Frizzled Beef.   Boiled Potatoes.

Graham Muffins.

Squash Pie.   Edam Cheese.

Tea or Cocoa.

No. 10.

Brown Soup.

Bread.   Butter.

Cold Roast Beef.   Baked Potatoes.

Sliced Tomatoes.

Ice Cream.   Cake.

Tea or Cocoa.

No. 11.

Beef Broth.

Bread.   Butter.

Sautéd Egg-Plant.   Breakfast Bacon.
Boiled Rice.   Whole Wheat Rolls.

Plum Pie.   Pine-Apple Cheese.   Wafers.
Tea or Cocoa.

No. 12.

Mixed Soup.

Bread.   Butter.

Cold Roast Turkey.   Cranberry Jelly.
Baked Potatoes.   Celery.

Rice Pudding.
Tea or Cocoa.

No. 13.

Tomato Soup.

Bread.   Butter.

Pork Chops.   Apple Sauce.
Boiled Potatoes.   Corn Crusts.

Snow Pudding.   Wafers.   Cheese.
Tea or Cocoa.

No. 14.

Bisque of Clams.

Bread.   Butter.

Sweetbread Salad.   Cold Boiled Ham.
French Rolls.   Raspberry Jam.

Pine-Apple Fritters.
Tea or Cocoa.

No. 15.

Purée of Potato.

Bread.   Butter.

Cold Roast Lamb.   Corn Oysters.
Potato Salad.   Graham Rolls.

Huckleberry Pie.   Edam Cheese.
Tea or Cocoa.

No. 16.

Hominy Soup.

Bread.   Butter.

Broiled Ham.   Creamy Omelet.
Stewed Apricots.   Lyonnaise Potato.

Peach Fritters.
Tea or Cocoa.

No. 17.

Purée of Peas.

Bread. Butter.

Fried Oysters. Cold Catsup.
Baked Potatoes. Tropical Toast.

Pine-Apple Pudding.
Tea or Cocoa.

No. 18.

Noodle Soup.

Bread. Butter.

Liver and Bacon. Fried Onions.
Boiled Hominy. Vienna Rolls.

Cherry Pie. American Cheese.
Tea or Cocoa.

No. 19.

Vegetable Soup.

Bread. Butter.

Beefsteak Pie. Tomato Salad.
Rice Croquettes.

Fruit. Saltines. Cheese.
Tea or Cocoa.

No. 20.

Clear Soup.

Bread.   Butter.

English Meat Pie.   Mixed Pickles.
French Rolls.   Orange Marmalade.

Strawberry Pudding.
Tea or Cocoa.

No. 21.

Clear Soup.

Bread.   Butter.

Sautéd Sweetbreads.   Radishes.
Breakfast Bacon.   Creamed Potatoes.

Fruits in Jelly.   Angel Cake.
Tea or Cocoa.

BILLS OF FARE FOR SUPPER.

No. 1.

Turkey Hash on Toast.   Cold Ham.
Baked Potatoes.   Raspberries.
Bread.   Butter.   Tea.

No. 2.

Broiled Beefsteak.   Breakfast Bacon.
Hashed Potato.   Dewberries.   French Rolls.
Bread.   Butter.   Tea.

No. 3.

Cold Roast Beef.   Cold Catsup.
Boiled Rice.   Blackberries.   Wheat Griddle Cakes.
Bread.   Butter.   Tea.

No. 4.

Cold Roast Veal.   Baked Potatoes.
Spiced Plums.   Corn Crusts.   Sponge Cake.
Bread.   Butter.   Tea.

No. 5.

Broiled Ham.   Scrambled Eggs.
Stewed Potato.   Milk Toast.   Peaches in Jelly.
Bread.   Butter.   Tea.

No. 6.

Fish Croquettes.   Breakfast Bacon.
Cottage Cheese.   Boiled Potatoes.
Corn-Bread.   Jelly Cake.
Bread.   Butter.   Tea.

No. 7.

Frizzled Beef.   Baked Potatoes.
Baking Powder Biscuit.   Strawberries.
Bread.   Butter.   Tea.

No. 8.

Broiled Chicken.   Tomato Salad.
Fried Potatoes.   Waffles.   Orange Layer Cake.
Bread.   Butter.   Tea.

No. 9.

Codfish Balls.   Cold Boiled Ham.
Apple Salad.   Vienna Rolls.   Peaches.
Bread.   Butter.   Tea.

No. 10.

Cold Roast Lamb.   Creamed Potatoes.
Ripe Currants.   French Rolls.   Ginger Wafers.
Bread.   Butter.   Tea.

No. 11.

Fried Oysters.   Cabbage Salad.
Cold Boiled Ham.   Olives.   Vienna Rolls.
Bread.   Butter.   Tea.

No. 12.

Cold Roast Chicken. Fried Potatoes.
Celery.   Olives.   Federal Bread.
Soft Ginger Cake.   Edam Cheese.
Bread.   Butter.   Tea.

No. 13.

Boned Turkey.   Fried Scollops.
Baked Potatoes.   Celery.   Vienna Rolls.
Bread.   Butter.   Tea.

No. 14.

Scrapple.   Cold Roast Mutton.
Onion Salad.   Scalloped Potatoes.
French Rolls.   Nut Cake.
Bread.   Butter.   Tea.

No. 15.

Veal Chops.   Deviled Crabs.
Lyonnaise Potato.   Graham Rolls.   Fruit Jam.
Bread.   Butter.   Tea.

No. 16.

Pressed Corned Beef.   Spiced Pickles.
Shirred Eggs.   Potato Croquettes.
Wheat Muffins.   Chocolate Cake.
Bread.   Butter.   Tea.

No. 17.

Broiled Quail.   Currant Jelly.
Welsh Rarebit.   Baked Sweet Potatoes.   Imperial Rolls.
Bread.   Butter.   Tea.

No. 18.

Cold Roast Turkey.   Scalloped Oysters.
Potato Croquettes.   Cranberry Sauce.   Celery.
Bread.   Butter.   Tea.

No. 19.

Lamb Chops.   Cress.
Fried Potatoes.   Pop-Overs.   Blackberries.
Bread.   Butter.   Tea.

No. 20.

Cold Boiled Tongue.   Panned Oysters.
Potato Salad.   Fruit Jam.   Rice Muffins.
Bread.   Butter.   Tea.

No. 21.

Pork Chops.   Hot Apple Sauce.
Scalloped Potatoes.   Corn Griddle Cakes.
Bread.   Butter.   Tea.

INDEX.

Almonds, baked	63
" to blanch	63
Anchovy sauce	133
Angel cake	247
Apple fritters	141
" jelly	174
" pie No. 1	217
" " No. 2	217
" " No. 3	217
" " English, No. 1	218
" " " No. 2	218
" " New England	218
" pudding, baked, No. 1	239
Apple pudding, baked, No. 2	239
Apple pudding, steamed, No. 1	236
Apple pudding, steamed, No. 2	236
Apple roly-poly	237
" salad No. 1	272
" " No. 2	272
" " No. 3	272
" sauce	95
" " cider	97
" strudels	218
" tapioca pudding	238
" tart	224
" water	158
Apples, fried	139
" to bake, No. 1	62
" " No. 2	62
" to prepare	28
" to sauté	149
Apples, to stew dried	99
" " " fresh	95
Apricot tapioca pudding	238
Apricots, to stew dried	98
Arrow-root blanc-mange	229
Asparagus broth	107
" cream of	116
" peas	92
" purée of	122
" salad	275
" stock	103
" to boil	72
" to can	167
" to stew	92
" to wash	25
Aspic jelly	305
Bacon, to prepare	23
" to sauté	148
Baked chicken pie	225
" corn-meal pudding No. 1	232
Baked corn-meal pudding No. 2	233
Baked custard	231
" sago custard	232
" tapioca custard	232
" tapioca pudding	238
Baking	46
Baking powder biscuit No. 1	197
Baking powder biscuit No. 2	197
Baking powder biscuit No. 3	197

Banana cream	258	Beef, to roast	49
" fritters	141	" to select	10
" ice	261	" to stew	86
" pudding	257	Beefsteak pie	224
" salad No. 1	271	" to sauté	151
" " No. 2	271	" to toast	162
" " No. 3	271	Beet salad No. 1	274
" sauce	245	" " No. 2	275
" shortcake	203	" and potato salad	275
Bananas, to bake	63	Beets, purée of	124
" to sauté	150	" to boil	73
Barley gruel	157	" to stew	90
" rolled, to cook	77	Berries, to pick over	29
" soup	113	" to select	16
Batter pudding, steamed	233	" to wash	29
" " to steam a	83	Beverages	77
Bavarian cream	256	Bills of fare	319
" " chocolate	256	Bird, to bone a	309
" " with eggs	256	" to draw a	21
Beans, purée of, No. 1	123	Biscuit, baking powder, No. 1	197
" " " No. 2	123	Biscuit, baking powder, No. 2	197
" " " No. 3	123	Biscuit, baking powder, No. 3	197
" to bake	62	
" to boil green string	72	
" to can	167	
" to select	16	Biscuit, beaten	197
" to stew dried	91	Bisque of clams	121
" to stew green	90	" " lobster	121
" to string	25	" " oysters	121
Beaten biscuit	197	" " tomato	120
Beef broth No. 1	108	Bisques	120
" broth No. 2	108	Black tea, to make	79
" extract	109	Blackberry jam	173
" frizzled	291	" jelly	174
" stock	103	" mush	162
" tea No. 1	108	" pie	219
" " No. 2	108	" pudding	237
" to boil corned	70	Blanc-mange, arrow-root	229
" to boil spiced	70	" cornstarch	229
" to prepare a roast of	22	" farina	229

Blanc-mange, farinose . . 230	Bread-making 182
" Iceland moss 228	Breakfast bacon, omelet
" Irish moss . 228	with 314
" rolled wheat 229	Breakfast bacon, to prepare 23
" sea moss . 228	
Boil, how to 67	Breakfast bacon, to sauté 148
Boiled custard No. 1 . . . 230	Breakfast hash 295
" " No. 2 . . . 230	Broil, how to 35
" " No. 3 . . . 230	Broiling 34
" " No. 4 . . . 231	" griddle 41
" " No. 5 . . . 242	" oven 43
" " No. 6 . . . 243	Broth, asparagus 107
" frosting No. 1 . . 252	" beef, No. 1 108
" " No. 2 . . 252	" " No. 2 108
" " No. 3 . . 253	" celery 106
Boiling 65	" chicken, No. 1 . . 107
Boned meats 307	" " No. 2 . . 108
Boston brown bread . . . 206	" " No. 3 . . 108
Braising 89	" clam, No. 1 107
Bread, Boston brown . . 205	" " No. 2 107
" cakes 200	" mutton, No. 1 . . . 109
" compressed yeast 189	" " No. 2 . . . 109
" corn 210	" oyster 107
" crumbs, to prepare 27	" salsify 107
" entire wheat flour 205	" toast 162
" federal 195	" veal 109
" French 189	Brown bread, Boston . . 206
" graham 204	Brown butter No. 1 . . . 127
" grease in 191	" " No. 2 . . . 127
" liquid yeast . . . 192	" " No. 3 . . . 127
" sauce No. 1 . . . 132	" sauce No. 1 . . . 128
" " No. 2 . . . 132	" " No. 2 . . . 128
" sugar in 191	" " No. 3 . . . 129
" to toast 40	" soup No. 1 117
" Vienna . . . 189, 191	" " No. 2 118
" whole wheat flour 205	" " No. 3 118
Bread and butter pudding No. 1 237	Browned flour gruel . . . 158
	" hashed potato . 296
Bread and butter pudding No. 2 238	" potato cakes . . 297
	" sliced potatoes . 297

354 Index.

Buckwheat cakes No. 1 . .	201
" " No. 2 . .	202
Buns	195
Butter, brown, No. 1 . .	127
" " No. 2 . .	127
" " No. 3 . .	127
" clarified	147
" drawn	127
" parsley, No. 1 . .	127
" " No. 2 . .	127
" and sugar, creamed	243
Cabbage, pickled	175
" salad	273
" to boil	73
" to prepare . .	25
" to select . . .	15
" to stew	92
Cake, angel	247
" citron	250
" coffee	196
" delicate	249
" nut	250
" pans	248
" pound	249
" rich fruit	249
" soft ginger	250
" sponge	248
" sunshine	248
Cake-making	247
Cakes, bread	200
" browned potato . .	297
" buckwheat, No. 1	201
" " No. 2	202
" corn griddle, No. 1	211
" " " No. 2	211
" flannel	200
" potato and fish . .	297
" wheat griddle, No. 1	199
" " " No. 2	199
Cakes, wheat griddle, No. 3	199
Calf's brains, to sauté .	152
" head, to prepare a .	296
Canning, preserving, and pickling	163
Caper sauce No. 1 . .	130
" " No. 2 . .	130
Caramel custard	232
" sauce	243
Carrots, purée of	124
" to boil . .	73
" to prepare . . .	24
" to select	15
" to stew	91
Carving	316
Catsup, cold	176
" cucumber	176
Cauliflower, to boil . . .	72
" to prepare .	25
" to select . .	15
Celery broth	106
" cream of, No. 1 . .	115
" " " No. 2 . .	116
" salad	273
" sauce	131
" stock	103
" to prepare	26
" to select	16
" to stew	92
Cereals	74
" to cook	75
Ceylon tea, to make . . .	79
Charlotte Russe No. 1 . .	255
" " No. 2 . .	256
Cheese, cottage	228
" soufflé No. 1 . .	302
" " No. 2 . .	302
" straws No. 1 . .	304
" " No. 2 . .	304
Cherries, to can, No. 1 . .	166

Cherries, to can, No. 2 . . 166	Chocolate frosting . . 253
" to preserve . . 170	" to make . . 80, 161
Cherry pie 220	Chops, fried veal 146
" pudding, steamed 236	" to broil 37, 42
" sauce 245	" to prepare 23
Chestnuts, purée of . . . 124	" to sauté pork . . . 151
Chicory, to prepare . . . 25	" " veal . . . 150
Chicken broth No. 1 . . . 107	Chowder, clam 120
" " No. 2 . . . 108	" fish 120
" " No. 3 . . . 108	Cider apple sauce 97
" cream of 116	Cinnamon rolls 196
" creamed 283	Citron cake 250
" creamy 297	Clam broth No. 1 107
" croquettes No. 1 144	" " No. 2 107
" " No. 2 144	" chowder 120
" " No. 3 144	Clams, bisque of 121
" " No. 4 145	" deviled 289
" fricasseed . . . 291	" to steam 82
" fried 145	Clarified butter 147
" jellied 306	Clear soup 109, 110
" patties 226	" " with curry . . 110
" pie, baked . . . 225	" " " dainty dump-
" salad No. 1 . . . 277	lings 110
" " No. 2 . . . 277	Clear soup with fancy vege-
" " No. 3 . . . 277	tables 111
" " with lettuce 278	Clear soup with macedoine
" soufflé 302	vegetables 111
" stock 104	Clear soup with mixed
" to boil a 68	flavoring 111
" to broil a 38	Clear soup with poached
" to fricassee a . . 89	eggs 110
" to roast a . . . 54	Clear soup with sliced
" to sauté 151	lemon 110
" to stew a . . . 84	Clear soup with tapioca . 110
" and oyster hash 293	Coal fire, management of 30
" with mushrooms,	Cocoa No. 1 161
stewed 86	" No. 2 161
Chicken, with truffles,	" No. 3 161
stewed 86	" to make 80
Chocolate Bavarian cream 256	Codfish balls 144

Codfish cakes, to sauté .	154
" creamed	285
" scalloped	287
" and oysters, scalloped	288
Coffee cake	196
" crust	158
" hygienic	79
" ice cream	262
" to make, No. 1 . .	77
" " No. 2 . .	78
" " No. 3 . .	78
Cold catsup	176
Compound stock	104
Compressed yeast	186
" " bread .	189
Cooked frosting	251
" mayonnaise dressing	281
Cookery, sick-room . . .	156
Cooking, methods of . . .	33
Corn, cream of	117
" crusts	210
" dodgers	209
" fritters	141
" griddle cakes No. 1 .	211
" " " No. 2 .	211
" muffins No. 1 . . .	210
" " No. 2 . . .	210
" " fried . . .	140
" oysters	153
" soup	113
" to bake, No. 1 . . .	61
" " No. 2 . . .	61
" to boil	72
" to can	167
" to select green . . .	16
" to steam	82
" to stew	91
Corned beef, pressed . . .	306
Corned beef, to boil . . .	70
Corn-bread	210
" fried	140
Corn-meal	207
" granulated . .	208
" gruel	157
" mush	211
" pudding, baked, No. 1	232
Corn-meal pudding, baked, No. 2	233
Cornstarch blanc-mange, No. 1	229
Cornstarch blanc-mange, No. 2	229
Cottage cheese	228
Crab-apple jelly	175
Crabs, deviled	289
" to sauté	152
Cracked wheat muffins .	207
" " rolls . .	207
" " to cook .	77
Cracker crumbs, to prepare	27
Cranberries, to stew, No. 1	96
" ' " No. 2	96
Cranberry jelly	96
" tart	224
Cream, banana	258
" Bavarian	256
" " with eggs	256
" chocolate Bavarian	256
Cream dressing	281
" ice, No. 1	262
" ice, No. 2	262
" ice, No. 3	262
" mock	242
" orange	257
" pie, lemon . . .	223

Index

Cream pie, orange	223
" " vanilla	223
" pine-apple	257
" plain	241
" strawberry	258
" whipped	241
Cream of asparagus	116
" " celery No. 1	115
" " " No. 2	116
" " chicken	116
" " corn	116
" " salsify	116
" " veal	117
Creamed asparagus patties	226
" butter and sugar	243
" celery patties	226
" chicken	283
" codfish	285
" fish	283
" green pea patties	226
" lobster	284
" macaroni	285
" mock terrapin patties	226
Creamed mushroom patties	226
Creamed oyster patties	226
" oysters No. 1	284
" " No. 2	284
" potatoes	285
" rice	234
" sago	234
" salmon	285
" shrimps	284
" sweetbread patties	226
Creamed sweetbreads	284
" tapioca	284
" toast	285
Creamy chicken croquettes	297
Creamy omelet	312
Crescents	195
Cress, to prepare	26
Croquettes, chicken, No. 1	144
" " No. 2	144
" " No. 3	144
" " No. 4	145
" creamy chicken	297
" fish	143
" hominy	143
" lobster	143
" potato, No. 1	299
" " No. 2	299
" " No. 3	300
" rice, No. 1	143
" " No. 2	300
" shrimp	144
" sweetbread	145
" veal	145
Crumbs No. 1	27
" No. 2	27
" No. 3	27
Crust, coffee	158
Crusts, corn	210
Cucumber catsup	176
" pickles	177
" salad	273
" and fish salad	279
Cucumbers, to prepare	26
" to select	16
" to stew	91
Currant jam	173
" jelly	175
" salad	270
Curried oysters	288
" rice	286
" toast	286
Custard, baked	231
" boiled, No. 1	230
" " No. 2	230

Custard, boiled, No. 3	230
" " No. 4	231
" " No. 5	242
" " No. 6	243
" caramel	232
" pie	222
" sago	232
" tapioca	232
Custards, to bake	64
Cutlets, lobster	298
Damson pie	220
Damsons, spiced	177
Delicate cake	249
" desserts	254
Deviled clams	289
" crabs	289
" eggs	290
" lobster	290
Diamonds, graham	205
Dipped toast	286
Dodgers, corn	209
Dough, the proper consistency of	189, 191
Dough, when sufficiently light	190
Doughnuts, fried	139
Drawn butter	127
Dressing, cooked mayonnaise	281
Dressing, cream	281
" French, No. 1	280
" " No. 2	280
" mayonnaise	280
Duck, to roast wild	55
Egg nog	159
Egg pastry	216
" plant, to sauté	147
" " to select	16

Egg salad No. 1	279
" " No. 2	279
" sauce	128
" to boil an	70, 311
" to poach an	311
" to sauté an	311
" whips	159
" " with syrup	160
Eggs, deviled	290
" scalloped, No. 1	288
" " No. 2	288
" scrambled, No. 1	312
" " No. 2	312
" shirred, No. 1	312
" " No. 2	312
" to select	13
" to steam	83
" and omelets	311
English apple pie No. 1	218
" " " No. 2	218
" breakfast tea	79
English meat pie	226
Entire wheat flour bread	205
" " " gruel	158
Entreés and side dishes	283
Farina blanc-mange	229
" gruel	157
" how to cook	77
Farinose blanc-mange	230
" gruel	157
" how to cook	77
Federal bread	195
Fig pudding	240
Fish balls	144
" cakes	154
" chowder	120
" creamed	283
" croquettes	143
" deviled	290

Fish fried	146
" hash	292
" pie	225
" sauce	130
" scalloped, No. 1	287
" " No. 2	287
" stuffing for	28
" to bake a	56
" to boil a	69
" to bone a	22
" to broil a	39, 45
" to prepare a	21
" to prepare salted	24
" to sauté	152
" to select	14
" to steam a	81
" turbans	299
Flaky pie crust	215
Flannel cakes	200
Flour	184
" gluten in	184
" graham	205
" nitrogenous matter in	184
Flour, pastry	186
" patent	184, 185
" spring wheat	186
" strength of	185
" winter wheat	186
Foamy sauce No. 1	244
" " No. 2	244
Food materials	17
" " care of	18
" " preparation of	20
Fowl, to boil a	69
" to bone a	309
" to carve a	317
" to draw a	20
" to pick a	20

Fowl, to wash a	20
French bread	189
" dressing	280
" pancakes	199
" pudding	234
" rolls No. 1	193
" " No. 2	193
" " No. 3	194
" toast	304
Fricasseed chicken	291
" oysters	290
" salt pork	291
Fricasseeing	88
Fried apples	139
" chicken	145
" corn-bread	140
" corn muffins	140
" doughnuts	139
" fish	146
" mush	146
" onions	139
" oysters	146
" potatoes	138
" prairie chicken	145
" quail	145
" veal chops	146
Fritters, apple	141
" banana	141
" corn	141
" oysters	142
" peach	141
" pine-apple	141
" plain	140
" sweetbread	142
Frizzled beef	291
Frosting	251
" boiled, No. 1	252
" " No. 2	252
" " No. 3	253
" chocolate	253

Frosting, uncooked	251
Fruit cake	249
" pudding, steamed	236
" salads	269
" toast	162
" and bread puddings	238
" " rice puddings	238
Fruits, to cook fresh	94
" " dried	97
" to select	16
" in jelly	258
Frying	136
Gems, graham	205
" " with eggs	206
" " " sour milk	206
Gems, graham, with sweet milk	206
German coffee cake	196
Giblets, stewed, with mushrooms	292
Ginger cake	250
" wafers	250
Glaze	134
Gluten	184
" gruel	158
Gooseberries, to stew green	96
Gooseberry marmalade	174
" pie	220
Graham bread	204
" diamonds	205
" flour gruel	158
" gems, plain	205
" " with eggs	206
" " with sour milk	206
Graham gems with sweet milk	206

Granulated corn-meal	208
Grape jelly	175, 254
" marmalade	174
" pie	220
Grease in bread	191
Green pea patties	226
" tea	79
" tomato pickles	176
" turtle soup	119
Griddle broiling	41
" cakes, corn, No. 1	211
" " " No. 2	211
" " wheat, No. 1	199
" " " No. 2	199
" " " No. 3	199
" to broil chops on a	42
" " oysters on a	43
" " steaks on a	42
Grouse, to broil	39
" to sauté	152
Gruel, barley	157
" browned flour	158
" corn-meal	157
" farina	157
" farinose	158
" gluten flour	158
" graham flour	158
" Irish moss	158
" oatmeal	157
" peeled wheat flour	158
" rice	157
" rolled wheat	157
" sea moss	158
" white flour	157
" whole wheat flour	158
Gruels	156
Gumbo soup	118
Ham, for baking or boiling, to prepare a	23

Index.

Ham omelet	313
" to boil a	69
" to broil	40
" to prepare	23
" to sauté	148
" to select	13
Hamburg steak, to sauté	151
Hash, breakfast	295
" chicken and oyster	293
" fish	292
" mutton	295
" to sauté	154
" turkey	293
" turkey and oyster	293
" veal	294
Hashed potato	296
Heart, to bake a	55
" to braise a	90
Hollandaise sauce No. 1	133
" " No. 2	133
Hominy croquettes	143
" muffins	212
" rolls	212
" soup	113
" to cook	77
" to sauté	153
Huckleberry pie	220
" pudding	238
" pudding, steamed	237
Hygienic coffee, to make	79
Ice, banana	261
" lemon	261
" orange	261
" strawberry	261
Ice cream No. 1	262
" " No. 2	262
" " No. 3	262
" " coffee	262
" " pine-apple	262
Ice cream, strawberry	262
Iceland moss blanc-mange	228
Imperial rolls	193
Irish moss blanc-mange	228
" " gruel	158
Jam, blackberry	173
" currant	173
" raspberry	172
" strawberry	172
Jams	94
Jellied chicken	306
Jellies	94
Jelly, apple	174
" aspic	305
" blackberry	174
" crab-apple	175
" cranberry	96
" currant	175
" fancy fruits in	258
" grape	254
" lemon	254
" mock peach	255
" nectarine	255
" orange	254
" peach	255
" peaches in	258
" pine-apple	255
" plum	255
" quince	175
" raspberry	174, 255
" sauce No. 1	129
" " No. 2	129
" " No. 3	130
" strawberry	174, 255
Joint, to carve a	317
Junket No. 1	228
" No. 2	228
Koumiss, to make	80

Lamb chops, to broil	37
" " to sauté	150
" to boil a leg of	69
" to bone a leg of	309
" to fricassee	89
" to prepare a leg of	23
" to roast	52
" to roast a leg of	52
" to select	12
" to stew	88
Lemon cream pie	223
" ice	261
" jelly	254
" pie No. 1	222
" " No. 2	223
" sauce	245
" sherbet	260
Lemonade No. 1	160
" No. 2	160
" No. 3	160
Lemons, to wash	30
Lentils, purée of	125
Lettuce salad	272
" to prepare	26
" to select	16
Light omelet	314
Lima beans, to can	167
Liquid sauce	245
" " transparent	244
" yeast	192
" " bread	192
Liver, to bake a	55
" to broil	38
" to prepare	24
" to sauté	155
Lobster, bisque of	121
" creamed	284
" croquettes	143
" cutlets	298
" deviled	290
Lobster salad	274
" sauce No. 1	133
" " No. 2	133
" scalloped	289
Lyonnaise potato	297
Macaroni, creamed	285
" soup	113
" to boil	72
Mace sugar	245
Marketing	7
Marmalade, gooseberry	174
" grape	174
" orange	173
" peach	174
" pine-apple	173
" plum	174
Marmalades	94
Mayonnaise dressing	280
" " cooked	281
Meat, how to select	10
" pie, English	226
" " scrap	224
" sauces	126
Meats, to braise	89
Mixed fish salad	279
" fruit sherbet	260
" salads	275
" soups	115
" soup stock No. 1	104
" soup stock No. 2	105
Mixing	179
Mock cream	242
" peach jelly	255
" terrapin	295
" " patties	226
" turtle soup	118
Muffins, corn, No. 1	210
" " No. 2	210
" " fried	140

Muffins, cracked wheat	207
" hominy	212
" oatmeal	207
" rice	198
" wheat	207
" " No. 1	198
" " No. 2	198
" " No. 3	198
Mush, blackberry	162
" corn-meal	211
" fried	146
" to sauté	148
Mushroom patties	226
" sauce	128
" " fresh	128
Mushrooms, stewed chicken with	86
Mushrooms, to stew	91
Mutton broth No. 1	109
" " No. 2	109
" chops, to broil	37
" hash	295
" to boil a leg of	69
" to fricassee	89
" to prepare a leg of	23
" to roast	51
" to roast a leg of	52
" to select	12
" to stew	87
Nectarine jelly	255
New England apple pie	218
Noodle soup	114
Nun's puffs	142
Nut cake	250
Oatmeal gruel	157
" how to cook	77
" muffins	207
" rolls	207
Oats, rolled, how to cook	77
Okra soup No. 1	113
" " No. 2	114
" " No. 3	115
" to stew	92
Omelet, creamy	312
" ham	313
" light	314
" orange	314
" soufflé	314
" with breakfast bacon	314
Onion salad	273
Onions, fried	139
" to bake	61
" to sauté	147
" to select	16
" to stew	92
Oolong tea, to make	79
Orange cream	257
" " pie	223
" ice	261
" jelly	254
" marmalade	173
" omelet	314
" pie	223
" pudding	257
" salad	270
" sauce	244
" sherbet	260
" shortcake	203
Orangeade	160
Oranges, to wash	30
Oven broiling	43
" how to test temperature of	49
Oven, temperature for baking bread	190
Oven, temperature for baking cake	48

Oven, temperature for roasting meats	49
Oven, temperature for roasting poultry	48
Oven, to broil a chicken in	44
" to broil a fish in	45
" to broil a quail in	44
" to broil a rabbit in	45
" to broil a squirrel in	45
Ox-tail soup	115
Oyster broth	107
" fritters	142
" patties	226
" pie	225
" sauce	131
Oysters, bisque of	121
" creamed, No. 1	284
" " No. 2	284
" curried	288
" fricasseed	290
" fried	146
" panned	288
" raw	275
" stewed	284
" to broil	39
" " on a griddle	43
" to sauté	153
" to scallop, No. 1	57
" " " No. 2	57
" to steam	81
Pancakes, French	199
Panned oysters	288
Parsley butter No. 1	127
" " No. 2	127
" sauce No. 1	130
" " No. 2	130
Parsnips, purée of	124
" to boil	73
" to sauté	150
Parsnips, to select	15
" to stew	93
Paste, puff	213
Pastry, egg	216
" potato	217
" suet	216
" and pie	213
Patties, creamed asparagus	226
" " celery	226
" " chicken	226
" " green peas	226
" " mock terrapin	226
Patties, creamed mushroom	226
Patties, creamed oyster	226
" " sweetbread	226
Patty cases	215
Pea soup	113
Peach fritters	141
" jelly	255
" marmalade	174
" pie	221
" tapioca pudding	238
Peaches in jelly	258
" spiced	177
" to can	165
" to pare	28
" to preserve	168
" to remove the skins from	28
Peaches, to stew dried	99
" to stew fresh	97
Pears, to bake	63
" to can	166
" to preserve	169
" to stew	96
Peas, purée of	122
" to can	167

Peas, to select	16
" to shell	25
" to stew	93
Peeled wheat flour bread	205
" " " gruel	158
Pickled cabbage	175
" cucumbers	177
" green tomatoes	176
Pie, apple, No. 1	217
" " No. 2	217
" " No. 3	217
" baked chicken	225
" beefsteak	224
" blackberry	219
" cherry	220
" crust, flaky	215
" custard	222
" damson	220
" English apple, No. 1	218
" " " No. 2	218
" English meat	226
" fish	225
" gooseberry	220
" grape	220
" huckleberry	220
" lemon, No. 1	222
" " No. 2	223
" lemon cream	223
" New England apple	218
" orange	223
" orange cream	223
" oyster	225
" peach	221
" pie-plant	220
" plum	220
" potato	222
" pumpkin	221
" raspberry, No. 1	219
" " No. 2	219
" scrap meat	224
Pie, squash	222
" strawberry, No. 1	219
" " No. 2	219
" sweet potato	221
" sweetbread and mushroom	225
Pie, vanilla cream	223
Pie-plant pie	220
" to stew	96
Pine-apple cream	257
" fritters	141
" ice cream	262
" jelly	255
" marmalade	173
" salad	271
" sauce	245
" sherbet	261
" shortcake	204
Pine-appleade	161
Pine-apples, to can	165
" to preserve	169
Piquant sauce No 1	129
" " No. 2	129
Plain cream	241
" fritters	140
" soup	106
Plum jelly	106, 255
" marmalade	174
" pie	220
" pudding No. 1	240
" " No. 2	240
" " No. 3	241
Plums, to can	166
" to preserve	170
" to remove the skins from	28
Plums, to stew	97
" to stew dried	99
Pop-overs	202
Pork chops, to broil	38

Pork chops, to sauté	151
" fricasseed salt	291
" to bone a leg of	310
" to roast fresh	53
" " a leg of	53
" to select	13
Potato, browned hashed	296
" " sliced	297
" cakes, browned	297
" croquettes No. 1	299
" " No. 2	299
" " No. 3	300
" hashed	296
" Lyonnaise	297
" pastry	217
" pie	222
" purée of	122
" salad No. 1	274
" " No. 2	274
" soufflé	302
" timbales of	301
" and fish cakes	297
Potatoes, browned sliced	297
" creamed	285
" fried	138
" scalloped, No. 1	286
" " No. 2	286
" to bake	58
" to boil	71
" to prepare	24
" to sauté	149
" to select	15
" to steam	82
" to stew	93
Poultry, stuffing for	27
" to braise	89
" to select	13
Pound cake	249
Prairie chicken, fried	145
" " to broil	39

Prairie chicken, to sauté	152
Pressed corned beef	306
" veal	306
Prunellas, to stew	99
Prunes, to stew dried	98
Pudding, baked apple, No. 1	239
Pudding, baked apple, No. 2	239
Pudding, baked corn-meal, No. 1	232
Pudding, baked corn-meal, No. 2	233
Pudding, baked sago	238
" " tapioco	238
Pudding, banana	257
" bread and butter, No. 1	237
Pudding, bread and butter, No. 2	238
Pudding, fig	240
" French	234
" fruit and bread	238
" " and rice	238
" huckleberry	238
" orange	257
" plum, No. 1	240
" " No. 2	240
" " No. 3	241
" sauces	227, 241
" snow	257
" soufflé	233
" steamed, No. 1	235
" " No. 2	235
" " No. 3	235
" " No. 4	235
" " apple, No. 1	236
Pudding, steamed apple, No. 2	**236**

Pudding, steamed batter	233
" " blackberry	237
Pudding, steamed cherry	236
" " fruit	236
" " huckleberry	238
Pudding, suet	235
Puddings	227
Puffs, nun's	142
Pumpkin pie	221
Purée of asparagus	123
" beans No. 1	123
" " No. 2	123
" " No. 3	123
" beets	124
" carrots	124
" chestnuts	124
" lentils	125
" parsnips	124
" peas	122
" potato	122
" salsify	124
" sorrel	125
" spinach	124
" tomato No. 1	122
" " No. 2	122
" " No. 3	122
" turnip	124
Purées	121
Quail, fried	145
" roast	55
" to broil	39
" to sauté	152
Queen Ann rolls	195
Quince jelly	175
Quinces, to can	165
" to preserve	169
Rabbit, to sauté	152
" to stew	88
Raisin sauce	245
Raisins, to stew	99
Rarebit, Welsh, No. 1	303
" " No. 2	303
" " No. 3	304
Raspberries, to preserve	172
Raspberry jam	172
" jelly	174, 255
" pie No. 1	219
" " No. 2	219
" shortcake	203
Rice, creamed	234
" croquettes No. 1	143
" " No. 2	300
" curried	286
" gruel	157
" muffins	198
" pudding	64
" soup	113
" timbales of	301
" to boil	74
" to steam	82
" to wash	30
Roast, how to carve a	317
" turkey	53
Roasting	46
" meats, temperature of oven for,	47, 48, 50
Roasting poultry	47
Rolled barley, how to cook	77
Rolled oats, how to cook	77
" wheat blanc-mange	229
" " gruel	157
" " how to cook	77
Rolls, cinnamon	196
" cracked wheat	207
" French, No. 1	193

Rolls, French, No. 2	193
" " No. 3	194
" hominy	212
" imperial	193
" oatmeal	207
" Queen Ann	195
Roly-poly, apple	237
" fruit	237
" to steam a	83
Russe, Charlotte, No. 1	255
" " No. 2	256
Sago, creamed	234
" custard, baked	232
" pudding, baked	238
Salad, apple, No. 1	272
" " No. 2	272
" " No. 3	272
" asparagus	275
" banana, No. 1	271
" " No. 2	271
" " No. 3	271
" beet, No. 1	274
" " No. 2	275
" " and potato	275
" cabbage	273
" celery	273
" chicken, No. 1	277
" " No. 2	277
" " No. 3	277
" " with lettuce	278
" cucumber	273
" " and fish	279
" currant	270
" dressing, cooked	281
" " cream	281
" " French, No. 1	280
Salad dressing, French, No. 2	280
Salad dressing, mayonnaise	280
Salad dressings	280
" " seasoning for, No. 1	282
Salad dressings, seasoning for, No. 2	282
Salad dressings, seasoning for, No. 3	282
Salad, egg, No. 1	279
" " No. 2	279
" fish	276
" lettuce	272
" lobster	276
" mixed fish	279
" onion	273
" orange	270
" oyster	275
" pine-apple	271
" potato, No. 1	274
" " No. 2	274
" salmon	276
" shrimp	276
" spinach	275
" strawberry	270
" sweetbread, No. 1	278
" " No. 2	278
" tomato, No. 1	273
" " No. 2	274
" " and fish	279
Salad-making	268
Salads, fruit	269
" mixed	275
" vegetable	272
Salisbury steak, to sauté	151
Salmon, creamed	285
" salad	276
" scalloped	289
Salsify broth	107
" cream of	116

Salsify, purée of		124	Sauce, parsley, No. 2		130
"	sauce	131	"	pine-apple	245
"	soup	113	"	piquant, No. 1	129
"	stock	103	"	" No. 2	129
"	to prepare	24	"	raisin	245
"	to sauté	150	"	salsify	131
"	to select	15	"	shrimp	132
"	to stew	92	"	strawberry	245
Salt codfish, scalloped		287	"	tartare	133
" pork, fricasseed		291	"	tomato, No. 1	134
Sauce, anchovy		133	"	" No. 2	134
"	banana	245	"	" No. 3	134
"	bread, No. 1	132	"	" No. 4	134
"	" No. 2	132	"	" No. 5	135
"	brown, No. 1	128	"	transparent liquid	244
"	" No. 2	128	"	white, No. 1	132
"	" No. 3	129	"	" No. 2	132
"	caper, No. 1	130	"	" No. 3	132
"	" No. 2	130	"	" No. 4	132
"	caramel	243	Sauces, meat		126
"	celery	131	" white		131
"	cherry	245	Sausage, to sauté		154
"	egg	128	Sautéing		146
"	fish	130	Scalloped eggs No. 1		288
"	foamy, No. 1	244	"	" No. 2	288
"	" No. 2	244	"	fish No. 1	287
"	fresh mushroom	128	"	" No. 2	287
"	Hollandaise, No. 1	133	"	fresh fish and oysters	288
"	" No. 2	133	Scalloped lobster		289
"	jelly, No. 1	129	"	oysters No. 1	57
"	" No. 2	129	"	" No. 2	57
"	" No. 3	130	"	potatoes No. 1	286
"	lemon	245	"	" No. 2	286
"	liquid	245	"	salmon	289
"	lobster, No. 1	133	"	salt codfish	287
"	" No. 2	133	"	tomatoes	60
"	mushroom	128	Scollops, to sauté		152
"	orange	244	Scrambled eggs No. 1		312
"	oyster	131	"	" No. 2	312
"	parsley, No. 1	130			

Scrapple	296
" to sauté	148
Sea moss blanc-mange	228
" " gruel	158
Seasoning	263
" for salad dressings No. 1	282
Seasoning for salad dressings No. 2	282
Seasoning for salad dressings No. 3	282
Seedless raisins, to stew	99
Serving and garnishing	315
Shells	161
" tart	224
Sherbet, lemon	260
" mixed fruit	260
" orange	260
" pine-apple	261
" strawberry	260
Shirred eggs No. 1	312
" " No. 2	312
Shortcake, banana	203
" orange	203
" pine-apple	204
" raspberry	203
" strawberry	203
Shrimp croquettes	144
" salad	276
" sauce	132
Shrimps, creamed	284
Sick-room cookery	156
Small puddings, to steam	83
Smear-case	228
Snow pudding	257
Soft ginger cake	250
Sorrel, purée of	125
Soufflé, cheese, No. 1	302
" " No. 2	302
" chicken	302
Soufflé, omelet	314
" potato	302
" pudding	233
Soup, barley	113
" brown, No. 1	117
" " No. 2	118
" " No. 3	118
" clear	109
" " with curry	110
" " with dainty dumplings	110
Soup, clear, with fancy vegetables	110
Soup, clear, with mixed flavoring	110
Soup, clear, with poached eggs	110
Soup, clear, with sliced lemon	110
Soup, clear, with tapioca	110
" corn	113
" green turtle	119
" gumbo	118
" hominy	113
" macaroni	113
" mixed	115
" mock turtle	118
" noodle	114
" okra, No. 1	114
" " No. 2	114
" " No. 3	115
" ox-tail	115
" pea	113
" plain	106
" rice	113
" salsify	113
" tomato, No. 1	113
" " No. 2	117
" transparent tomato, No. 1	117

Soup, transparent tomato,
    No. 2 117
Soup, vegetable, No. 1 . . 114
  "   "   No. 2 . . 114
  "   "   No. 3 . . 114
  "   "   No. 4 . . 114
Soup-bones, to prepare . 22
Soup-making 100
Spaghetti, creamed . . . 285
Spiced beef, to boil . . . 70
  "   damsons 177
  "   peaches 177
Spinach, purée of 124
  "   salad 275
  "   to boil 73
  "   to prepare . . . 25
  "   to select 16
Sponge cake 248
Squash pie 222
  "   summer, to stew . 94
  "   to bake, No. 1 . . 61
  "   "   "   No. 2 . . 61
  "   to prepare 24
  "   to sauté 147
  "   to select 15
  "   to steam 82
  "   winter, to stew . . 93
Squirrel, to sauté 152
  "   to stew 88
Steak, Hamburg 151
  "   Salisbury 151
  "   to broil 36, 42
  "   to prepare 23
Steamed apple pudding
    No. 1 236
Steamed apple pudding
    No. 2 236
Steamed batter pudding . 233
  "   blackberry pudding 237

Steamed cherry pudding . 236
  "   fruit pudding . . 236
  "   huckleberry pudding 237
Steamed pudding No. 1 . 235
  "   "   No. 2 . 235
  "   "   No. 3 . 235
  "   "   No. 4 . 235
Steaming 81
Stewed chicken with mushrooms 86
Stewed chicken with truffles 86
Stewed giblets with mushrooms 292
Stewing 84
Stock, asparagus 103
  "   beef 103
  "   celery 103
  "   chicken 104
  "   compound . . . 104
  "   mixed, No. 1 . . 104
  "   "   No. 2 . . . 105
  "   mutton 103
  "   salsify 103
  "   simple vegetable . 102
  "   veal 103
  "   vegetable 102
Strawberries, to can . . . 164
  "   to hull . . . 29
  "   to preserve, No. 1 170
Strawberries, to preserve, No. 2 171
Strawberries, to preserve, No. 3 171
Strawberry cream 258
  "   ice 261
  "   ice cream . . 262
  "   jam 172

Strawberry jelly . . . 174,	255	
" pie No. 1 . . .	219	
" " No. 2 . . .	219	
" salad	270	
" sauce	245	
" sherbet . . .	260	
" shortcake . .	203	
Strawberryade	160	
Straws, cheese, No. 1 . .	304	
" " No. 2 . .	304	
String beans, to boil . . .	72	
" " to can . . .	167	
" " to prepare .	25	
Strudels, apple	218	
Stuffing for fish	28	
" for poultry . . .	27	
" for veal	27	
Suet pastry	216	
" pudding	235	
Sugar, mace	245	
Sultana raisins, to stew .	99	
Sunshine cake	248	
Sweet potato pie	221	
Sweet potatoes, to bake .	59	
" " to boil .	73	
" " to sauté .	149	
" " to steam	82	
Sweetbread croquettes .	145	
" fritters	142	
" patties	226	
" salad No. 1 .	278	
" " No. 2 .	278	
" and mushroom pie	225	
Sweetbreads	12	
" creamed . .	284	
" to broil . . .	38	
" to prepare .	24	
" to roast . . .	55	
Syrup	243	

Tapioca, creamed	234	
" custard, baked .	232	
" pudding, baked	238	
Tart, apple	224	
" cranberry	224	
" shells	224	
Tartare sauce	133	
Tea, beef, No. 1	108	
" " No. 2	108	
" to make black . . .	79	
" " Ceylon . . .	79	
" " English breakfast	79	
Tea, to make green . . .	79	
" " oolong . .	79	
" toast	158	
Terrapin, mock	295	
" veal	294	
Timbales	300	
" of potato	301	
" of rice	301	
To bake almonds	63	
" apples No. 1 . .	62	
" " No. 2 . .	62	
" bananas	63	
" beans	62	
" bread 48,	190	
" cake	48	
" corn No. 1 . . .	61	
" " No. 2 . . .	61	
" custards	64	
" a fish	56	
" a heart and liver .	55	
" onions	61	
" pears	63	
" potatoes	58	
" rice pudding . . .	64	
" squash No. 1 . .	61	
" " No. 2 . .	61	
" sweet potatoes .	59	

To bake tomatoes	60	To broil chops on a griddle 42
" tongue	56	
To boil asparagus	72	To broil a fish 39
" beets	73	" " in the oven 45
" cabbage	73	" grouse 39
" carrots	73	" ham 40
" cauliflower	72	" liver 38
" a chicken	68	" oysters 39
" corn	72	" " on a griddle 43
" corned beef	70	
" an egg ... 70,	311	To broil prairie chicken . 39
" a fish	69	" quail 39
" a fowl	69	" " in the oven . 44
" a ham	69	" a rabbit 45
" a leg of lamb	69	" a squirrel 45
" macaroni	72	" steak 36
" mutton	69	" " on a griddle 42
" parsnips	73	" sweetbreads . . 38
" potatoes	71	" tomatoes 40
" rice	74	" tripe 38
" spiced beef	70	To can asparagus 167
" spinach	73	" cherries No. 1 . . 166
" string beans	72	" " No. 2 . . 166
" sweet potatoes	73	" corn 167
" turkey	69	" lima beans 167
" turnips	73	" peaches 165
" vegetables	71	" pears 166
To bone a fish	22	" peas 167
" a fowl	309	" pine-apples 165
" a leg of lamb	309	" plums 166
" " pork	310	" quinces 165
" " veal	309	" strawberries ... 164
" a turkey	307	" string beans ... 167
To braise a calf's heart	90	" tomatoes No. 1 . . 168
" meats	89	" " No. 2 . . 168
" poultry	89	" " No. 3 . . 168
To broil chicken	38	To carve a joint 317
" " in the oven	44	" a roast 317
		" a turkey 316
To broil chops	37	To cook cereals 75

374   *Index.*

To cook coarse hominy	.	77
" " oatmeal	.	77
" cracked wheat	.	77
" dried fruits	. . .	97
" farina	. . . . .	77
" fine hominy	. . .	77
" fresh fruits	. . .	94
" rolled barley	. .	77
" " oats	. . .	77
" " wheat	. .	77
To fricassee a chicken	. .	89
" lamb	. . . .	89
" mutton	. . .	89
" veal	. . . .	89
To make black tea	. . . .	79
" Ceylon tea	. . .	79
" chocolate	. . 80,	161
" cider apple sauce		97
" cocoa	. . . . .	80
" " No. 1	. .	161
" " No. 2	. .	161
" " No. 3	. .	161
" coffee No 1	. .	77
" " No. 2	. .	78
" " No. 3	. .	78
" cranberry jelly	. .	96
" English breakfast tea	. . . .	79
To make green tea	. . . .	79
" hygienic coffee	.	79
" koumiss	. . . .	80
To preserve cherries	. . .	170
" peaches	. . .	168
" pears	. . . .	169
" pine-apples	.	169
" plums	. . .	170
" quinces	. . .	169
" raspberries	.	172
" strawberries No. 1	. . . .	170
To preserve strawberries No. 2	. . . .	171
To preserve strawberries No. 3	. . . .	171
To roast beef	. . . . . .	49
" chicken	. . . . .	54
" fresh pork	. . .	53
" lamb	. . . . . .	52
" a leg of lamb or mutton	. . . .	52
To roast mutton	. . . . .	51
" quails	. . . . . .	55
" sweetbreads	. . .	55
" turkey	. . . . .	54
" veal	. . . . .	52
" wild duck	. . . .	55
To sauté apples	. . . . .	149
" bananas	. . . .	150
" beefsteek	. . . .	151
" breakfast bacon		148
" calf's brains	. .	152
" calf's liver	. . .	155
" chicken	. . . .	151
" corn oysters	. .	153
" egg-plant	. . .	147
" eggs	. . . . . .	311
" fish	. . . . . .	152
" fish cakes	. . .	154
" grouse	. . . . .	152
" ham	. . . . . .	148
" Hamburg steak		151
" hash	. . . . . .	154
" hominy	. . . . .	153
" lamb chops	. . .	150
" liver	. . . . . .	155
" mush	. . . . .	148
" onions	. . . . .	147
" oysters	. . . . .	153
" parsnips	. . . .	150
" pork chops	. . .	151

To sauté potatoes	149	To stew dried apples 99
" prairie chicken	152	" " apricots 98
" quail	152	" " beans 91
" rabbit	152	" " peaches 99
" Salisbury steak	151	" " plums 99
" salsify	150	" " prunellas 99
" sausage	154	" " prunes 99
" scollops	152	" green gooseberries 96
" scrapple	148	" " shelled beans 90
" soft-shell crabs	152	" lamb 88
" squash	147	" mushrooms 91
" squirrel	152	" mutton 87
" sweet potatoes	149	" okra 92
" tomatoes	148	" onions 92
" tough beefsteak	151	" oysters 284
" veal chops	150	" parsnips 93
To steam a batter pudding	83	" peaches 97
" clams	82	" pears 96
" corn	83	" peas 93
" eggs	83	" pie-plant 96
" fish	81	" plums 97
" oysters	81	" potatoes 93
" potatoes	82	" rabbit 88
" rice	82	" raisins 99
" a roly-poly	83	" salsify 92
" small puddings	83	" squirrel 88
" squash	82	" sultana raisins 99
" sweet potatoes	82	" summer squash 94
To stew apples	95	" tomatoes 93
" asparagus peas	92	" veal 86
" beef	86	" vegetables 90
" beets	90	" winter squash 93
" cabbage	92	To stuff a leg of lamb 309
" carrots	91	" " " pork 310
" celery	92	" " " veal 309
" chicken	84	" a turkey 307
" corn	91	To toast bread 40
" cranberries No. 1	96	Toast, beefsteak 162
" " No. 2	96	" broth 162
" cucumbers	91	" creamed 285

Toast, curried	286
" dipped	286
" French	304
" fruit	162
" oyster	162
" tea	158
" tropical	305
Tomato, bisque of	120
" purée of, No. 1	122
" " No. 2	122
" " No. 3	122
" salad No. 1	273
" " No. 2	274
" sauce No. 1	134
" " No. 2	134
" " No. 3	134
" " No. 4	134
" " No. 5	135
" soup No. 1	113
" " No. 2	117
" " transparent, No. 1	117
Tomato soup, transparent, No. 2	117
Tomato and fish salad	279
Tomatoes, to bake	60
" to broil	40
" to can, No. 1	168
" " No. 2	168
" " No. 3	168
" to prepare	26
" to sauté	148
" to scallop	60
" to select	16
" to stew	93
Tongue, to bake a	56
" to prepare a dried	23
Transparent liquid sauce	244
" tomato soup No. 1	117
Transparent tomato soup No. 2	117
Tripe, to broil	38
Tropical toast	305
Truffles, stewed chicken with	86
Turbans, fish	299
Turkey hash	293
" roast	53
" to boil a	69
" to bone a	307
" to carve a	316
" to roast a	54
" and oyster hash	293
Turnips, purée of	124
" to boil	73
" to prepare	24
" to select	15
Vanilla cream pie	223
Veal broth	109
" chops, fried	146
" cream of	117
" croquettes	145
" hash	294
" pressed	306
" stuffing for	27
" terrapin	294
" to bone a leg of	309
" to fricassee	89
" to roast	52
" to sauté	150
" to select	12
" to stew	86
Vegetable soup No. 1	114
" " No. 2	114
" " No. 3	114
" " No. 4	114
" stock	102
" soups	111

Vegetables, fancy	111
" macedoine	111
" to boil	71
" to select	15
" to stew	90
Vermicelli, creamed	285
Vienna bread	189, 191
Vol-au-vents	215, 284
Wafers, ginger	250
Waffles No. 1	201
" No. 2	201
" No. 3	201
Water, hard	66
" soft	66
Welsh rarebit No. 1	303
" " No. 2	303
" " No. 3	304
Wetting	179
Wheat griddle cakes No. 1	199
Wheat griddle cakes No. 2	199
Wheat griddle cakes No. 3	199
Wheat muffins No. 1	198
" " No. 2	198
" " No. 3	198
Whey	228
Whipped cream	241
Whips, egg	159
" " with syrup	160
White flour gruel	157
" sauce No. 1	132
" " No. 2	132
" " No. 3	132
" " No. 4	132
" sauces	131
" soups	115
Whole wheat flour bread	205
" " " gruel	158
Wild duck, to roast	55
Winter squash, to stew	93
Yeast, compressed	186
" liquid	192
" proper quantity of	191

www.ingramcontent.com/pod-product-compliance
Lightning Source LLC
Chambersburg PA
CBHW030407230426
43664CB00007BB/781